HISTORIC GOVAN

HISTORIC GOVAN

Archaeology and development

Chris Dalglish and Stephen T Driscoll
with contributions by Irene Maver, Norman F Shead
and Ingrid Shearer

THE SCOTTISH BURGH SURVEY

Published by the Council for British Archaeology and Historic Scotland
First published in 2009

Copyright © 2009 Historic Scotland
The moral right of the authors has been asserted.
British Library Cataloguing in Publication Data
A catalogue for this book is available from the British Library

Edited by Catrina Appleby, CBA and Mark Watson, Historic Scotland

Page design and typesetting by Carnegie Publishing Ltd

Printing and binding: Information Press, Oxford

ISBN: 978-1-902771-62-5

Council for British Archaeology
St Mary's House,
66 Bootham,
York YO30 7BZ
www.britarch.ac.uk

Historic Scotland
Longmore House
Salisbury Place
Edinburgh
EH9 1SH
Tel. 0131 668 8600
Fax. 0131 668 8669
www.historic-scotland.gov.uk

Front cover: Aerial view of Govan (2005) looking east over Fairfield shipyard © crown copyright RCAHMS; Constantine Sarcophagus in Govan Old Parish Church © crown copyright Historic Scotland; inset Water Row (Mitchell Library)

Contents

Acknowledgements.. vii

Figures...viii

Synopsis xv

1 The purpose of this survey 1

2 Setting the scene...7
   The scope of the Govan Burgh Survey 7
   The natural environment 9
   Before Govan: prehistory and earliest history 14
   Sources 18

3 Early historic and medieval Govan 28
   Historical background 28
   Archaeological evidence 31
   Discussion 48

4 Early modern to early industry (sixteenth to early nineteenth centuries)...51
   Introduction 51
   The economy and the Clyde... 52
   The road network... 54
   The decline of agriculture and the rise of manufacturing 59
   Early industry 62
   The changing community... 65
   Architectural traditions... 67
   The post-Reformation Church 73
   Discussion 77

5 The Burgh of Govan (c 1850–1912) 80
   Introduction 80
   Industrialisation 81
   Population and housing... 99
   The Burgh of Govan 103
   The social environment... 110
   Discussion 121

6 Developing Govan's cultural heritage.......................................123
   Historic Govan in the twentieth century............................. 123
   Current statutory designations 127
   The archaeological potential of Govan 130
   Historic Govan: the significance of a place 142

Glossary 149

References 153

    Primary sources 153

    Published primary sources 153

    Secondary sources 154

Index.. 165

Broadsheet

Acknowledgements

During the course of this project we received help and encouragement from a great many people, whose contributions have significantly enhanced the final result. The archaeologists would like to thank the historians, Irene Maver and Norman Shead, for their guidance and forbearance. The West of Scotland Archaeological Service provided advice and support which allowed us to develop the GIS used for the mapping. The various members of Historic Scotland's staff have been understanding and helpful during the prolonged gestation of the report, especially the sequence of inspectors who have overseen and contributed to this effort: Olly Owen, Ann MacSween, Martin Brann and Mark Watson. As the project neared completion John Hume generously read a draft and his comments saved us from various errors and drew our attention to historic images we had overlooked, including some of his own.

At a late stage in the preparation of this volume (after the 'final' draft had been submitted to Historic Scotland) GUARD was commissioned by Glasgow City Council to conduct an archaeological evaluation of the Water Row area, which was undertaken in autumn 2007 (Driscoll *et al* 2008). The opportunity has been taken to incorporate some of the results of the fieldwork and accompanying map work into this study.

Finally, we must acknowledge a special debt to Tom Davidson-Kelly, formerly minister of Govan Old, who in many respects paved the way for this study. He is responsible for revitalising interest in Govan's medieval past, through the conference on *Govan and its early medieval sculpture* (Ritchie 1994) and the subsequent establishment of the Friends of Govan Old, which promotes the historical investigation of the church and its burgh. His activities inspired the excavations of the 1990s and during the course of this study his advice on ecclesiastical history has been invaluable.

Figures

Chapter 1

1.1 Location map and extents of old parish boundary and survey area (Based on OS mapping © crown copyright. All rights reserved, Historic Scotland Licence No. 100017509 [2009]) 2

1.2 The area selected for this survey in relation to Glasgow, showing phases of development, some key sites and the conservation area boundary 3

1.3 Excavations in progress at the southern boundary of the kirkyard during 1994..........................4

1.4 Analysis of the development history of the block bounded by Govan Road, Pearce Street, Pearce Lane and Water Row as represented in various editions of the Ordnance Survey 4

Chapter 2

2.1 Aerial view of central Govan, looking west down the Clyde (2005)................8

2.2 View of Govan from the east by Joseph Swan, c 1824 12

2.3 Distribution map of finds of prehistoric and Roman date............................15

2.4 Detail of Govan from Timothy Pont's manuscript map......................22

2.5 Detail of Partick from Timothy Pont's manuscript map 22

2.6 The survey of Scotland made under the direction of General Roy after the Jacobite rising of 1745 23

2.7 Detail from Thomas Richardson's 1795 *Map of the town of Glasgow & country seven miles around* 23

2.8 Detail from John Ainslie's *Map of the County of Renfrew* (1800) 24

2.9 Detail from William Forrest's *Map of the County of Lanark* (1816) 24

2.10 George Martin's *Map of the City of Glasgow* (1842)............................24

2.11 First edition Ordnance Survey 1:10,560 map, 1857–58 25

2.12 Second edition Ordnance Survey 1:10,560 map, 1893–94................................25

2.13 Third edition Ordnance Survey six inch map, survey 1909, published 1914 ...25

2.14 Kyle's Clyde Navigation Survey of 1842 26

2.15 Map of the *Village of Govan* drawn by W D Barles in 1906, showing Govan as it was imagined to be in 1837 27

Chapter 3

3.1 Aerial photograph of Govan Old churchyard from the north during the excavations of 1994 29

3.2 The 'Sun Stone', so-called because of its boss with spiralling snakes' heads 30–31

3.3 The Govan sarcophagus, cut from a single block of sandstone 32

3.4 Hogback no. 2, shown here on display in the church, is thought to be the earliest of the Govan hogback tomb stones 33

3.5 Both ends of hogback no. 5, shown here on display in the church, are carved to resemble the decorative binding of church-shaped reliquary casket 33

3.6 Recumbent cross-slab no. 18, reused in the seventeenth and eighteenth centuries 33

3.7 The shaft of the finely executed freestanding Jordanhill cross 33

3.8 Plan of Govan Old churchyard showing position of sculptured stones in 1899 34

3.9 Map showing the locations of 'Govan School' sculpture, and the approximate extent of the medieval parishes 35

3.10 Map showing the locations of the archaeological excavations, conducted 1994–2007 36

3.11 Plan of trench C showing the stone foundations interpreted as a church structure, 1996 37

3.12 View from the south of the massive drystone foundations of the possible church in trench C, 1996 37

3.13 Sequence of medieval churches at Govan as reconstructed by Chris Jopson in 2001 38

3.14 Plan of trenches A and B dug across the churchyard boundary 39

3.15 View from the south of metalled road in south-east of churchyard, trench G, 1996 39

3.16 Section cut across the churchyard boundary revealing the depth of deposits within the interior and the scale of the external ditch, trenches A and B, 1994 40

3.17 'A view of the banks of the Clyde taken from York Hill' by Robert Paul, 1758 43

3.18 The excavation searching for Doomster Hill in 1996 44

3.19 Govan Manse in 1857 from the Ordnance Survey 1st edition Town Plan, 1:500 46

3.20 View of Partick Castle from the east side of the Kelvin from A MacGeorge's *Old Glasgow*, 1880 47

Chapter 4

4.1   View of Govan village approaching from the south at the junction of Harmony Row and Kittle Corner by T Fairbairn, 1848 51

4.2   Govan Ferry from Partick by David Allan, 1820s 53

4.3   Ford at Linthouse as imagined by T C F Brotchie 54

4.4   Stepping stones over the lower Kelvin, with Partick Bridge in the background 55

4.5   Old Bridge of Partick 55

4.6   Photograph of Water Row from the south-east c 1910, with the shipyards of Partick in the background 56

4.7   Plans of the old houses on the west side of Water Row made in 1911, prior to demolition 56

4.8   View along Manse Lane (now Pearce Lane) by J P Main, 1870 57

4.9   View of Pointhouse and its ferry slip from the east, 1815 (MacGeorge 1893) 58

4.10 Entrance to Govan Shipbuilding yard and Sheephead Inn looking west along Govan Road 58

4.11 The Bunhouse Inn by Old Dumbarton Road in Kelvinhaugh on the eastern approach to Partick Bridge 59

4.12 Fairfield farmhouse in Elder Park, the oldest building to survive in Govan ... 59

4.13 View of Govan waterfront from the east showing fishermen at work in front of their hut on the shore 60

4.14 An engraving of the silk factory from the north shore by Swan c 1840, taken from the letterhead of Morris Pollok, silk throwster 62

4.15 Buchanan's Waverley Tavern dominates the lower end of the east side of Water Row 62

4.16 The Bunhouse Mill on the east side of the Kelvin 63

4.17 The Bishop Mills on the eastern approach to Partick Bridge in 1978 prior to restoration and development as flats 64

4.18 Thatched cottage on Govan Road at Shaw Street opposite the entrance gates to Govandale 68

4.19 Photograph of the same seventeenth-century thatched cottage on Main Street, c 1900, before it was replaced by the Lyceum Theatre 68

4.20 The Ordnance Survey first edition map (1857) reveals a dense spread of grand houses in their own policies throughout Govan's rural hinterland 69

4.21 The entrance to Holmfauldhead House, photographed c 1900 71

4.22 Linthouse, photographed c 1870 71

4.23 Moore Park house seen from its gardens, c 1870 72

4.24 Thornbank, *c* 1870..72

4.25 The spire of the 1826 Govan Old Church designed by James Smith of Jordanhill 74

4.26 Photograph *c* 1910 of the first parish school, which stood on the north side of Govan Cross..76

4.27 Photograph of Govan Manse, 1858, from the south.....................................77

Chapter 5

5.1 Map showing the location of industry in Govan...82

5.2 Meadowside Yard, 1912, looking north from the Govan side..........................83

5.3 Scotway House, former offices of Meadowside yard.......................................83

5.4 View of the Barclay Curle yard across the river from Linthouse, 1933...........84

5.5 Mackie and Thomson's Old Govan Yard, also known as the Govan Shipbuilding Yard, 1891..85

5.6 Advertisement for Mackie and Thomson Shipbuilders, *Scotland's Industrial Souvenir*, 1905 85

5.7 Aerial view of the Harland and Wolff yard, *c* 1930, which dominated the Water Row area from 1911 to the 1960s.....................................86

5.8 Aerial view of Fairfield shipyard and Govan Road, *c* 1930, before enlargement of Meadowside Granary, opposite, in 1938.................................87

5.9 Survey drawing by Geoffrey Hay (1980) of the Fairfield Yard.........................87

5.10 Clocking off at Fairfield Yard 88

5.11 Fairfield's fitting-out basin, showing the sheerlegs that were to be replaced by a Titan crane in 1911 88

5.12 The Titan cantilever crane was built in Fairfield's fitting-out basin in 1911 and demolished in 2005 88

5.13 The office block of the Linthouse Yard, built 1914, now occupied by Govan Workspace and others...88

5.14 The Linthouse engine shop which was dismantled in 1987 and re-erected at the Scottish Maritime Museum in Irvine..................................88

5.15 Aerial photograph of Govan and Partick taken by the Luftwaffe in 1939 and marked with targets...90

5.16 Aerial view of the Scottish Co-operative Wholesale Society works at Shieldhall, 1913..92

5.17 The cabinet factory within the Scottish Co-operative Wholesale Society works at Shieldhall...92

5.18 The Luma Lamp Factory is the only surviving major element of the SCWS Shieldhall works, 1939..93

5.19 Queen's Dock in 1936, showing a fixed steam crane on the left and the new Finnieston electric cantilever crane on the right.......................94

5.20 Cessnock (Prince's) Dock, c 1965...95

5.21 Aerial view of eastern Govan looking east (2005)..............................95

5.22 Three paddle steamers in No. 3 Dry Dock, Govan Graving Docks, c 1910 96

5.23 Aerial view of the Govan Graving Docks in their current abandoned state, opposite the *Glenlee* and the Anchor Line transit sheds 96

5.24 Merklands Lairage, c 1930 97

5.25 Meadowside Granary c 1970, reputedly the largest brick building in Europe in 1955 97

5.26 Govan Ferry, c 1890..97

5.27 The variable-level vehicular ferry to Govan..98

5.28 Govan Cross subway station was entered through a public house.................99

5.29 Copland Road subway station 99

5.30 The concentration of housing in the nineteenth century shows the strong zoning between residential areas and those occupied by manufacturing sites 100

5.31 Neptune Street in a rare view of a tenement back court, c 1920 102

5.32 Langlands Road, c 1910...102

5.33 Tenements, Govan Road and Burghead Place 102

5.34 Tenements, Govan Road and Cressy Street...102

5.35 Terraced houses on St Kenneth Drive 103

5.36 Napier House, Govan Road, c 1960, built as a model lodging house in 1898–99 103

5.37 Govan municipal buildings of 1868..106

5.38 Govan Town Hall...106

5.39 Southern General Hospital (formerly Govan Combination Hospital) 107

5.40 Elder Cottage Hospital 107

5.41 Elder Cottage Hospital nurses' home 107

5.42 Aerial view of the Shieldhall sewage works, c 1930, from the south 108

5.43 Hill's Trust School, c 1964..109

5.44 Greenfield Street School, c 1964 109

5.45 Gilbert Street drill hall 109

5.46 Govan Cross from the west facing Govan New Church (St Mary's).............112

5.47 Statue of William Pearce, 2007 112

5.48 Unveiling of statue of William Pearce in 1894 113

5.49 Map showing how the churches, municipal institutions and philanthropic establishments are spread across the residential areas and away from the riverfront... 114

5.50 View of Elder Park looking east, *c* 1891 115

5.51 The portico to the Elder Park Library carries the burgh crest which features shipbuilding imagery and bears the motto *nihil sine labore*, 'nothing without labour'.. 115

5.52 Unveiling the statue of John Elder in 1888 115

5.53 Statue of Isabella Elder 116

5.54 The Lyceum Theatre, built 1899 116

5.55 a) The Lyceum Cinema in February 1939; b) Snow White and the seven dwarves illustrated in a mural in the foyer of the Lyceum cinema 116

5.56 The main stand of Ibrox Park, in 1935, from the Copeland Road end 116

5.57 The Pearce Institute, photographed in 1959 by David Walker for the Scottish National Building Record 116

5.58 Postcard showing the British Linen Bank, 1897, on the south-west corner of Govan Cross and the YMCA, 1905 117

5.59 Norman-style church of Linthouse St Kenneth's by Peter Macgregor Chalmers opened in 1900, demolished in 1982 118

5.60 The Romanesque-style tower of St Anthony's RC church 119

5.61 Rowand Anderson's Govan Old Parish Church, about twenty years after it was built in 1888, showing the condition of the churchyard prior to its modern decline 119

5.62 Drawing of Govan Old Parish Church with the great tower that was never built.. 120

5.63 The Gothic appearance and enormous scale of the Govan Old Parish Church were intended to inspire worship, but perhaps also to emulate Glasgow's medieval Cathedral.. 120

Chapter 6

6.1   Reconstruction of Govan and Partick *c* AD 1000, showing the link between the church and Doomster Hill with the royal estate of Partick on the north shore 133

6.2a Taransay Street back court, *c* 1970 138

6.2b Taransay Street back courts after reinstatement of drying greens by ASSIST 138

6.3   Visitors to the excavation open day 1994 contemplate a nineteenth-century burial 143

6.4   Filming an evening news broadcast about the 1994 excavations 143

6.5   Excavations undertaken in conjunction with Time Team in 1996 143

6.6a Govan Cross, 1969 145

6.6b Govan Cross, 2007 145

6.7   Aerial view of western Govan, 2005 147

Historic Govan: synopsis

Historic Govan aims to assess the present character of Govan's heritage and the state of knowledge of its historical development from the earliest settlement to its annexation by Glasgow in 1912. This synthesis of previous scholarship and recent fieldwork has produced new insights into the value and potential of Govan's cultural resources. They are presented to inform the appropriate management of the historic environment, to establish future avenues of research, and to encourage public understanding and appreciation of Govan's heritage.

Govan is a remarkable place. Over the centuries it has enjoyed two periods of great importance. The recent era of significance, when the name Govan was synonymous with Clyde-built ships, is the most familiar. But a millennium earlier, Govan forged a reputation from different raw materials: royal power and religious belief. During and after the Viking Age, Govan developed into a centre of political authority, utilising the ancient religious foundation as a platform for a revitalised British kingdom. Superficially, it may seem that few connections exist between medieval and industrial Govan, but upon closer analysis it can be seen how the ancient organisation of the settlement influenced subsequent development. Most profound has been the stability of Govan Cross, which has remained the focus of the community as a place of assembly and public activity despite the sweeping changes introduced by industrial and urban development. Modern Govan's strong community identity may owe something to this deeply grounded sense of place.

Medieval Govan was constructed around three essential elements: a major river crossing, a regionally significant church, and a centre of royal power. The existing Govan Old Parish Church was built in part from the proceeds of shipbuilding and stands upon one of the oldest Christian sites in western Scotland. The raised, heart-shaped churchyard has protected the ancient site from encroachment by shipyards and tenements. The collection of early historic sculpture found at Govan, dating from the tenth to the twelfth centuries AD, numbered at least 46 pieces when first discovered. Some 30 survive today, making it one of the largest collections in Scotland.

Little is known about the early settlement that grew up around the river crossing at Water Row, so finding out about the community which produced the sculpture is one of the most pressing goals of future archaeological research. By contrast, with the benefit of more documentation, we know that the village which emerged in the post-medieval period was a thriving craft centre, focused on handloom weaving. Far from being an isolated rural backwater, as has been suggested in the past, Govan and its textile industry were tied to the developing importance of the Clyde as a commercial avenue. Govan could boast of global connections, working with raw materials from the American colonies and the Far East.

The nationally significant collection of burial monuments in Govan Old Parish churchyard, dating from the fifteenth to twentieth centuries AD and spanning the ages of Reformation, Imperialism and Industrialism, reveals the fluid nature of society in the post-medieval period. Through these memorials, Govan's established resident landowners competed with an incoming class of colonial merchants, who saw the area as a suitable place for a country retreat, and with emergent groups of artisans, notably the weavers, vying for recognition and position. Unexcavated archaeological remains together with under-studied archive sources have the potential to expand greatly our understanding of this time in history.

From the early nineteenth century, slowly at first but with increasing impact, Govan underwent a massive transformation with the coming of heavy industry and the change from rural village to urban townscape. The Govan shipyards have an acknowledged and prominent position in the history of the Clyde shipbuilding industry, an industry that was once dominant in global terms. Robert Napier, who ran Govan's oldest shipyard from 1841, is known as the 'Father of Clyde Shipbuilding' for his tutelage of many of the industry's leading figures in his yard – the 'kindergarten of Clyde shipbuilders'.

Complementing and often conflicting with our appreciation of Govan's global position in the industrial era, and the achievements of individuals like Napier, is Govan's built heritage. The importance of this has recently been acknowledged through designation as a conservation area. This heritage gives us insight into the environment, daily lives, routines and actions of the majority of the urban population. The surviving buildings, parks, statues and other built features create a complex urban environment. Collectively, this townscape allows appreciation not only of the daily realities of industrial and urban life, but also the dynamic politics and social relationships that defined what it meant to be a Govanite of the time. There is wide scope for gaining further knowledge of the genesis and development of modern Govan from a reappraisal of existing archive sources, surviving buildings, and archaeological remains. While this material is vital for understanding the daily environment of the industrial population, it also has wider global importance. To investigate and record Govan's industrial environment is, simultaneously, to inform historical knowledge of Glasgow, the Clyde, Scotland and, indeed, those many parts of the world that saw Govan's ships and other products with increasing regularity through the nineteenth century and beyond.

1   The purpose of this survey

This third series of burgh surveys is intended as a guide for the general reader in understanding and researching the rich history and archaeology of Scotland's historic towns. It is also intended to furnish local authorities with reliable information to help protect and manage the archaeology and historic environment of our urban centres (see Owen, MacSween and Ritchie 2000).

Historic Govan is an introduction to and summary of Govan's history and archaeology. It is the first synthesis of Govan's history and heritage since T C F Brotchie's *The History of Govan*, written a century ago in 1905 and reprinted in 1938.

The volume discusses the significance and potential of Govan's heritage. It is a guide to the archaeological and architectural history of the former burgh which aims to inform the management of these cultural resources. During the research for this volume, a complementary Geographical Information System (GIS), a map-based digital resource containing a database of archaeological and other historic sites and buildings, was developed.

Further preliminary research into the archaeological potential of a site can be gleaned from local and national libraries and archives. The PASTMAP website (http://www.PASTMAP.org.uk) can also be consulted. This interactive website, supported jointly by Historic Scotland and the Royal Commission on the Ancient and Historical Monuments of Scotland, allows anyone with internet access to search data on Scotland's historic environment including the statutorily protected sites, scheduled ancient monuments and listed buildings.

Both the present survey and PASTMAP provide information only. In all cases where development is being considered, advice should be sought from the Local Authority planning department and from their archaeological advisors: for Glasgow, contact should be made with the West of Scotland Archaeology Service (Charing Cross Complex, 20 India Street, Glasgow, G2 4PF; telephone 0141 287 8333).

The approach to Govan taken here has been holistic in terms of the historical periods considered, the material consulted, and the geographical area studied (**figs 1.1 & 1.2**).

Govan's historic environment – its archaeology, historic buildings, and historic townscape – is a palimpsest formed over the last 1500 years. The significance of early historic Govan is clear from the sculpture now housed in Govan Old Parish Church and from recent archaeological excavations (**fig 1.3**). It has therefore been important for us to consider that period in depth. We also pay close attention to the medieval period. In order to understand the

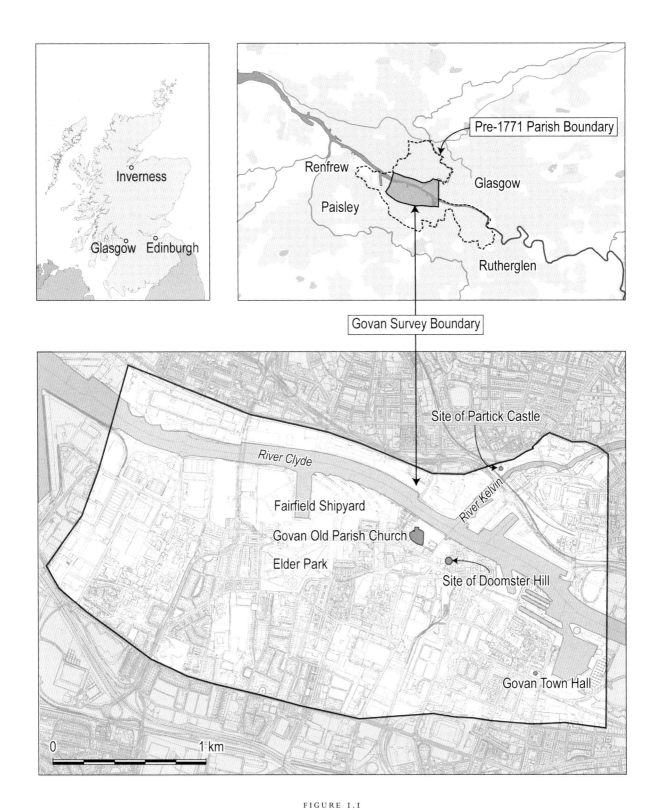

FIGURE I.I

Location map and extents of old parish boundary and survey area (Based on OS mapping © crown copyright. All rights reserved, Historic Scotland Licence No. 100017509 [2009])

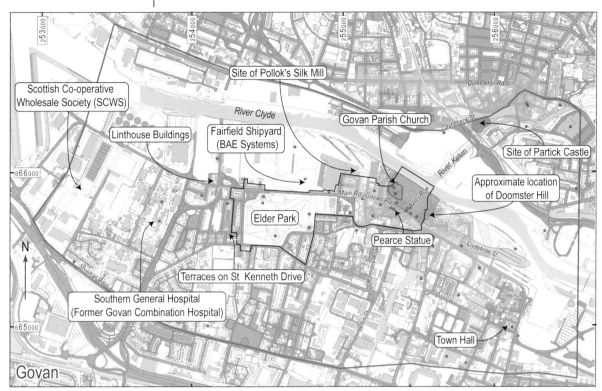

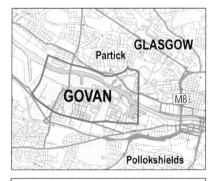

This map is based on Ordnance Survey material with the permission of Ordnance Survey on behalf of the Controller of Her Majesty's Stationery Office © Crown copyright. Unauthorised reproduction infringes Crown copyright and may lead to prosecution or civil proceedings.

Development at a glance:

Approximate extent of Medieval settlement core
Approximate extent of Post-Medieval settlement based on Forrest's map (1816)
Extent of mid-nineteenth century settlement based on OS 1st Edition (1857-58)
Course of Clyde and Kelvin Rivers (1838)
Modern course of Clyde and Kelvin Rivers (at High Water Mark)

Key:

Listed buildings within survey area
Scheduled Ancient Monument (Govan Old Churchyard)
Approximate location of Doomster Hill
Survey boundary area
Conservation area

FIGURE I.2
The area selected for this survey in relation to Glasgow, showing phases of development, some key sites and the conservation area boundary

particular historic character of Govan, however, it was necessary to extend the period under study forward to 1912, to include the major transformations of the industrial era – a period of great significance in the present context. In 1912 Govan was united with Glasgow, and ceased to exist as a municipal entity, at which point it was the fifth largest burgh in Scotland.

Consideration of the most recent past entailed the study of a wealth of historical documents, maps and plans, and a large number of sites,

FIGURE 1.3
Excavations in progress at
the southern boundary of
the kirkyard during 1994

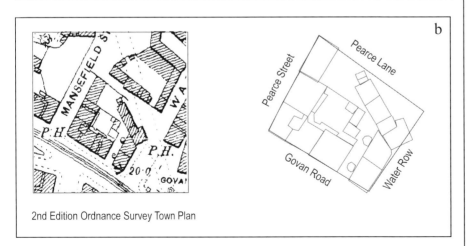

1st Edition Ordnance Survey Town Plan

2nd Edition Ordnance Survey Town Plan

a

b

FIGURE 1.4
Analysis of the development
history of the block bounded
by Govan Road, Pearce
Street, Pearce Lane and
Water Row as represented
in various editions of the
Ordnance Survey (a) 1st
edition 1857–58, (b) 2nd
edition 1893–94, (c) 3rd
edition 1913, (d) 4th edition
1933. The earlier maps
show that the corner of
Water Row and Pearce Lane
splayed out in a manner
characteristic of medieval
market places and we might
expect a similar splay to have
originally existed on the
north side of Pearce Lane

buildings, and other aspects of the townscape. From an early stage, the Geographical Information System (GIS) proved essential in managing the relatively large amount of data encountered. These digital data are a core resource for managing Govan's heritage, but are too detailed to be published conventionally. The distribution maps published here are generated from GIS (**figs 2.3, 5.1, 5.30 & 5.49**) and present a simplified snapshot of the state of knowledge at the time of the study. Any paper publication is only a partial representation, since the GIS is intended to be a dynamic resource, capable of being updated. As a result, this volume does not contain a gazetteer of all of Govan's historic sites and buildings – the GIS aims to serve that function and may be accessed at the West of Scotland Archaeology Service.

When used in conjunction with the historic map resources, GIS is a powerful tool in charting how a particular site has developed over time. The value of such an approach can be seen in the regression analysis undertaken for the block bounded by Govan Road, Pearce Street, Pearce Lane and Water Row (**fig 1.4**). Such fine-grained analysis is beyond the scope of this study,

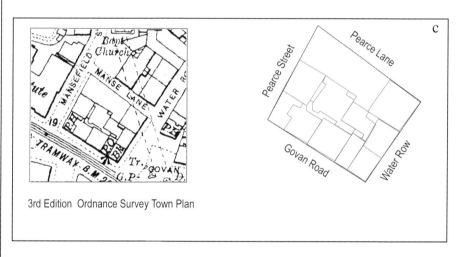

3rd Edition Ordnance Survey Town Plan

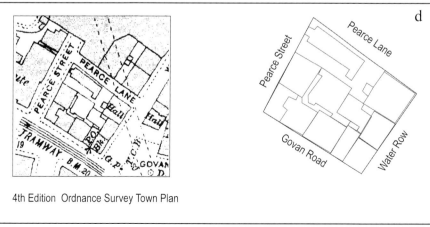

4th Edition Ordnance Survey Town Plan

but the example shows how helpful this approach can be for assessing the significance of a particular site.

The overall study area is not based upon a medieval burgh: Govan did not achieve burgh status until 1864. In defining the study area, careful consideration was given to the extent of the medieval settlement, which compelled us to include Partick, and to the extent of the modern industrial burgh. This has led to the examination of a substantial portion of the medieval parish and to the inclusion of areas which remained in the rural hinterland of the town until the nineteenth century (see **fig 1.2**).

Chapter 2 of this book sets the scene, outlines the scope of the survey, and explains its spatial and temporal confines. It contains sections on the character and development of the natural, physical environment and on the archaeology of the Govan area prior to the earliest known development of the town. Finally, it summarises the nature of the available historical and archaeological evidence.

Chapters 3 to 5 detail the history of Govan and the character of its built heritage by historical period. They aim to provide a synthetic history of the town: a discussion of elements of its built heritage, and the historical context necessary for assessing the significance of that heritage. Chapter 3 is concerned with the early historic period (a term used in preference to 'the early medieval period' or 'the Dark Ages' for the sixth to eleventh centuries AD) and the medieval period (twelfth to sixteenth centuries). Chapter 4 is concerned with the early modern and pre-industrial era (to the mid-nineteenth century). Chapter 5 covers industrial Govan (from *c* 1850 to 1912). The structure of this three-chapter section of the text is weighted towards the recent centuries due to the wealth of historical information and relatively high level of survival of material remains for that period.

Chapter 6, the concluding chapter, is aimed particularly at planners and professional heritage managers, but it is also hoped that it will be of wider interest. The chapter provides a summary assessment of Govan's built heritage, outlines the interest and importance of the historic built environment, including details of significant sites, buildings and areas of potential. It also discusses the potential of the built heritage and archaeological resource to inform our understanding of the history of Govan and its community.

A glossary of technical terms, a list of the references cited in the text, and an index conclude the book.

2   Setting the scene

This chapter sets out spatial, temporal, and thematic bounds for the survey; the natural environment and its cultural impact; the prehistoric and Roman archaeological background; and the nature of the available evidence.

The scope of the Govan Burgh Survey

Delimiting the temporal scope of the Govan survey means defining a start date and an end date. Unlike many of the other subjects of the *Scottish Burgh Survey*, which were accorded burgh status in the medieval period, Govan did not technically become a burgh until 1864. Yet Govan's significance as far back as the early historic period has long been recognised. This is most strikingly illustrated by the significant corpus of tenth- and eleventh-century sculptured stones now inside Govan Old Parish Church and by the fact that excavations in the churchyard have produced evidence dating back to the fifth or sixth century AD. The antiquity of any settlement around the church site is at present unknown, but the earliest establishment there of the church seems a reasonable starting point for the survey, as this church has formed a continuous and important focus for settlement throughout its history (**fig 2.1**).

Govan went on to become the fifth largest Scottish burgh with the annexation of the neighbouring Linthouse district in 1901. It was not long before Govan lost its independence to Glasgow in 1912. The latter year was chosen as the end date of the survey for several reasons. Firstly, this allows a full treatment of the history of the independent burgh. Secondly, it addresses the industrial period in depth. To many, Govan's history means its industrial history, and there is a widely held association between the town and shipbuilding. The industrial significance of Govan continues, but taking 1912 as an end date allowed attention to be given to the processes whereby modern Govan was created. Conveniently, this end date corresponds with the end date of the second volume of a recent three-volume history of Glasgow (Fraser and Maver 1996a). By taking this study into the early twentieth century we can include the period when Govan and Glasgow were at the peak of their prosperity (Fraser 1996, 1).

Definition of the scope of the survey in spatial terms was, equally, not a straightforward issue. A reasonable approximation of the likely extent of the medieval town can be drawn from post-medieval maps, but one of the main features of Govan's early history is its close association with Partick across the Clyde. From the twelfth century, Govan pertained to the bishops of Glasgow, who had a 'castle' on their lands at Partick, and it is likely that

the early church at Govan was closely associated with a royal estate of the British kingdom of Strathclyde, also centred on Partick. To take account of this historical association, a decision was taken to include a portion of the north bank of the Clyde around its confluence with the River Kelvin (**fig 2.4**). The northern edge of the survey area runs along Castlebank Street and Dumbarton Road, taking in the Partick and Whiteinch shipyards and a number of other features.

Considering that the second main focus of the survey was the industrial period, it was decided that the bounds of the survey should extend far beyond the probable limits of medieval Govan. While many of the main shipyards fall within that limit, others lie further to the west. Other types of industry, significant areas of housing and key elements of the modern urban landscape developed in areas to the south and west of the medieval core. Thus, a somewhat arbitrary line had to be taken in defining the limits of the survey area. However, these limits were set to allow inclusion of the larger part of Govan's pre-1912 development and to ensure that the main strands of Govan's recent history were covered. The southern edge was the railway to Greenock. To the east, the limits essentially lie just beyond the built-up extent

FIGURE 2.1
Aerial view of central Govan, looking west down the Clyde (2005). The Gothic form of Govan Old Parish Church within its ancient curvilinear kirkyard occupies the centre of the view, with Water Row towards the bottom running alongside the ad hoc car park to the former ferry terminus (Crown copyright: Royal Commission on the Ancient and Historical Monuments of Scotland)

of the town as defined on the second edition Ordnance Survey maps of the 1890s. At that time, Govan had yet to be engulfed within the urban sprawl that is present-day Glasgow. To the west is included the Southern General hospital complex and the former site of the Scottish Co-operative Wholesale Society works at Shieldhall.

An important factor in defining the spatial bounds of the survey was the need to treat Govan's industrial period in a holistic manner. The character of this period and the significance of its built heritage cannot properly be understood by isolating one aspect, its industry, from the wider urban context. The geographic bounds of the survey have been extended to address this.

The natural environment

The paradoxical saying 'the Clyde made Glasgow, and Glasgow made the Clyde' sums up the inter-relationship between the development of city and river (Gilfillan 1958, 18). It applies equally to Govan, whose development was also tied to the character of the wider natural environment.

The geological development of the region can be considered, for present purposes, with reference to two broad eras. The first extends over the very long period from before 570 million years ago to around 250 million years ago and concerns the initial formation of the major rock and mineral deposits (see Cameron and Stephenson 1985; Lawson 1992; Neville George 1958; 1973). The second, known as the Quaternary, extends from around two million years ago until the present and is characterised by repeated climatic fluctuations between temperate and arctic conditions, or Ice Ages, ending in the present post-glacial period (see Cameron and Stephenson 1985; Gilfillan 1958; Jardine 1973, 1992; Neville George 1973; Riddell 1979, 2–8).

Govan lies within the Midland Valley of Scotland, the relatively low-lying central part of the country between the Grampian Highlands and the Southern Uplands, both composed of rocks formed over 400 million years ago. Once established, the Highlands and Uplands acted to channel subsequent processes of erosion and sedimentary deposition.

Between around 410 and 360 million years ago, the sandstones that line the flanks of the Valley were formed in a time of heavy rainfall and powerful and fast-flowing streams. These rocks were created from a sequence of flood-plain sediments and their lower layers are inter-bedded with volcanic deposits. The ensuing period, from around 360 million to 290 million years ago, was one of humid equatorial conditions. This saw the development of a huge fluvio-deltaic complex, the deposition of large quantities of sand and mud, and occasional flooding by the sea resulting in the formation of thin limestones and calcareous mudstones.

Luxuriant forest growth resulted in rich deposits of coal, and in ironstones, oil shales and fireclays. Volcanic activity formed the line of hills – the

Renfrewshire, Kilpatrick and Gargunnock Hills and the Campsie Fells – that now sweep around Glasgow from south to north. These volcanic rocks are relatively hard and so have persisted through subsequent episodes of erosion.

The period to around 250 million years ago was one of sand deserts and further volcanic activity, when the marine / estuarine environment changed to a continental one. Volcanic and wind-borne deposits of this period probably extended across much of the Midland Valley, but subsequent erosion has left only isolated examples. Geological features of the period from around 250 to two million years ago are also largely absent from the Glasgow area because of the erosion of existing deposits by the glaciers of the period from around two million to 10,000 years ago. This period saw a sequence of at least six major cold intervals, interspersed with warmer periods when the ice melted and retreated. The visible effects of glaciation in the Glasgow area today derive mostly from the last cold stage and we live today in the subsequent post-glacial era.

The last cold period began between 125,000 and 70,000 years ago and ended about 10,000 years ago. Massive ice sheets spread into the Midland Valley from the Highlands and Southern Uplands, eventually submerging the entire region beneath a cover of ice between 1.5 and 1.8km thick. Climatic amelioration caused the ice to melt and the Valley was largely free of ice by around 13,000 years ago. However, an ensuing climatic deterioration between about 11,000 and 10,300 years ago resulted in the re-formation of the ice sheets. This time the ice sheets only extended a limited distance beyond the margins of the Midland Valley and certainly not as far as Govan. This final stage of glaciation was brought to an end by rapid improvement of the climate around 10,000 years ago.

Erosion by the ice sheets and their associated melt-waters transformed the landscape, scouring and eroding the existing rocks and other deposits. Channels formed beneath the ice later filled with deposits of sand, gravel, clays and silts, and similar deposits were laid across most of the valley floor. The more resistant of the older rocks project through this mantle of glacial till as hills and mountains. In places, the till was formed into low, pear-shaped mounds, known as drumlins, and these are a prominent feature of the Glasgow townscape today, with examples near Govan at Yorkhill and Partickhill.

At the end of the last glaciation there was no sharp and simple change from glacial to present-day conditions and several thousand years of further changes to the physical landscape ensued. With glaciation, worldwide sea level dropped to at least 100m below its present level and the landmass was depressed by the weight of the ice. As the ice melted, sea levels rose substantially and the land rebounded. In the Glasgow area, the combined effect of these processes was a sequence of episodes in which the land was submerged beneath the sea, resulting in the creation of now-raised fossil beaches and the deposition of water-borne sediments.

Between about 13,000 and 11,000 years ago, one of these marine transgressions formed fossilised shorelines nearby at Anniesland and Jordanhill. Marine and brackish-water clays, sands and silts were laid down. After this, the Glasgow area was submerged by a greater marine transgression which reached its maximum extent around 6500 years ago, and which has left various higher fossil beaches relating to the rising and falling water levels. Silt and sand deposits from this time occupy the low carse lands bordering the Clyde and account for the very flat, low-lying ground on the river fringes in and around Glasgow – the topography of Govan is a case in point. As the climate improved, the area was also gradually colonised by woodland. A climatic optimum was reached between around 5000 and 3000 years ago, and conditions have since become cooler and wetter.

A key feature of the post-glacial landscape, and one of signal importance in the history of Govan and Glasgow, is the River Clyde. This has a catchment area of some 740 square miles (1916km^2) and a length approaching 100 miles (160km) from its source in the Southern Uplands. River becomes estuary just upstream of Glasgow and transforms into the Firth as the channel swings south by Greenock.

Initially, the Clyde drained from its source in the Southern Uplands through the Biggar Gap and into the Tweed to the south. At some point, and it is not known exactly when or how, the river broke the watershed near Biggar and took a new course to the west. A gap in the line of the volcanic Kilpatrick and Renfrewshire hills between Dumbarton and Langbank has allowed the river to pass out to the sea along its current line. Over the years, the river has silted up, and this process is still continuing with the transportation of between 50,000 and 200,000 tons of sediment downstream each year.

The waters of the Firth run to a great depth, with channels up to 90m deep. This deep water ends abruptly at the Tail of the Bank off Greenock, where the seabed swings suddenly upward. From Dumbarton upstream to Glasgow and beyond, the river was relatively shallow until recent times. As late as the eighteenth century, and prior to substantive efforts to deepen the river, a ford existed at Govan, where the low-water depth was as little as 0.4m (Riddell 1979, 22).

This, in broad outline, is the development of Govan's physical environment up to recent times. Understanding the character of this environment is important in understanding historic Govan. Two issues are expanded here to illustrate this point: the relationship of the town to the river, and the resources provided by the local and regional environment.

From its earliest historical period, Govan has developed in close association with the Clyde. The river formed a convenient transport route but not necessarily a barrier, given the presence of various fords. This route allowed

FIGURE 2.2
View of Govan from the
east by Joseph Swan (c 1824)
showing the semi-improved
character of the river before
steam-powered dredging and
straightening had canalised
the waterfront. River traffic
is carefully located so as not
to obscure the key features
of Govan: in the distance
the silk factory and the spire
of Govan Old, in front the
cottages at the end of Water
Row next to the ferry slip,
the ferry itself is setting out
from the north bank at Point
House. To the left Doomster
Hill can be glimpsed
through a gap in the foliage.
The gable of a two-storey
building peeks over the
summit

movement, but it also meant that Govan was strategically significant. The important early church at Govan was located close by the river at a fording point (**fig 2.2**), and across from the site of an important early royal estate at Partick. The early historic capital of Dumbarton lay a relatively short distance down the Clyde.

Govan, as a place, was not unique in both its access to the Clyde and the presence of a ford – until relatively recent times there were many such fording places across the river. What made the crossing at Govan particularly attractive was the confluence of the Clyde with the River Kelvin. Because the Kelvin is a substantial tributary, it deposits significant amounts of silt into the Clyde, which makes for a relatively shallow, dependable ford. In addition, the Kelvin valley was an important communication route in its own right. Although it is not navigable for a significant distance, the valley provides a useful land route.

These geographical factors had an influence on how people moved around and where they settled from prehistoric times. The Kelvin valley served as the principal overland route north during the Middle Ages and the significance of the fording point at Govan is evident as far back as the earliest mention of the place in AD 756, when a large Northumbrian and Pictish army chose to cross the Clyde at this point after an assault on Dumbarton, suggesting that Govan was the first suitable crossing place to the east (see Chapter 3). As a consequence of being a place through which people moved, Govan may also have developed organically into a place where people gathered. What seems certain is that the River Clyde was not seen as a serious impediment to movement between the north and south shore, so that conceptually the two areas could be considered as one, as was the case with the medieval parish which embraced both banks of the Clyde (see **fig 3.9**).

The shallowness of the Clyde at Govan, which prevented large ships from navigating up river to this point, may also have had a positive influence on the development of the place. The numerous islands, such as White Inch and the King's Inch at Renfrew, and the sandbars will have made reaching the middle stretch of the Clyde hazardous for those unfamiliar with the river. During the Viking Age (AD 800–1000), the difficulties of navigation may have provided a welcome degree of security for Govan and may go some way to explain its emergence as an important centre at that time.

In due course, however, the shallowness of the river also became an obstacle to be overcome. In more recent times, the Clyde became synonymous with the commercial and industrial development of Govan, and of wider Glasgow. In particular, Govan was characterised by its prominent place in the shipbuilding industry. The relationship of town and river at this time, however, was not straightforward. The shallow depth of the Clyde limited the size of vessel that could navigate to and from Glasgow and numerous schemes were developed to 'improve' the river (see Riddell 1979). The first known attempt to deepen the river occurred in 1556, when the towns of Renfrew, Dumbarton and Glasgow each supplied labour for a six-week attack on a major shoal at Dumbuck (*ibid*, 8). This met with little success, and a century later Cromwell's commissioner, Thomas Tucker, recorded that no vessel of any size could venture upstream of Dumbuck. Increased efforts to deepen the Clyde commenced in the later eighteenth century and gradually transformed it into the river we know today. These deepening efforts allowed the passage of the increasingly massive ships built in Govan's yards.

Just as the industrialisation of Govan and Glasgow was accompanied by the transformation of the river, it also transformed the rocks and other natural features of the region into economic resources (see, for example, Loudon *et al* 1958, 141–9). Industrial production was fuelled at first by waterpower, and then by coal derived from the rich coal seams of the Midland Valley. Coal was mined as close to Govan as Drumoyne. Iron deposits were processed to provide the materials for industrial manufacture. Limestone was used to increase the productivity of the fields, helping to feed the growing urban population. Other raw materials, like cotton from the Americas or silk, were brought in via the Clyde to supply the developing textile industries.

Govan's built heritage must also, in part, be understood with reference to the resources to hand in the surrounding natural environment (see Lawson 1990). Until the relatively recent deepening of the Clyde, there were no easy means of transport for bulky, low-value building materials. Even with the period of river engineering, local building materials remained significant until the coming of the railways in the mid-nineteenth century.

From these considerations and from what we know through archaeological excavation in Scotland's other medieval towns, it is likely that many of Govan's early buildings were constructed from impermanent local materials such as turf, wood or clay. More enduring materials could be quarried from local rocks, and sandstone has been of particular value in the Glasgow area. Sandstone quarries are known to have existed as near to Govan as Partick Bridge, Kelvingrove, Dowanhill and other sites just across the river on its north bank. Local clays were used in brick manufacture and, although brick was used in many buildings, its presence is often not immediately apparent, as there has been a preference for the use of stone for the externally visible parts of buildings. Many other local materials, such as the abundant sands and gravels, will also have gone into the building of Govan. However, these very sands and gravels also sometimes posed a problem, hindering the excavation of some of the Clyde's docks and shipyards (Gilfillan 1958, 25).

Before Govan: prehistory and earliest history

If this, in outline, is the environmental background to Govan's development, what then was the background of human occupation of the Govan area before the foundation of the town? At present, the patchy nature of the evidence means this can only be discussed in a superficial way and with reference to finds and sites outwith, but reasonably close to, the present area of study.

Evidence for a human presence in Scotland is mainly confined to the post-glacial period. Thus, at Govan as elsewhere, the potential evidence of human activity relates to the period of the last 10,000 or so years, and certainly extends back no farther than 13,000 years ago. This is the potential, but centuries of agricultural activity followed by urbanisation and industrialisation have had a significant adverse effect on the survival of any early archaeological features and deposits. As the evidence we have consists largely of stray finds of objects forming no coherent sequence, we can arrive at no continuous narrative for this long period. All that will be attempted here is a brief overview of what has been found (**fig 2.3**).

In 1851, a dugout canoe was unearthed on the north side of the Clyde, just west of its confluence with the Kelvin (Buchanan 1855, 44; Duncan 1883, 122; Mowat 1996, 40, 110, 120, 133, no. 62). The find was made during work with an excavating machine within the Meadowside shipyard, which had been established some four years earlier. This canoe is just one of a large number that have been found along and inland from the Clyde, in and around Glasgow. One of the first recorded discoveries was encountered at a depth of *c* 7.5m below the ground surface when the foundations of St Enoch's church were excavated in 1780 (Duncan 1883, 121). This find lay some 150m back from the present riverbank (Mowat 1996, 40). More canoes were found in the

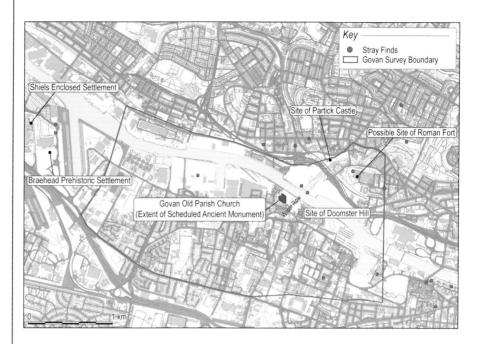

centre of the city, in the late eighteenth and early nineteenth centuries as far from the river as Drygate just south of the cathedral (Duncan 1883, 121–2).

Excavations associated with the construction of shipyards and docks along the Clyde, and with the deepening of the river, produced numerous further examples of such vessels in the mid- to late nineteenth century, and some examples emerged in the twentieth century (see Mowat 1996, 120). The character of each of these boats differs, and some may be of greater antiquity than others. At least some of the Clyde logboats are 5000 years old. A number have been found in deep deposits laid down when the area was submerged by the sea. Others have been found on terraces far back from the present river, suggesting they too were deposited at a time when water coverage was far greater.

Our first evidence of people actually living on the lands bordering the Clyde in the Govan area comes indirectly through a further series of stray finds. These include several stone and bronze axe heads and a number of pottery vessels and fragments of pots, sometimes accompanied by pieces of bone, representing cremation burials. A stone 'hammer' found on the banks of the Clyde at Linthouse was exhibited at the Glasgow International Exhibition of 1901 (Glasgow International Exhibition 1901, 21). Stone axe heads have been found nearby at Shiels, Shields Road, and the Kingston and Princes Docks (Roe 1966, 242, no. 395; 1967, 78, no. 130; Clough and Cummins 1988, 237–8, nos LNK 11 and LNK 30; Glasgow International Exhibition 1888, 22; Mitchell and Anderson 1890, 4, 5). It is normally assumed that such stone axes date to the Neolithic period, from c 4000 to 2000 BC (Ashmore 1996, 92). The finer examples are likely to have been more than just tools, perhaps holding some form of symbolic significance or ceremonial purpose. Unfortunately, we do not know if any of these examples were deliberately buried or discarded in special circumstances.

A bronze axe has also been discovered relatively close to Govan, in the Clyde at York Street Ferry (Coles 1960, 70; Henderson 1938, 170, no. 201; Schmidt and Burgess 1981, 198, no. 1163). This is of late Bronze Age date, the Bronze Age commonly referring to the period between *c* 2000 and 500 BC. Most weapons of this period in Scotland have been found in rivers, lochs or boggy areas, and it seems that there was some form of religious or ritual practice that involved throwing metal objects into watery places (Ashmore 1996, 116). The fact that the York Street bronze axe came from the river may suggest that it was deposited in this way.

For most of these stray finds, we have no information on the activities that led to their deposition. Several prehistoric pots with associated materials, discovered in the nineteenth century, have a more certain interpretation – as containers for human burials. Several pottery vessels, including a Beaker, two food vessels and a collared urn, the last containing cremated bones and a stone axe, were found in 1886 during quarrying works in Victoria Park (Clarke 1970, 519, no. 1703; Clough and Cummins 1988, 238, no. LNK 32; Longworth 1984, 310, no. 1959; Morrison 1968, 119; Ritchie 1970, 143, 146; Ritchie and Shepherd 1973, 24; Roe 1966, 242, no. 396; Roe 1967, 78). The pottery types associated with this group of artefacts span the entirety of the Bronze Age, a period of over 1000 years. There are a few other examples of discoveries where the descriptions of the pottery are less precise, but which nonetheless also probably date to the Bronze Age. Of particular note here are an urn found while digging the foundations of Springfield Quay in 1877 and several urns found on Gilmorehill in 1832 (Anderson and Black 1888, 351; Glasgow International Exhibition 1888, 24; 1901, 25; Mitchell and Anderson 1890, 10; Roger 1857, 216).

Despite this wealth of finds we have no evidence from Govan or its immediate area about the character of settlement in the Bronze Age, or indeed earlier. For the Iron Age, from approximately 750 BC to the Roman presence in the early centuries AD, the excavations at Shiels and Braehead tell us a great deal. Neither of these sites was visible on the ground surface, but the fact that significant archaeological remains lay below ground was identified from cropmarks appearing on aerial photographs. The cropmarks at Shiels represented an Iron Age settlement, comprising a single, circular enclosure ditch with several roundhouses inside (Scott 1996). The excavator suggested that the site had seen reuse in the medieval period. At nearby Braehead, three large ditches, numerous palisades and a sequence of structures, some of which were certainly houses, represented the remains of an Iron Age settlement whose form had been altered several times (Ellis 2000; 2001). To the south is a circular earthwork in the North Woods of Pollok Park, which survives as a prominent bank and ditch enclosing a relatively small area (20 by 15m), capable of containing no more than two or three roundhouses. It has been investigated on two occasions by the Glasgow Archaeological Society (Johnson 1959, 1960; Driscoll and Mitchell 2008), but at the time of writing there are no scientific dates so it is tentatively dated to the Iron Age on the basis of the scant artefacts and the form of the monument.

The evidence for the Roman period, the first and second centuries AD, is similar to that for earlier periods in that it consists largely of stray finds. Roman coins have been found at various times in Govan and along the Clyde. Some of these are likely to have been lost from modern collections, and so do not tell us much about any actual Roman presence in the past. Others may well have been deposited in the first or second centuries AD, but for most finds we do not know the circumstances of deposition.

One exception to this is a possible Roman fort on Yorkhill, directly across the Clyde from Govan (see Hanson 1980, 63–4; Napier 1873, 1–5). There is a tradition of an earthwork there and finds including Roman pottery, glass and coins have been recovered from the site (Buchanan 1877, 257). Topographically, Yorkhill is a good location for a fort, being relatively high ground overlooking the Clyde at its confluence with the Kelvin and at a point where the river was fordable until relatively recent times (Buchanan 1877, 256). A first-century Roman coin has also been found nearby at Partick (Macdonald 1918, 244). This all makes Yorkhill a candidate for the site of a Roman fort, although it can be debated whether or not this is to be ascribed to the first-century campaigns of the general Agricola or occupation in the second century, at the time of the Antonine Wall, which runs nearby to the north of Glasgow and through Bearsden.

Given the present sketchy understanding we have of the prehistory and earliest history of the Govan area, there can be little coherent discussion of this long period. However, a few important points are worth drawing out. What evidence there is highlights that the Govan area represented an attractive locale for several millennia before the development of the town. The Clyde estuary and its carse lands would have provided significant resources in fishing and farming. The river probably also facilitated transport and communication along its length but, being fordable at this point, it was not an impediment to movement across it. The Govan area had strategic importance for this reason.

The fact that many of the archaeological discoveries were made in the nineteenth century during major engineering works gives an indication of the massive transformation of the environment in the industrial period – processes discussed in depth in Chapter 5. Added to this, the processes of industrialisation and urbanisation have also had a significant impact on the survival of archaeological remains and buildings dating from the earlier centuries of the town itself. But this does not mean that there is no potential for the survival of important archaeological remains from early periods – indeed, a few discoveries of such remains have recently been made, as will be discussed in the following chapters.

Sources

Throughout *Historic Govan*, discussion is channelled by the nature of the available sources, which primarily consist of documents, maps, and archaeological remains.

Documentary sources

Medieval documentation is limited. As discussed in more detail in the next chapter, the earliest reference to Govan (as *Ovania*) has recently been noted in *Historia Regnum Anglorum* as an incidental detail within an account of an assault by the combined Northumbrian and Pictish armies on Dumbarton in AD 756 (Breeze 1999). The author of this account, Simeon of Durham, was a Northumbrian monk who utilised contemporary records including sources with first-hand knowledge of the geography of the northern British people, possibly drawing upon a Pictish source (Forsyth 2000, 29–31), so the account is considered highly reliable. By the eighth century, there is archaeological evidence for the presence of a church at Govan, but we may suppose that Govan was mentioned primarily because it was a good place for a large army to cross the Clyde.

The next reference to any part of the parish of Govan appears to be in the *Vita Kentigerni* (Life of Kentigern), where it is stated that King Rederech (Rydderch Hael of Dumbarton) died in the royal *vill* of Pertnech (Partick) (Forbes 1874, 118, chapter xlv). Although the *Vita*, by Jocelin of Furness, was written in the last quarter of the twelfth century, the chapter which mentions Rydderch's death contains Brittonic forms of names; this information could therefore go back to a Life of Kentigern written as early as the late seventh or early eighth century in the ancient British tongue (Macquarrie 1997, 133, 135, 137).

The *Inquisitio David*, the survey of the lands of the church of Glasgow made between 1114 and 1124 at the instigation of the future King David I, makes no mention of Govan or Partick, for they were still in royal hands (Barrow 1999, 60–1, no. 15). David, with his son Earl Henry, granted Govan with its bounds to Glasgow Cathedral between 1128 and 1136, in an 'exasperatingly laconic' act which makes no mention of the church (*ibid*, 17, 72, no. 34). Also granted to the cathedral, in 1136, was that part of Partick that Archdeacon Ascelin held of David and which had formerly been royal demesne (ie estates); these lands were to remain with the cathedral after Ascelin's death (*ibid*, 80–1, no. 56). Bishop Herbert (1147 x 1164) created a prebend in the cathedral for

Helya, his clerk, from Govan parish, the land in Partick given by King David I, and the islands lying between Govan and Partick (Innes 1843, 11, no. 7).

Thereafter, until the sixteenth century, there are only scattered references to Govan parish, most of which are printed in the collections of documents *Charters and other documents relating to the City of Glasgow* (Marwick and Renwick 1894–1906) and *Registrum Episcopatus Glasguensis* (Innes 1843). These are: an act of Robert Bruce, Earl of Carrick, on behalf of himself and John Comyn as Guardians (1298), and an act of Bishop William Rae (1342), both dated at Govan; and an act of Maurice, Lord of Luss (1277) and an act of Bishop Robert Wishart (1297), both given at Partick. An agreement between Bishop Rae and his chapter (1362) refers to the bishop's *manerium* at Partick (Innes 1832, 204; 1843, volume 1, 191–2, 251, 265–70, nos 229, 287, 299, 300; Simpson 1960, 64, no. 415). Bishop John (either Lindsay or Wishart, 1329 x 1337) granted half of his land of Little Govan (ie the Gorbals) to Polmadie hospital, and in 1485 there occurs the first reference to St Ninian's hospital near the southern end of Glasgow Bridge, and thus in Govan parish (Innes 1843, volume 1, 229, no. 269; Marwick and Renwick 1894–1906, volume 2, 465–7). The *Auchinleck Chronicle* records a major flood in 1454, which destroyed houses, barns and mills, and forced the inhabitants of Govan to sit on the roofs of their houses (printed in MacGladdery 1990, 163–4). The Protocol Book of Mr Cuthbert Simon (1499–1510) has a few references to Govan, including a note that a ship might be brought up river as far as the ford there (Bain and Rogers 1875, volume 1, 375–6, no. 233). More plentiful evidence, if of a specialised nature, becomes available with the Rental Book of the archbishops of Glasgow, 1509–70 (Bain and Rogers 1875). The list of those in the Regality of Glasgow who paid rent to the archbishop provides the first known names of the inhabitants of the parish of Govan, including well-known names such as Rowand and Maxwell of Pollok, and the earliest reference to a fulling mill in Partick in 1517 (*ibid*, 174).

For the period from the sixteenth to early nineteenth centuries, the records of Glasgow contain some references to Govan church, the chaplain's manse, houses, mills, paths, some of the lands and landowners, and occupations such as brewing and fishing (Marwick and Renwick 1876–1916; 1894–1906; Renwick 1894–1900). Most evidence relates to Partick, however, as the City owned the mill there. Hence there is information on hiring millers, the state of the mill and associated buildings, disputes with other mill-owners, the supply of water, and roads and bridges between Glasgow and Partick.

The contract for the rebuilding of Partick Castle in 1611 survives and gives a detailed account of its structure (reproduced in MacGibbon and Ross 1892, 5–8 and Napier 1873, 23–9; commentary in McKean 2001, 68–9). The *Statistical Accounts* of the 1790s and 1845 give descriptions of Govan parish before industrialisation altered it radically and when it was in a state of transition (Leishman 1845; Pollock 1973). From the 1845 account, agriculture and handloom weaving were evidently still important, but a silk throwing factory (a powerloom factory), canals and a toll-bar are evidence that change had begun. The printed muniments of the family of Maxwell of Pollok cover the period from *c* 1200 to the later nineteenth century, but most of those relating to Govan parish are post-Reformation in date (Fraser 1863; 1875). They contain important information on land and landholding, and on personal and territorial names both south and north of the Clyde. Other sources relating to landholding and population include: the 1691 hearth tax returns for Lanarkshire, which allow the first approximation of the size of the population (Adamson 1981, 103); Webster's census of 1755 (Kyd 1975, 30); the archbishop of Glasgow's rental of the Barony of Glasgow, covering 1515–68 (Bain and Rogers 1875, volume 1, 72–194); and other Glasgow records (Marwick and Renwick 1894–1906; Renwick 1894–1900).

Records peculiar to Govan itself include the minutes of the kirk session (Glasgow City Archives, Mitchell Library CH2/1277/1–5). The earliest surviving volume covers 1651 to 1662, and the next four volumes cover 1710 to 1821. The session dealt mainly with moral discipline: censure of and fines for adultery, fornication and irregular marriages. Entries also cover the state of the poor and the care of orphans, such entries being more numerous for the late eighteenth and early nineteenth centuries. Attempts were made to board out such children, at the parish's expense but not always in the parish, and to apprentice boys of a suitable age to a trade (invariably weaving and, again, not always in the parish). There are occasional references to schools and the schoolmaster (the latter also usually the session clerk), and to the weather and the harvest. National and international events hardly impinge on these records, but examples of those that do include the Jacobite risings and the Battle of Waterloo; collections noted include one to build a Protestant church and schoolhouse in Breslau. The French Revolutionary and Napoleonic Wars are reflected in references to the wives and widows of servicemen and to the high price of provisions. The hardships are also shown by a petition from twelve weavers asking to be put on the poor roll of the parish because trade was so bad.

Of the separate cash books for the poor fund only one, covering 1703 to 1727, survives (Glasgow City Archives, Mitchell Library CH2/1277/10). The first few leaves record collections made at the church door; then there are lists of payments to named recipients. A few additional details include the salary of the schoolmaster of Partick and the purchase of bibles.

The Govan heritors' records begin in 1791 and are held by the National Archives of Scotland (series HR). The heritors' responsibilities included the church building, the school, and the care of the poor. These records can be used to supplement the kirk session minutes: the heritors' response to the weavers' petition of 1816 was to authorise a subscription for the weavers but also to criticise their lack of thrift and 'to recommend industry, good management and careful economy to the operative classes' (Cage 1981, 131).

The records of the Govan Weavers' Society begin in 1756, when the society was founded, and are held by the University of Glasgow Archives (archive ref. DC 52). The weavers' records begin with the first meeting of the society and deal with regulations, election of officials, admission of members, and payments to widows and families of members, membership in 1772 being restricted to those in the parish (Brotchie 1905, 138–57).

A certain amount of research has taken place into the history of Govan from the mid-nineteenth century, though virtually nothing has previously been published on the development of the Burgh between its inception in 1864 and its annexation to Glasgow in 1912. Brotchie's *History of Govan* (1905), for all its detail, is an assertively 'booster' history of Govan, written from an anti-annexationist point of view. It is heavily influenced by the majority views of the pre-1912 burgh commissioners. Brotchie perpetuates a nostalgia about 'independent' Govan, which is not borne out by the reality of considerable working class support for the Glasgow connection. More research on politics and power in Govan, on the role of women in the community, and other subjects in this period is urgently required. Up until 1912, Govan's history is distinctly blurred, because it was not technically part of Glasgow and so fell outside the remit of the city's historians. Yet many historians still assume that it was part of Glasgow, and it is thus uncomfortably tied to the Glasgow story.

Map sources

The earliest map showing Govan is that of Timothy Pont in the late sixteenth century (**figs 2.4 & 2.5**). Though stylised and lacking in detail, these give a valuable early depiction of the village stretching east from the church that accords well with later, more detailed sources. Pont also gives an indication of the state of the Clyde at that time, yet to undergo serious deepening works and still populated by small islands like White Inch. Partick Bridge is shown, as are the town of Partick itself and Partick Castle. Most of the available seventeenth-century maps, including Blaeu's *Atlas Novus* and those of Adair and Gordon, are derivatives of Pont's work.

The first detailed map of Govan is the *Military Survey of Scotland*, undertaken in the wake of the 1745 Jacobite rebellion under the leadership of General William Roy from 1747 to 1755 (**fig 2.6**). In comparison with earlier maps of the area the Roy map is by far the most detailed, accurate and precisely recorded cartographic survey. Roy's positioning of key elements of the village, such as roadways, major land divisions and larger buildings, holds up well when compared with the Ordnance Survey first edition of the 1850s, surveyed a hundred years later. However, Roy's map has obvious flaws, and caution must be exercised when examining the village in detail and attempting

to identify specific features. The purpose and historical context of the survey must always be borne in mind, and while Govan has long been a strategic point for fording the river, it is unlikely to have been considered a key military interest, perhaps resulting in a more rapid and therefore inaccurate survey.

The Roy map shows the morphology of the town clearly and the surrounding countryside in sufficient detail to allow the distinction to be made between enclosed farmland and the town commons. The majority of buildings are strung out along Main Street (which became Govan Road after the merger with Glasgow in 1912) in a roughly east–west arrangement, echoing Pont. Enclosed backlands are shown at the rear of most of these buildings. This map is of particular use for locating Doomster Hill and Partick Castle.

Numerous other maps were produced in the later eighteenth and nineteenth centuries (see Moore 1996 for an overview). Many of these are too stylised and general to be of any additional use, though examples like Thomas Richardson's *Map of the town of Glasgow & country seven miles around* of 1795 do give some useful information on the country estates surrounding Govan (**fig 2.7**). For the period between Roy's map and the OS first edition map (1857–58), cartographic sources for Govan are comparatively slight. While there was a flurry of cartographic activity during this period, the majority of maps were commissioned by, and focused on, the city of Glasgow. Many of these maps were incredibly detailed, but unfortunately few extended further west than Anderston, and when they did they contained only basic, heavily stylised information.

Ainslie's *Map of the County of Renfrew* (1800) (**fig 2.8**), Forrest's map of *The county of Lanark* (1816) (**fig 2.9**) and Thomson's *Map of Renfrewshire* (1820) are amongst the more detailed examples from this period, although even these maps are still sparse and impressionistic. Ainslie and Forrest both show Doomster Hill (named the 'Hillock' by Ainslie), but not in great detail. George Martin's *Map of the City of Glasgow* (1842) (**fig 2.10**) is the only reasonably accurate representation of the village published prior to the Ordnance Survey first edition map, and is critical for locating the site of Doomster Hill (see below).

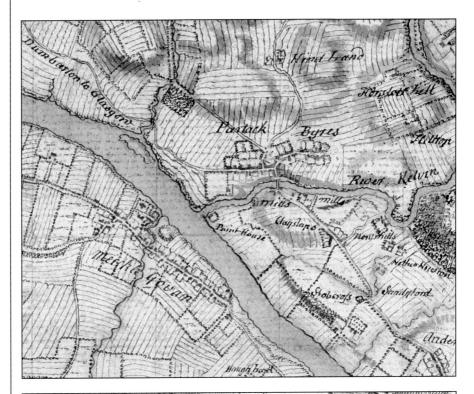

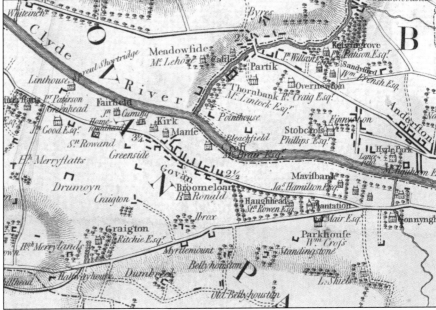

Of particular value are the early editions of the Ordnance Survey produced in the 1850s (first edition), 1890s (second edition) and the 1900s (third edition) (**figs 2.11, 2.12 & 2.13**). These maps were published at 1:10,560 scale, but the Ordnance Survey also produced more detailed Town Plans at 1:500 scale. The OS first edition shows Govan at the outset of industrialisation and

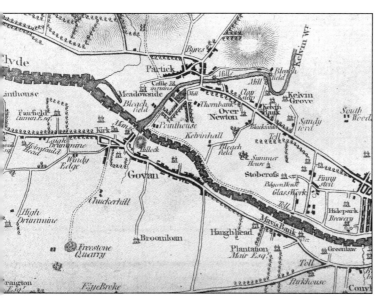

thus serves as a useful comparison with the Roy map in assessing the pre-industrial character of the town. The later editions are valuable for tracking the progress of industrialisation and urbanisation, and for identifying since-demolished buildings, industrial areas, and other features, but the pace of development was so rapid that significant changes took place in between surveys and therefore went unrecorded.

Despite the reliability of the Ordnance Survey, these maps have limitations as they were produced for a purpose and so lack detail in some areas. House plans are shown in some detail, but it is not easy to distinguish between different housing types. Public buildings are given most detail. Sanitation was a major reason for commissioning the first edition at 1:500 in urban areas and the maps give detail on this issue, identifying specific industries and even particular functions of buildings within a works and detailing water

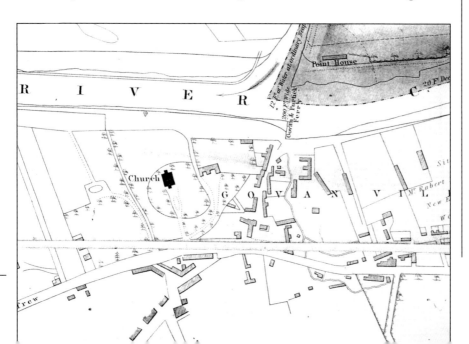

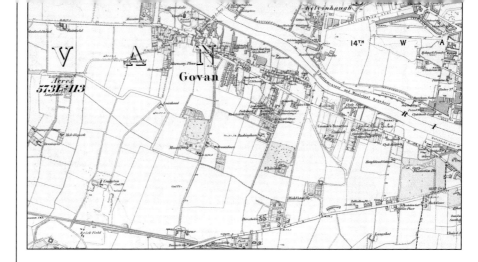

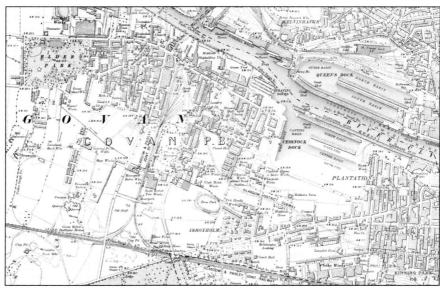

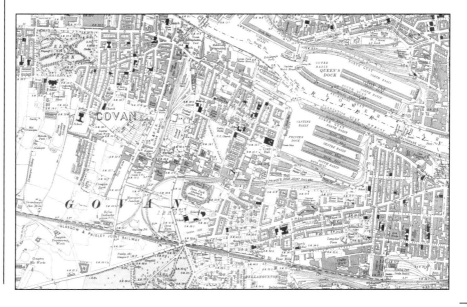

supply. Topography sadly is not indicated, so therefore Doomster Hill is not represented.

Detailed surveys of the Clyde before and during its transformation in the eighteenth and nineteenth centuries are held in the Clyde Port Authority archive in the Mitchell Library, Glasgow (**fig 2.14**), along with records of soundings and numerous other relevant reports and documents. The dykes projecting into the Clyde used to deepen the channel are a conspicuous feature of the early nineteenth-century maps (see **fig 2.8**) and the Roy map probably provides the last view of the unmodified course of the river.

A curious contribution to Govan's cartographic corpus is a map of the *Village of Govan* drawn by W D Barles in 1906 (**fig 2.15**). This map shows Govan as it was imagined to be in 1837 and supplies detailed information about the occupants and owners of various dwellings and buildings in the village, as well as showing old street names and street layout. The pictographic representations of many of the buildings appear to be fairly accurate. Barles's rendition of the three two-storey buildings at the north end of the west side of Water Row, the dye works and the area around Manse Lane corresponds reasonably well with contemporary illustrations and descriptions. The names of the residents and proprietors listed beside the buildings also appear to be accurate. While this is a useful comparative source, it cannot be relied upon, as we know little of its origins or how it was researched. It was apparently the product of antiquarian studies which were supported by the Old Govan Club, and may also have drawn on the memories of older Govan residents. The date of 1837 may also be telling; such a specific date would suggest the researchers drew on a primary source of this date, perhaps a valuation roll or parish records. The significance of the date 1837 is unknown.

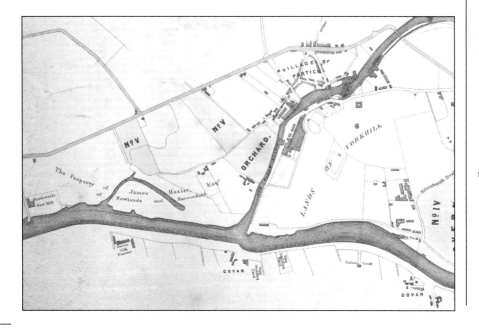

FIGURE 2.14
Kyle's survey of 1842 for the Clyde Navigation Survey not only provides fine-grained evidence for the course of the river during the period of its improvement but also included important topographical detail, such as the orchard which formed the grounds of Partick Castle (Reproduced by permission of the Mitchell Library, Glasgow)

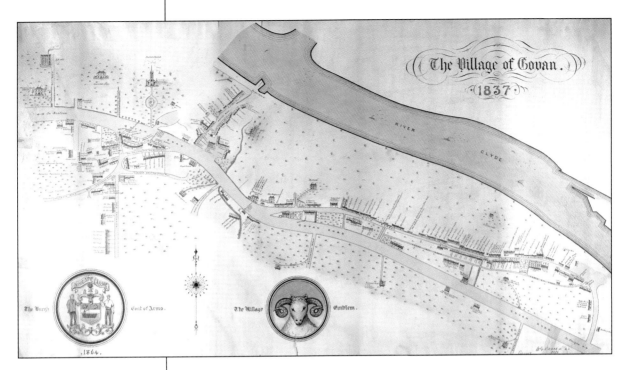

FIGURE 2.15
This map of the *Village of Govan* drawn by W D Barles in 1906 shows Govan as it was imagined to be in 1837. The detailed information about the various occupants and old street names is the product of antiquarian studies supported by the Old Govan Club (Courtesy of Govan Reminiscence Group and Govan Workplace Ltd)

Antiquarian and archaeological investigations

Antiquarian accounts of discoveries made in excavation works in the nineteenth and early twentieth centuries have proved useful in preparing this report. Govan spawned something of an industry in antiquarian description, illustration, and photography in the later nineteenth and early twentieth centuries, detailing now-lost buildings. In fact, almost all our information on the buildings of the pre-industrial town comes, at present, from these sources. The character of known and potential archaeological remains, historic buildings, and other built features is described in some detail in the following chapters.

Govan has seen limited, but informative, archaeological excavation in recent years, notably in and around Govan Old Parish Church and around Water Row (Cullen and Driscoll 1994; Driscoll 2003; Driscoll and Will 1996, 1997). Excavations were also undertaken by Helen Adamson (Glasgow Museums) in the 1970s to the south-east of Govan Old churchyard under the Manpower Services Scheme, but it has not been possible to locate records of these excavations. At a late stage in the preparation of this study Glasgow City Council sponsored an archaeological evaluation at Water Row (Driscoll, Will and Shearer 2008), the results of which have been incorporated.

3   Early historic and medieval Govan

Historical background

The early historic period (*c* AD 500–1118)

Although the origins of Govan can be traced back to the early historic period (sometimes described as the Dark Ages or early medieval period), the place is mentioned in relatively few medieval documents and none of these provides a narrative account. The linguistic form of the name Govan, however, provides important insights into the age and nature of the settlement. Despite the scant historical mention of Govan, it is clear that it was a place of some significance in the centuries prior to the foundation of Glasgow Cathedral in the twelfth century, a point reinforced by the large collection of sculpture from the pre-cathedral era housed in Govan Old Parish Church.

Place-names can be very revealing about the origins and character of a settlement and this is true for Govan. A folk etymology for Govan, based upon the Gaelic word for smith, *gobha*, has been widely circulated, but this interpretation is not supported by the earliest forms of the name found in the historical records associated with the creation of Glasgow Cathedral (eg *c* 1134, *Guuen*; Lawrie 1905, 82). An alternative derivation from the Gaelic *gobán* or 'promontory', proposed by Macquarrie (1994, 27), is also in conflict with the historical forms. Clancy (1996, 2–3) has argued that the name was coined when the local population still spoke a north British dialect (akin to Old Welsh). He proposes that the name incorporated two elements: *gwo-* /*go-*, meaning 'small' and *ban*, meaning 'hill', which he suggests refers to Doomster Hill. The identification of the settlement with its distinguishing feature – the great court hill (discussed below) – seems plausible given Govan's relatively flat topography. This coining of the name would mean that Doomster Hill had become the defining feature of the place before the British tongue was replaced by Gaelic. This linguistic change was probably underway in Strathclyde by the tenth century, although in the Glasgow area British speech probably survived a generation or so beyond the final collapse of the kingdom of Strathclyde at the end of the twelfth century (Broun 2004, 140; Taylor 2007, 2). If the identification of *Ovania* with Govan is correct (discussed above p.18), it would indicate that the hill was in existence by AD 756. A British origin for Govan's name is consistent with the recognised British linguistic origins for the name Partick, first recorded around 1150 as *Perthec* ('little grove'), and of course the name of Glasgow itself, which comes from the British for 'green hollow'.

Govan Old Church is dedicated to St Constantine (**fig 3.1**). This rare dedication should reveal something of Govan's origins, although there are

FIGURE 3.1
Aerial photograph of Govan
Old churchyard from the
north during the excavations
of 1994. The present church
(oriented south–north)
protrudes through the north
side of the ancient boundary

doubts as to the identity of the saint. Traditionally, he has been identified with a sixth-century saint-king known from south-western Britain and this is confidently proclaimed in the inscription on the plinth made to support the sarcophagus in the church. More recently Macquarrie has suggested that Govan's Constantine was an Irish martyr, commemorated in Kintyre, whose relics may have been moved to Govan for security during the Viking Age (1994, 31). There is no decisive evidence in support of either identification: the British possibility sits nicely with the overall British character of the region, while the Kintyre saint is geographically closer. Whatever the case, it is worth noting the popularity of the name Constantine amongst the early kings of Scotland, particularly those who claimed descent from the *Cenél nGabráin* dynasty of Dalriada. These royal associations are reinforced by the imperial aura of the original Constantine, the fourth-century Roman emperor, and must be borne in mind when considering the wider significance of Govan and its cemetery.

Stepping back to look at Govan's wider significance is difficult, because we know so little about northern British history. Although the kingdom of Strathclyde can claim to be the longest surviving British kingdom in the north, only a few of the kings are mentioned in contemporary historical records and there is little genealogical material to shed light on the composition of the ruling dynasty (Macquarrie 1993). The centuries after the destruction of Dumbarton by the Vikings in AD 870 are particularly obscure (Clancy 2006, 1818–21; Alcock and Alcock 1990). Despite the shortage of information, there has been no shortage of theories to explain the period leading up to the annexation of Strathclyde by the kings of Scots early in the twelfth century (Broun 2004). The most well-established narrative argues that during the political upheavals of the Viking Age (AD 800–1000) the northern British kingdom on the Clyde came to be dominated by Gaels (ie the Scots) and that it eventually was reduced to little more than a lordship held by the royal heir. Certainly David I (1124–53) was designated ruler (*princeps*) of the Cumbrians [ie British] prior to becoming king (Barrow 1999, no. 15), but the earlier political reality is much less tidy. Broun argues that, despite the assaults by Vikings and the continual presence of Hebridean Norse-Gaels (ie the Gall-Gaídil), there is every reason to suppose that a British kingdom survived until the 1060s (Broun 2004, 125–38). Thereafter it was conquered by the kings of Scots and its memory survived on in the guise of the diocese of Glasgow.

The medieval period (1118–1560)

The foundation of the See of Glasgow (between 1114 and 1118) had profound importance for the history of the west of Scotland, because the cathedral was the first institution to use writing on a large scale. Literacy was essential for the administration of the cathedral's vast holdings and a valuable tool for promoting interest in religious devotion, particularly activities associated with Glasgow's patron St Kentigern. Both the administrative and the devotional texts for Glasgow are important for the history of Govan.

It was common practice for medieval churches wishing to celebrate the accomplishments of their patron to produce biographical accounts of their saint. In the case of Glasgow, there are two different versions of the *Life of Kentigern* which survive from the twelfth century. These incorporate even earlier material which derives from a British source pre-dating the establishment of the cathedral (Macquarrie 1997, 117–44). The significant point for Govan is that this earlier stratum describes Partick as the royal *vill*, 'estate', of Rhydderch Hael, a well-attested seventh-century ruler of the kingdom of Dumbarton (Macquarrie 1993; 1997, 137).

The first contemporary historical notice relating to Govan is David I's grant of the lands of Govan to Glasgow Cathedral, made between 1128 and 1136 (Barrow 1999, 72): 'You are to know that I have given and granted to the church of St Mungo of Glasgu and to the bishopric of the same church Guven, with all its bounds'. Subsequently, Govan (including Partick) was made a prebendary of the cathedral by Bishop Herbert (1147–64). This in effect meant that the income from teinds (tithes) was channelled to support the household of the bishop (Davidson Kelly 1994b, 16). It also meant that the prebendary of Govan became a member of the cathedral chapter and had a manse in Glasgow, which lay immediately to the north of Provand's Lordship, while the work of the parish was undertaken by subordinates, a vicar and parish clerk.

FIGURE 3.2
(below and facing) The 'Sun Stone' is so-called because of its boss with spiralling snakes' heads (1.7m tall). On the reverse is an interlaced cross over a mounted warrior whose sword and spear are clearly visible. The top has been roughly shaped to accept a capping stone of some sort (now lost). The rough, irregular form of the cross-slab has led to the suggestion that it started out as a prehistoric standing stone (Stirling Maxwell 1899)

As a consequence of the loss of status following the establishment of the diocese, Govan rarely appears in medieval documents except in the context of activity associated with the business of the cathedral. In 1342, an episcopal act was issued from Govan and likewise, in 1362, an agreement between the bishop and chapter (Innes 1843 volume 1, nos 287, 299, 300). Exceptionally, in 1298 Govan was the setting for a meeting of national significance, when Robert Bruce issued an act on behalf of the Guardians of Scotland. Presumably Bruce had been staying in the Partick manor house of Bishop Robert Wishart, one of his most loyal supporters.

Archaeological evidence

Govan Old Parish Church and its sculpture

The oldest physical remains of medieval Govan are sculptured stones from the early Middle Ages which are preserved within Govan Old Parish Church. The assemblage of early historic sculpture known from Govan once consisted of 46 pieces, all of which were found in the churchyard. Unfortunately, sixteen stones have been 'lost' since first being recorded in the nineteenth century and they are presumed buried somewhere in the churchyard. Four of these sculpted stones come from upright crosses, only one of which, the 'Sun Stone' (**fig 3.2**), is complete. All of the remaining stones were burial monuments of one type or another and 27 are on display in the church today. All of these monuments are thought to date from between AD 900 and 1100, according to recent art-historical assessments (Ritchie 1994). In addition, one somewhat battered coffin-shaped gravestone of medieval date (possibly fifteenth century) remains outside in the churchyard.

Without question the most impressive monument is the unique monolithic sarcophagus (**fig 3.3**), the exterior of which is covered with interlace decoration and figurative panels. The most prominent scene displays a mounted warrior hunting, a symbolic motif which combines ideas of military prowess with the Christian quest for salvation. The elaborate decoration makes it clear that the sarcophagus was intended to be displayed prominently inside a church. Whether it was intended to hold the relics of a saint or the bones of a king is impossible to tell, but it is undoubtedly one of the most outstanding pieces of sculpture of its age.

The most substantial of the remaining burial monuments are the five so-called hogbacks, which are massive sandstone blocks carved to represent a house or a church with a pronounced curving roof ridge (**figs 3.4 & 3.5**). These monuments are found in areas of northern England settled by Vikings and on the southern Scottish mainland where there was a significant Norse presence. Together, the five Govan hogbacks form the largest known group in Scotland and include the largest such monument in Britain (Lang 1994). These

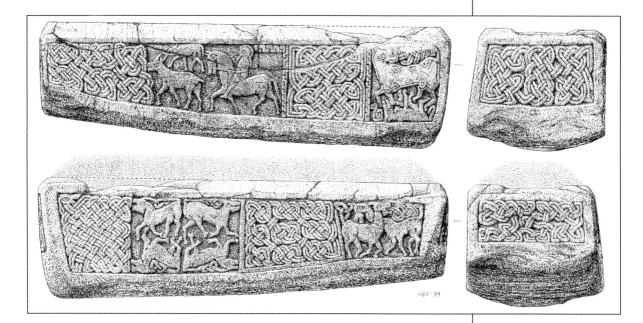

hogbacks may be dated to AD 925 to 1000 using art-historical criteria (Ritchie 2004), although interestingly two were subsequently modified suggesting that they remained active monuments for more than a single generation (*ibid*).

The largest group of burial monuments comprises recumbent slabs incised with interlace crosses, of which 38 are known to have existed (**fig 3.6**). Although these are part of a wider tradition of cross-slabs, the Govan type is highly distinctive and regionally specific. It appears to have been a long-lived tradition, perhaps having a currency from AD 900 to 1100 (Cramp 1994). Similar recumbent cross-slabs are found at only two other sites in Scotland, both on the Clyde and both with royal associations: Dumbarton Castle (two examples) and Inchinnan (two examples) (Driscoll, O'Grady and Forsyth 2005). These recumbent cross-slabs are now widely accepted as evidence of a major high-status cemetery at Govan. There is no external evidence to indicate whether these stones marked the graves of important churchmen or the secular elite. It is entirely possible that these monuments were used by both.

The four upstanding crosses, although executed to a high standard, are in some respects less impressive for being incomplete and in two cases heavily worn (**fig 3.7**). Three of these crosses survive only as shafts, yet the presence of four crosses in total is itself exceptional and underscores Govan's position as a major church.

This collection is one of the largest of early historic sculpture from Scotland. Iona and St Andrews have produced larger collections, but neither has as much material from the tenth and eleventh centuries as is known from Govan. The large quantity of burial monuments from Govan indicates a cemetery of considerable importance (**fig 3.8**). The size and quality of the hogbacks and the sarcophagus indicate patronage at the highest, probably

FIGURE 3.3
The Govan sarcophagus is cut from a single block of sandstone and ornamented with four figurative and six interlace panels. The elaboration of the carvings makes it clear that it was intended to be displayed inside Govan church. The main figurative panel features a mounted warrior, a stag and ?hound. The hunting motif is emphasised by the other panels populated by deer with fantastic antlers (Drawing by Ian Scott, Crown copyright: Royal Commission on the Ancient and Historical Monuments of Scotland)

FIGURE 3.4

(above left) Hogback no. 2, shown here on display in the church, is thought to be the earliest of the Govan hogback tomb stones, based upon the style of the decorative border. It dates to around AD 900 and may be the earliest of all the Govan sculpture (RCAHMS: Tom and Sybil Gray Collection, SC1137167)

FIGURE 3.5

(above right) Both ends of hogback no. 5, shown here on display in the church, are carved to resemble the decorative binding of church-shaped reliquary casket (RCAHMS: Tom and Sybil Gray Collection, SC1137181)

FIGURE 3.6

(far left) Recumbent cross-slab no.18 uses interlaced knotwork to highlight the cross in characteristic 'Govan School' fashion. Originally carved to mark a grave in the tenth or eleventh century, no. 18 has been reused on two occasions, first for R D in the seventeenth century and again in the eighteenth for William Bogle (RCAHMS: Tom and Sybil Gray Collection, SC1137236)

FIGURE 3.7

(left) The shaft of a finely executed freestanding cross, which has lost its head. Apart from the 'Sun Stone' this is the best preserved of the crosses (the shafts of the other two were used for grave stones and are much worn). It was given to James Smith of Jordanhill, who placed it in his garden where it stood for many years. Like the 'Sun Stone' and the sarcophagus, this cross features a mounted rider, which is has been carved with much less proficiency than the surrounding interlace panels (RCAHMS: Tom and Sybil Gray Collection, SC1137195)

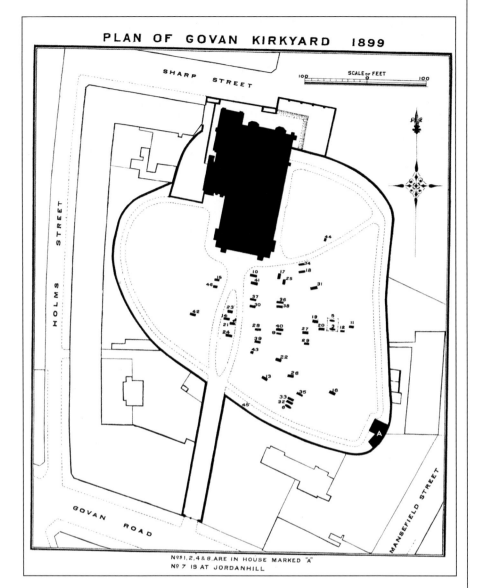

FIGURE 3.8
Plan of Govan Old
churchyard showing position
of sculptured stones in 1899
(Source: Stirling Maxwell
1899)

royal, level. There is an undeniable secular character to the sculpture, which
portrays the image of a mounted warrior on two of the upstanding crosses as
well as the sarcophagus. In recognition of the importance of these sculptures,
they are included on the Schedule of Ancient Monuments.

Although it is impossible to know precisely for whom this sculpture
was made, as there are no contemporary inscriptions, the sculpture of the
so-called 'Govan School' does reveal secular political influences (**fig 3.9**).
Current scholarly consensus is that the Govan assemblage is best accounted
for as evidence of a cemetery patronised by the kings of the Strathclyde
Britons. This observation has important implications for understanding the
royal associations of Doomster Hill and Partick Castle, which is explored
below.

Although it was the sculpture which first attracted antiquaries to Govan (Stuart 1856; Stirling Maxwell 1899; Allen 1902; Allen and Anderson 1903), in more recent times the archaeological significance of the churchyard itself has been recognised in a series of studies (Radford 1967a; Ritchie 1994). The curvilinear shape of the churchyard boundary wall is particularly suggestive, because round or oval churchyards are widely recognised as a sign of an ancient religious foundation in Scotland. The renewal of interest in Govan in the early 1990s inspired a programme of trial excavation in and around the churchyard between 1994 and 1996, which was intended to assess the archaeological integrity of the perimeter of the churchyard and its interior (**fig 3.10**) (Driscoll 1995; 1997; 2003). Although these excavations were too small to allow the site to be reconstructed in detail, they have confirmed the presence of an early historic cemetery and located the probable site of an early church, to the east of the existing one. Moreover, they have established that the entire churchyard contains deep archaeological deposits, which preserve evidence relating to every stage of Govan's development.

The earliest dating evidence comes from two burials oriented east–west (following Christian practice) found below the remains of a stone and

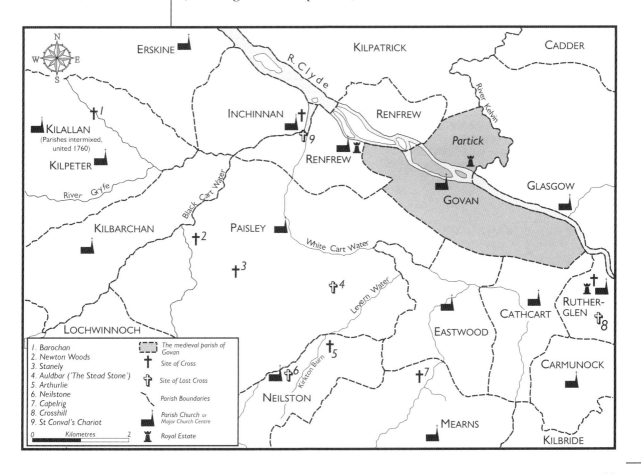

timber building, believed to have been a church. These graves have produced calibrated radiocarbon dates spanning the fifth to sixth centuries (samples GU-9024: AD 435–601 and GU-9025: AD 474–601). These are the earliest scientifically dated Christian burials in Strathclyde.

Fragments of a structure that are likely to represent a timber church with stone foundations were recovered in the 1994–96 excavations (**figs 3.11 & 3.12**), but too little was exposed to permit its form to be reconstructed. This church was replaced at some point in the Middle Ages by a stone-built church, which some have suggested was built in a Romanesque style, perhaps in the twelfth century. Although its form remains unknown, it appears to have stood on or near the site of the present church. Indeed, it is entirely possible that more than one stone church was erected during the medieval period. The first church about which any details are known was

FIGURE 3.10
Map showing the locations of the archaeological excavations, conducted 1994–2007, plotted against the 1st edition of the Ordnance Survey map (Based on OS mapping © crown copyright. All rights reserved Historic Scotland Licence No. 100017509 [2009])

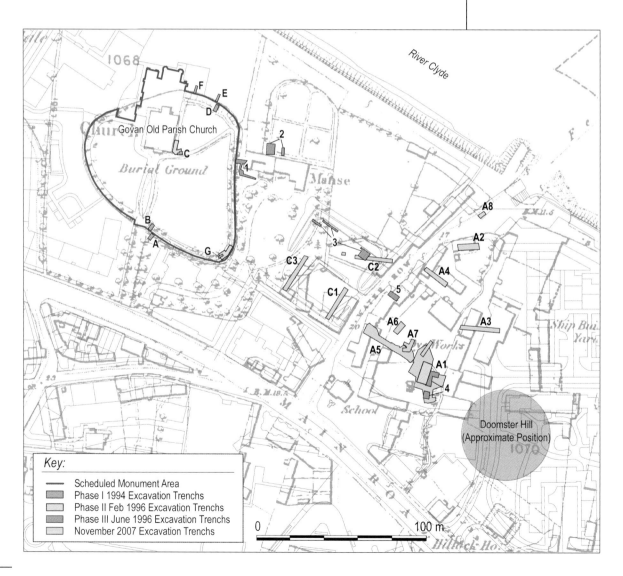

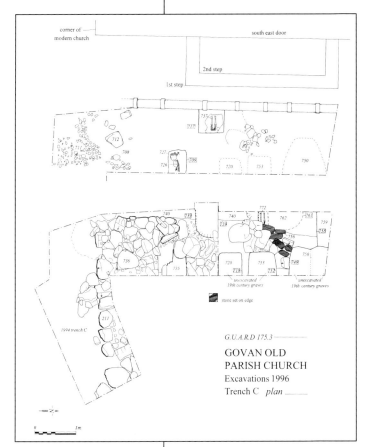

G.U.A.R.D 175.3

GOVAN OLD
PARISH CHURCH
Excavations 1996
Trench C plan

FIGURE 3.11
Plan of trench C showing the stone foundations interpreted as a church structure, 1996 (Source: GUARD)

FIGURE 3.12
View from the south of the massive drystone foundations of the possible church in trench C, 1996 (Source: GUARD)

erected in 1762 to replace the decrepit medieval structure. Archaeological evidence for the demolition of the medieval church, as well as for the demolition of the eighteenth-century one, was encountered in the 1994–96 excavations near the present church. A conjectural reconstruction of the sequence of churches known to have stood on the site was undertaken by Chris Jopson in 2001 (**fig 3.13**).

Apart from this trench outside the south-east corner of the existing church, investigations focused on the perimeter of the churchyard (**fig 3.14**). Traces of a dwelling or workshop near to the southern boundary included a hearth which has produced a calibrated date in the eighth or ninth century (GU-9021: AD 775–887). In the south-east of the churchyard, a metalled roadway was discovered that probably passed through the original entrance to the churchyard (**fig 3.15**). Charcoal incorporated in the metalled roadway produced a similar date range (GU-9022: AD 734–892). This roadway and lost entrance are important for understanding the relationship of the church to the wider settlement.

The excavations also confirmed that the elevated interior of the churchyard, which stands over 1.5m above the original ground level, was partially created by a large bank and ditch which formed the original churchyard boundary

700 - 1136

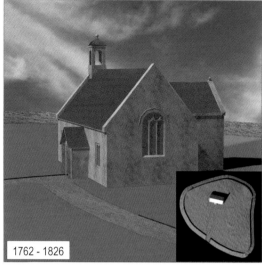

1762 - 1826

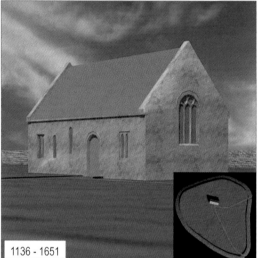

1136 - 1651

1826 - 1884

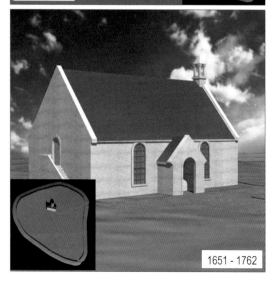

1651 - 1762

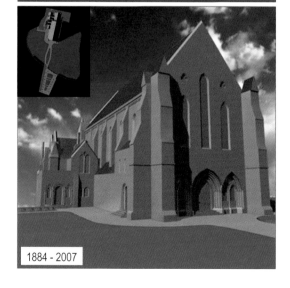

1884 - 2007

FIGURE 3.13

Sequence of medieval
churches at Govan as
reconstructed by Chris
Jopson as part of his
Glasgow School of Art
dissertation in 2001

(**fig 3.16**). This infilled ditch represents an important archaeological resource, because the accumulated fills contain artefacts and other material which has escaped disturbance from burials (in contrast to many areas of the interior of the churchyard). Charcoal recovered from the ditch fill has produced a calibrated date spanning the ninth to tenth centuries (GU-9023: AD 886–983) and discarded fragments indicate that shale jewellery was being manufactured here. This ditch was observed outside the modern churchyard wall on the south side and in two locations on the east, but could not be located in the two northern trenches. The ditch may not have extended to the river side of the church or it may have been eroded away. On balance, it is reasonable to conclude that the present churchyard preserves the sacred enclosure as laid out in the early historic period. However, because the infilled ditch runs outside

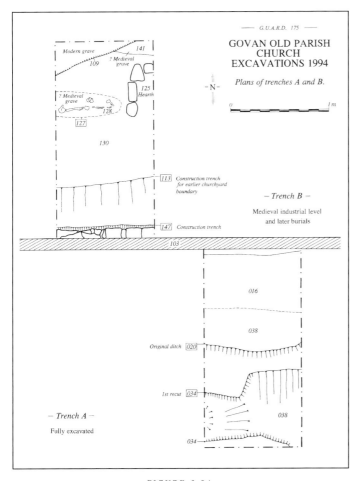

FIGURE 3.14

Plan of trenches A and B dug across the churchyard boundary (see fig 3.10). To the north, features such as a hearth indicate presence of a building within the enclosure, while outside of the wall the original boundary ditch was revealed, 1994 (Source: GUARD)

FIGURE 3.15

View of metalled road in south-east of churchyard, trench G, 1996
(Source: GUARD)

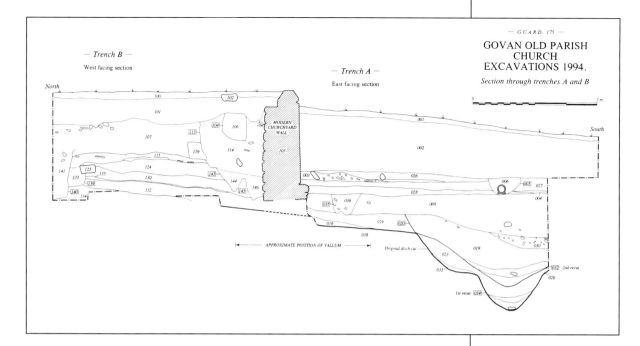

— Trench B —

West facing section

North

— Trench A —

East facing section

South

MODERN
CHURCHYARD
WALL

APPROXIMATE POSITION OF VALLUM

Original ditch cut

1st recut

2nd recut

the modern churchyard wall, it should be stressed that the archaeological deposits extend at least 5m *beyond* the modern boundary, which is outside the Scheduled Area.

Doomster Hill

Some 150m east of the churchyard stood a monument that provided a counterbalance to the religious centre. Until the mid-nineteenth century this flat-topped mound known as the Hillock or Doomster Hill loomed over the cottages of Water Row. Judging from its name and form it appears to have served as a court hill, that is, it served as a designated place where legal proceedings were conducted. It seems likely that the hill functioned more generally as place of popular assembly where all manner of public business might be conducted (elsewhere such monuments are known as moot hills). Unfortunately there is no contemporary medieval reference to Doomster Hill, but there are compelling post-medieval accounts which reveal its form and function, even if they do not reflect the monument's full importance. A critical assessment of these accounts already exists (Davidson Kelly 1994b, 1–18), which is complemented here by the archaeological excavations and more detailed map analysis.

Writing *c* 1795 for the *Statistical Account*, the Revd John Pollock noted that,

> In a bleachfield near to the village of Govan … there is an artificial mound of conical shape. Its perpendicular height is 17 feet. At the base, it is 150 feet in diameter, and at the top 102. It is commonly called the

FIGURE 3.16
Section cut across the churchyard boundary revealing the depth of deposits within the interior and the scale of the external ditch, trenches A and B, 1994 (Source: GUARD)

Hillock, and was probably one of the law hills upon which courts of justice used to be held in ancient times, which are to be met with in some other parts of Scotland. What chiefly favours this conjecture is, that the oldest people in the neighbourhood remember its being known by the name of Doomster Hill.

(Pollock 1973, 369).

By the time of the *New Statistical Account* the bleachfield had developed into a dye works and we are fortunate that the minister Revd Leishman had an interest in antiquities or we might not have such a clear report of excavations made into the hill.

This was the name [Doomster Hill] which was formerly given to a small circular hill on the south side of the Clyde, and immediately opposite the ferry-house. It is supposed to have been one of the law hills of the country. The utilitarian and the antiquary will be differently affected when they learn that a reservoir of the use of the adjoining dye-work has been formed on the top of this tumulus, or hillock, as it is called, in the oldest titles of the property. The depth of the reservoir is about 12 feet. The perpendicular height of the hill itself is about 17 feet, and the diameter of its base about 150 feet. When the reservoir was deepened a few years ago [in the 1830s], three or four rudely formed planks of black oak were dug out of it. Some small fragments of bones were likewise discovered, and a bed of what seemed to be decayed bulrushes. This proved the mound to be, at all events, an artificial one. And nothing forbids us to suppose that it may cover the ashes of some ancient hero, who now sleeps there unknown to fame.

(Leishman 1845, 690)

Leishman seems relatively well informed about prehistory, so this account must be taken at face value: there was apparently a burial chamber in the hill. One can only speculate on its age, however, and whether it was a primary feature. Not long after Leishman's account the mound was levelled either by the dye works or, more likely, when Old Govan shipyard took possession of the site in the 1850s.

Despite the hill's disappearance it is possible to reconstruct its appearance and location using contemporary figures and maps. While Pollock and Leishman's accounts agree as to the size of the mound (45m diameter and 5m high), these dimensions must be treated as approximations, not least because both fail to mention the prominent wide step or the massive ditch surrounding it. Both of these features are clearly visible in Robert Paul's engraving made in 1758, which also reveals how the massive hill dominated the houses of eighteenth-century Govan (**fig 3.17**).

The other important representation of Doomster Hill is found on the Roy map, surveyed soon after 1745. Here the mound is located in open ground by the river's edge north of Main Street, perhaps already in use as a bleachfield. The hill is of massive proportions (larger than the churchyard) but it is represented as a flat-topped oval without either step or ditch being represented (see **fig 2.6**). Interestingly the hill is shown almost twice as long as it is wide, with its long axis parallel with the river. If correct this could mean that the ministers' 150-foot diameter refers to the short axis, which would mean that the hill was something like 45 by 80m. Unfortunately, too few of the fixed points from Roy's day survive to allow it to be used to locate the site of Doomster Hill with precision.

This uncertainty has motivated a series of archaeological investigations beginning in the early 1990s to locate Doomster Hill with a view to obtaining a date for its construction and, more optimistically, to assess Leishman's report that it contained a burial. These excavations discovered a massive ditch in the waste ground/car park north of Govan New Parish Church (Driscoll and Will 1996, 15–17; Driscoll and Will 1997, 23–7), which was tentatively interpreted as the ditch shown in the Paul engraving. Reading the archaeological evidence was hindered by upwards of 2m of accumulated soil over the original ground surface, which had been generated by the demolition of the dye works, the shipyard, and a tenement block. Nevertheless, the massive scale of the ditch and the presence of fourteenth-century pottery encouraged the view that this was the site of Doomster Hill, although the ceramic dating was some centuries short of the expected construction date of *c* AD 900–1000.

In 2007 a larger archaeological evaluation was sponsored by Glasgow City Council as part of preparations for the redevelopment of the Water Row site. One of the main objectives of this evaluation (Driscoll *et al* 2008) was to locate Doomster Hill with greater confidence. The new archaeological evidence and more detailed examination of the map record have refined our understanding of the original location of Doomster Hill. The massive ditch was more completely exposed, making it clear that it was unlikely to have any relationship with Doomster Hill. Re-evaluation of the map evidence in the light of the excavations allows the site of Doomster Hill to be identified with greater certainty. Given the significance of the site for Govan's heritage the reasoning is presented in some detail.

The best visual record of Doomster Hill is provided in Robert Paul's *View of the banks of the Clyde taken from York Hill* (1758) which shows Doomster Hill as an enormous mound filling the space between the river and Main Street to the east of Water Row (**fig 3.17**). There are other, mid-nineteenth century, images representing Doomster Hill, but these post-date the dye works and provide no additional information about the form or location of the hill. The Paul engraving reveals two crucial details that are otherwise unknown. It shows that the mound was composed of two levels and that

FIGURE 3.17

'A view of the banks of
the Clyde taken from York
Hill' by Robert Paul, 1758.
Yorkhill on the north bank
now carries a hospital.
Dooomster Hill and Water
Row are on the left (Source:
Mitchell Library, Glasgow)

it was surrounded by a ditch, from which the mound had presumably been quarried. Unfortunately the perspective on this view is skewed, so it cannot be used to locate the mound with precision, although the visible landmarks allow the relative position of the mound to be established. The west side of Water Row and the ferry area can be clearly distinguished, with the Old Parish Church shown amongst trees to the west. Unfortunately, the east side of Water Row is more difficult to discern; the gable ends of buildings running perpendicular to the Main Street alignment can be seen to the west of the mound, but it is impossible to gauge where they are in relation to the rest of the street which is obscured by trees in the foreground.

The critical maps for locating the site of Doomster Hill are the Roy map (**fig 2.6**), Martin's map of 1842 (**fig 2.10**) and the OS first edition of 1857–58 (**fig 2.11**). Although the Roy map has too many internal contradictions to allow it to be transposed accurately onto the modern map, it provides valuable information, not least the indication that Doomster Hill might have been elongated rather than perfectly round (something that is yet to be verified). More importantly, with respect to its location, the Roy map clearly shows that the hill stood to the east of a burn that flowed parallel to Water Row and entered the Clyde around the ferry landing. The relationship to the burn is the key to locating its position.

While Doomster Hill remained of some interest to antiquaries in the mid-nineteenth century, such as Revd Leishman, surveyors stopped indicating its presence from the 1840s. The otherwise exemplary mid-nineteenth-century maps by Martin (1842) and the Ordnance Survey do not provide any topographic information nor do they label the hill, so the position must be identified with respect to the positions of buildings associated with the dye works and the burn. Roy's map shows a pronounced crook in the burn as it passes the west side of the mound, which pre-dates the major modifications that the burn underwent in the nineteenth century. Over time the burn was straightened and gradually disappeared from maps (and memory) as it was culverted. The most detailed representation of the burn is found on Martin's map (**fig 2.10**), which shows two branches flowing from the east and joining as it heads north towards the Clyde. It seems that the crook shown by Roy is still visible as a less pronounced bend between the 'V' and 'A' of the label 'GOVAN'.

FIGURE 3.18
The excavation searching
Doomster Hill in 1996. The
site is now believed to have
stood under Napier Street,
beyond the Land Rover

The burn was utilised and modified by the dye works, and it is most likely the expansion and development of the dye works which heralds the demise of Doomster Hill. The dye works shown on Martin's map consists of four buildings on the east side of the burn – the most conspicuous as an E-shaped one near the river – scattered across the premises. This small-scale works could happily accommodate Doomster Hill and even capitalise on its height to provide water pressure. By the time of the OS first edition (1857–58), however, the works had greatly expanded and the mound may have become an inconvenience.

Since the hill itself is not named, Doomster Hill must be located by identifying the reservoir mentioned by Leishman. The Martin map does not even name the dye works, but by working back from the OS first edition one can identify it and recognise that in 1842 the dye works was confined to the east of the burn. The legend 'Dye Works' on the first edition Ordnance Survey 1:500 scale map straddles the burn, because by 1857–58 the works had expanded west across the burn, which was now partially culverted. Unfortunately none of the dye works buildings are labelled, so identification of the reservoir cannot be certain.

Looking to the east of the burn on the Martin map, the mostly likely reservoir is a large squarish building (approximately 10 by 12m) surrounded by considerable open ground, which could comfortably have accommodated a mound the scale of Doomster Hill. This identification is reinforced by the position of 'Hillock House', constructed some time between Martin's survey and the OS first edition 1:500 scale map by the owner of the dye works. Pollock and Leishman report that Doomster Hill was known locally as the 'Hillock' by Govan folk and it is labelled as such on Ainslie's map of 1800 (**fig 2.8**). The adoption of this name for the house reinforces the view that Doomster Hill stood in this area and the construction of the house seems to have involved the diversion of the northern branch of the burn. This water management activity could well be linked to the construction of the reservoir.

This identification does not allow the position to be precisely located, but it does allow the site of Doomster Hill to be located around modern Napier Street (see **fig 3.10**). Only further archaeological investigation can establish its location with greater precision (**fig 3.18**).

Despite the lack of contemporary evidence for the function of Doomster Hill, its name suggests that it was a site where legal proceedings were held. The radical reformation of the court system following the Jacobite rising took place within the lifetime of Revd Pollock's informants, which strengthens the reliability of his description in the *Statistical Account*. Although court hills are a common feature throughout medieval Scotland (Barrow 1981), such hills are still confused with the remains of earthen castles. Such confusion between the court hills and castle hills was characteristic of early antiquaries who were sometimes misled by the coincidental similarity of the words moot, motte and moat, but this never seems to have happened at Govan. The distinctive step visible in Paul's view reinforced the interpretation of Doomster Hill as a court hill and assembly place, because stepped mounds are known to have been built to serve these functions in Viking Dublin (FitzPatrick 2004) and the Tynwald on the Isle of Man, where the Manx Parliament still meets (Darville 2004). Closer to home, and on a much more modest scale, the small stepped mound on Ward Law Hill, Rutherglen, appears to be the ancient burgh court hill, which apparently was fashioned from a prehistoric barrow (RCAHMS 1978, 151, NS623615). Perhaps the most relevant comparison is to be made with Scone, Perthshire, where, from at least AD 906, popular assemblies met to inaugurate their king on a low, flat-topped mound. Many of the issues relating to sovereignty and royal assemblies recently discussed in the context of Scone and the Stone of Destiny are relevant for Govan (Welander *et al* 2003). Given the immense scale of Doomster Hill and its proximity to the royal seat at Partick, it seems reasonable to suggest that the court of the king of the northern Britons met here.

Settlement location and layout

The location of the churchyard, Doomster Hill and the ferry crossing can be used to triangulate the general location of the medieval settlement to the Water Row and Govan Cross area. The map evidence suggests that there was a direct link between the church and Doomster Hill via Manse (Pearce) Lane. The medieval settlement may have originated immediately around the church, which some believe may have included a monastic community (Radford 1967a, 1967b), but the archaeological evidence is inconclusive. The ferry crossing seems an equally likely origin for settlement. Late medieval pottery has been recovered both from within the churchyard and towards the southern end of Water Row, but no definite medieval dwellings.

It is certain that there was a manse in Govan, but there is some doubt about its original position. The Roy map seems to indicate that the manse was to the south of the church, but by the 1780s/1790s it was located to the east. It seems most likely that the medieval manse lay under or near the manse represented on the first edition Ordnance Survey Town Plan of the 1850s (**fig 3.19**; see Chapter 4). This could not be verified archaeologically because when the area nearest to the site of the manse was investigated, it proved to have been truncated and all archaeological deposits removed (Driscoll and Will 1996, 13–15). It is thought that the manse stood on slightly elevated ground, which was levelled when the Harland and Wolff shipyard was built in 1911. However, the site of the manse is not completely sterile. Archaeological investigations revealed areas where deposits and structures survived within the grounds of the manse and traces of the manse may yet survive. This is a significant observation because it means that other pockets of extant archaeological deposits may be expected where minor topographical variations have allowed them to survive. On the basis of existing evidence, the locations of these pockets cannot be predicted with precision prior to excavation. More generally, the construction of the Harland and Wolff shipyard involved levelling up and revetting the sloping riverbank, thereby sealing the old ground surface, particularly towards the river edge.

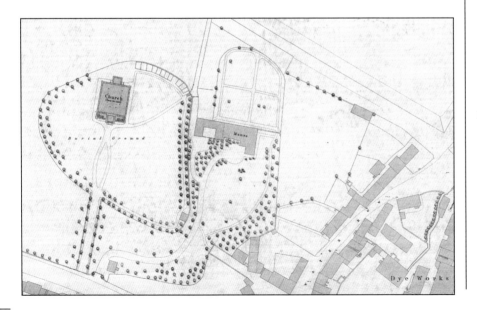

FIGURE 3.19
Govan Manse in 1857 from the Ordnance Survey 1st edition Town Plan, 1:500 (Reproduced by permission of the Trustees of the National Library of Scotland)

Partick Castle

The earliest historical references to Partick make it clear that prior to the twelfth century there was a royal *vill*, or estate, at Partick (Barrow 1999, 72). Although little is known about the form and design of early historic royal estates in Scotland, a comparable royal centre at Yeavering in Northumbria has been extensively excavated (Hope-Taylor 1977, Frodsham and O'Brien 2005). Yeavering was a significant royal estate, but only one of several and not the principal seat of the kings of Northumbria in the seventh and eighth centuries. Hope-Taylor excavated a complex series of timber buildings which sprawled over an area greater than 250m by 130m, at the heart of which stood a great hall over 30m in length. Over a dozen ancillary structures provided domestic accommodation for the local community and visitors, as well as space for agricultural storage and working. While it may be thought unlikely that Partick was as extensive, it is interesting that on the Roy map (**fig 2.6**), the village of Partick from the castle to the crossroads occupies an area similar to Yeavering. What is important to recognise is that, during the medieval period, a royal (later ecclesiastical) estate consisted of a collection of buildings (lesser dwellings and outbuildings) alongside the lord's accommodation.

There is no historical evidence relating to the form of the Partick estate after it came into the hands of the bishops of Glasgow between 1128 and 1136, but it is presumed that at some point in the Middle Ages a stone building was erected on the site. From the historical record, there is no way of knowing whether this was a castle or an unfortified manor house. The only possible reference to the bishop's *manerium* is found in a building contract of 1611 for the erection of the tower house known as Partick Castle, which specifies the demolition of a pre-existing structure prior to construction (MacGibbon and Ross 1892, volume 5, 5; see Chapter 4). It is probable that the seventeenth-century tower house was built on the site of the bishop's manor house using stones from the old structure. Following its abandonment in the eighteenth century, the tower house of 1611 came to be known erroneously as the Bishop's Castle.

The seventeenth-century tower house, built for George Hutcheson (one of the founders of Hutchesons' Hospital), was in effect a country house set in a park which ran along the west bank of the Kelvin, which was known as the Bishop's Orchard. Hutcheson's castle is known both from the detailed building contract and from two drawings made of it as a ruin. The earlier sketch, made in 1799, shows the entrance from the north-west, but reveals little of its landscape setting (MacGibbon and Ross 1892, volume 5, 4). A drawing of the castle made in 1828 gives a better impression of the setting of the building (MacGeorge 1880, 121). It shows the ruined castle perched on the crest of the bank of the River Kelvin, with Govan in the background across the Clyde (**fig 3.20**). The L-shaped plan of the tower house and the tree-lined enclosure of the orchard are clearly represented on the Roy map (see **fig 2.6**). The castle was demolished in the 1830s and was replaced by a dye works and then by an engineering works (see Chapter 4).

It is highly likely that Partick Castle was the final successor to the early historic royal estate and that the Bishop's Orchard, as represented on Kyle's plan of 1842, was also at the core of the estate (see **fig 2.14**). The Orchard and Castle Green are noted by Napier (1873, 46 and vaguely represented in his figure opposite p 57). Given that the parish church and Doomster Hill both lay to the south across the Clyde, it seems likely that the grounds of Partick estate also reached south towards the Clyde.

Discussion

All consideration of the significance of medieval Govan must still begin with the sculpture. As can be seen from the summary presented above, the archaeological investigations have been limited in scale and purpose. Although these excavations have provided dating evidence and confirmed the presence of archaeological deposits, below-ground archaeology has yet to contribute much detail to the understanding of Govan's past. By comparison, the sculpture in the churchyard continues to provide insights into Govan's position in early historic Scotland, over 100 years since it began to be appreciated as a major historical resource (Stuart 1856; Stirling Maxwell 1899). Despite the loss and decay of early historic sculpture over the past millennium, it is possible to use this evidence to reconstruct the outlines of the wider socio-political landscape (see **fig 3.9**). Indeed, detailed consideration of the sculpture in its regional context only serves to emphasise the pre-eminent position of Govan within Strathclyde.

As a group, the early historic sculpture from the region is remarkably homogeneous in style, so much so that it has been argued that there was a 'school' of stone carving based at Govan which produced or influenced all the sculpture within a zone stretching from Dumbarton to Hamilton (Macquarrie 1990; Driscoll, O'Grady and Forsyth 2005). Outside Govan, sculpture appears to have been used in three ways: to enhance the settings of important churches, to mark ecclesiastical boundaries on major routeways, and to commemorate the dead of the elite. All of these uses imply a high degree of secular patronage. The sudden appearance of this sculpture around AD 900 reinforces the historical indications that a significant reorganisation of the political landscape took place during the tenth century. While the hogback monuments are an unambiguous indication of Norse patronage, it is the recumbent burial monuments that are particularly revealing of this new political order. They are only found at sites with royal associations – Dumbarton and Inchinnan (near Renfrew), as well as Govan – which not only suggests they marked the graves of the ruling elite, but also that the significance of the older royal centre at Dumbarton had not completely disappeared. The volume of sculpture alone would indicate that Govan was an important Viking Age political centre, but the stepped form of Doomster Hill invites comparison with other major Viking centres of the Irish Sea: Tynwald and Dublin. Taken collectively, the sculpture, Doomster Hill and the estate of Partick mark Govan out as the *principal* royal centre of the last British kingdom in 'Scotland'.

Govan church was perhaps a natural choice as the spiritual centre for the political landscape laid out around AD 900, because it is one of the oldest Christian sites in the west of Scotland. There is a certain geographic logic underpinning Govan's selection. It commands a nodal position within the regional communication system and would have been particularly suitable as a place of popular assembly. It is worth stressing that the other two components of this political centre (Doomster Hill and the Partick estate) were as important as the church with its sculpture.

From what is known of popular assembly or court sites, Doomster Hill emerges into the first rank. Only Scone in Perthshire or Finlaggan on Islay can lay claim to greater historical significance. Whether the surviving archaeological evidence fulfils Doomster Hill's historical potential can only be determined by more extensive excavations.

Royal centres from early historic Scotland are better documented than assembly places, but none from the Viking Age (800–1000) has been examined extensively. Within Strathclyde, Govan/Partick may well be the only surviving

British centre from this era. Dumbarton was destroyed in AD 870 and it may be doubted whether the early historic levels have survived the intensive late medieval and early modern fortification of Clyde Rock (Alcock and Alcock 1990). At Renfrew, the site of the royal castle on the King's Inch (near Braehead shopping complex) was obliterated to build a lorry depot (Speller 1995). Much of the royal centre at Hamilton (historic Cadzow) now lies under the M74 motorway (Dennison Torrie and Coleman 1996, 42).

One of the most arresting aspects of Govan's early history is its rapid decline, which is best accounted for as the result of a deliberate policy on the part of David I (1124–53), king of Scots. Early in the twelfth century the British kingdom in Strathclyde was annexed by the Scots and thereafter a new diocese was established upriver at Glasgow, apparently snubbing Govan. It would appear that David sought to diminish the previous British regime by ignoring the existing ecclesiastical centre presumably to undermine its strong associations with the previous dynasty (Driscoll 1998). Partick's change of ownership reveals that not only was ecclesiastical jurisdiction transferred to Glasgow, but some of the British royal estates were as well. This interpretation of the process of annexation is based upon thin and partial evidence, but it serves to emphasise the potential significance of Govan's archaeological resources. The archaeology could make a real contribution to understanding the annexation of Strathclyde, which was a major event in the creation of the medieval kingdom of Scotland.

One final observation arising from the archaeological excavations of the 1990s and 2007 concerns the condition of the archaeological remains and their accessibility. As one moves away from the churchyard, the likelihood that the archaeological levels have been disturbed increases, but it is impossible to predict with confidence where deposits have survived or have been lost. As the Water Row excavations make clear, well-stratified archaeological deposits have survived the most intensive of industrial uses.

In our view, small-scale, piecemeal excavations will not yield intelligible results for the areas outside the churchyard, if only because of the large scale of monuments themselves. Moreover, the excavators believe that the archaeological resource is likely to survive in patches and pockets, which means that work will need to be undertaken on a large scale in order to make sense of the archaeological evidence and to realise Govan's potential. Large-scale excavations would involve civil engineering operations and probably will only be undertaken in the context of major urban redevelopment.

4 Early modern to early industry (sixteenth to early nineteenth centuries)

Introduction

Apart from the churchyard of Govan Old Parish Church, and with one or two other exceptions, little is now visible of Govan as it was in the period from the sixteenth to the early nineteenth century. However, increased documentary survival after the medieval period, the existence of maps of the town from the sixteenth century onwards, and the efforts of antiquaries in the nineteenth and early twentieth centuries to describe, illustrate, and photograph Govan's pre-industrial heritage mean that a reasonable outline of the town's history can be given. To a limited extent, recent archaeological excavations have added to the picture and have certainly indicated archaeological potential for the period. Such archaeological remains lying below the ground surface are a principal potential resource for future improvements in our understanding of this period in Govan's history.

In this chapter, these various forms of evidence are used to undertake a much-needed reassessment of sixteenth- to nineteenth-century Govan. In the later nineteenth and earlier twentieth centuries, it was normal to characterise pre-industrial Govan as something of an isolated, rural idyll (**fig 4.1**). Brotchie actually referred to it as 'sleepy hollow' (Brotchie 1905, 94). Revisiting the sources, however, suggests that this was not in fact the case. While the legacy of the medieval farming community remained strong, the period was also

51

one of change in connection with wider social and economic processes. The hinterland of the town became a country retreat for Glasgow's merchant class, many of them dispersing new-found wealth from their colonial ventures by creating landed estates. The Clyde was massively transformed from the eighteenth century to allow for Glasgow's commercial expansion, and Govan found renewed significance as a strategic communication nexus. It was on the main land route between Glasgow and the major Clyde ports at Greenock and Port Glasgow. Govan's economy became tied to the growing textile industries, fed by imported colonial products. New population groups, especially the weavers, emerged beside the old, and the social hierarchy was in a state of flux. All of these new developments and tensions were played out through the material environment.

The economy and the Clyde

The paucity of documentary and visible built evidence for medieval Govan makes it impossible, at present, to document economic activities before the sixteenth century. From that point, and more particularly from the eighteenth century, greater survival of sources allows a fuller assessment.

From the eighteenth century, the Clyde saw the first real phases of its transformation to the deep channel we know today. The first attempt to deepen the river was in 1556, when efforts were made to remove a shoal at Dumbuck, but this had little effect (Riddell 1979, 8–10). Further works followed in the seventeenth century with similarly poor results, and an outport was eventually established at Port Glasgow in 1668. It was not until the mid-eighteenth century that the imperative to deepen the river re-emerged, with the substantive engagement of Glasgow's merchants in colonial trade (*ibid*, 12–13).

Increasing pressure from Glasgow's tobacco merchants and others led to the first sustained attempt to deepen the river, between 1736 and 1762 (*ibid*, 15–30). Trial shoal removal works were funded and the construction of a series of locks and dams undertaken, but both to little avail. The first successful deepening programme was undertaken from *c* 1770, and this involved the construction of protruding jetties to narrow the channel and to funnel the natural scouring action of the river (*ibid*, 32–53). Where such dykes were constructed, an initial deepening of *c* 3 feet (*c* 1m) was achieved. Special ploughs were introduced to break up harder sections of the riverbed. By 1775, a depth at high tide of 7 feet (*c* 2m) had been achieved throughout. The task of training and deepening the river continued through the 1780s and 1790s, and depths at low tide of 5–7 feet (*c* 1.5–2m) became usual.

In the 1800s, it was realised that the scouring action of the river as trained by the jetties had reached its limits, and a programme to join the jetties by longitudinal walls was put in place (Riddell 1979, 57–9, 63–9). Much of the

land behind these walls was reclaimed by natural flood deposition or by the dumping of material removed from the channel, and this reclaimed land began to be colonised for agriculture or industry. The lengths of the jetties were manipulated to straighten the channel. By the 1820s, the effective limit of the river's natural scouring action had been reached and a new and different approach centred on the dredging and widening of the river was put in place (see Chapter 5).

These changes to the Clyde affected Govan: in 1755 the low water depth at Pointhouse was as little as 15 inches (*c* 0.4m) and the high water depth as little as 3 feet 3 inches (1m) (Riddell 1979, 22; Young 1899, 98). Even by 1770, the level of the river at this point had not changed much (Leishman 1845, 670). As we have just seen, however, low water depths along the length of the Clyde soon reached between 5 and 7 feet.

Two major fords had existed at Govan until this time, between Water Row and Pointhouse and between the east end of Govan and Kelvinhaugh, with a third at the western end of the parish near Braehead (Brotchie 1908, 220; Leishman 1845, 670). The people of Partick formerly used the Pointhouse ford to reach pastures on the south bank and the Kelvinhaugh ford was used by Highland drovers, resulting in the street name of Highland Lane (MacGeorge 1893, 56; Smart 2002, 80).

These fords soon became impassable and, as a result, the ferry crossing at Govan became all the more important (**fig 4.2**). A ferry had long been established between Water Row and Pointhouse, first recorded in the sixteenth century (Hume 1974, 107; Smart 2002, 75). From the early eighteenth century, a regular vehicular ferry was provided alongside the existing passenger crossing (Brotchie 1905, 286; Young 1899, 103). By the time of the mid-

YE LUNT HOUS GOVEAN IN 1662
SHAWYN YE AUNCIENT FOORD &
STEPPYN STANES TO YE WHYT INCH
AND SAE TO YE SYDE CALIT PERTYCK

T.C.F.B.

FIGURE 4.3
Ford at Linthouse as
imagined by T C F Brotchie
(*Transactions of the Old Govan
Club* 1923)

nineteenth-century Ordnance Survey map, a second ferry was running to Kelvinhaugh from Govan's east end.

Land along the riverbanks was reclaimed as the training jetties and longitudinal walls were built. Widening and straightening works from the 1820s reversed this process in places, but around Govan this reversal was constrained by the fact that shipyards had become established there from the 1830s onward. Indeed, at White Inch, reclamation continued in the 1840s with the dumping of dredged material, and the islands there were joined with the shore and consumed within expanding farmland (Brotchie 1905, 208; Leishman 1845, 695–6).

This reclamation process had the unintended consequence of preserving archaeological deposits in reclaimed ground bordering the Clyde. Excavations for new building berths in the Linthouse shipyard in 1913 revealed a line of buried boulders, interpreted as former stepping stones crossing to White Inch (**fig 4.3**), the remains of a building, and a section of former roadway leading to the river, indicating the site of another ford (Burnett 1919). These discoveries raise the possibility that earlier features are present behind the revetted waterfront elsewhere.

The road network

The continued concern with river crossings in this period should not be seen in isolation from the growing network of roads linking Glasgow with other towns (Hume 1974, 108). In 1753, two Turnpike Acts were passed, aiming at the improvement of the principal roads to aid commerce and, in the wake of the 1745 Jacobite rebellion, 'the convenient marching of his majesty's troops' (*ibid*, 108; see also Galbraith 1958, 314). The Roy map of *c* 1745 shows that,

FIGURE 4.4
Stepping stones over the
lower Kelvin, looking
upstream with Partick Bridge
in the background
(Source: Fairbairn 1885)

at that time, Govan still comprised a long, thin ribbon of houses on either side of the one main road (**fig 2.6**). Notable offshoots led down to the river at the east end and at Water Row, and to the south to what would become Langlands Road. By the 1850s and the first edition Ordnance Survey map, Main Street, as it was then called, had been bypassed to the south by a much straighter road – called Main Road then and Govan Road now. This new toll road between Glasgow and Renfrew had been built sometime after the 1753 Turnpike Acts, and as late as the 1840s and 1850s a tollhouse was still in operation at Govan Cross (Davidson 1923, 14; Leishman 1845, 700).

The Roy map shows that the main road from Glasgow through Partick took the line of the present Old Dumbarton Road and Castlebank Street.

FIGURE 4.5
Old Bridge of Partick
(Reproduced by permission
of the Mitchell Library,
Glasgow)

FIGURE 4.6
Photograph of Water Row
from the south-east *c* 1910,
with the shipyards of Partick
in the background. The large
two-storey building with
crow-stepped gables is the
Ferry Inn (Reproduced by
permission of the Mitchell
Library, Glasgow)

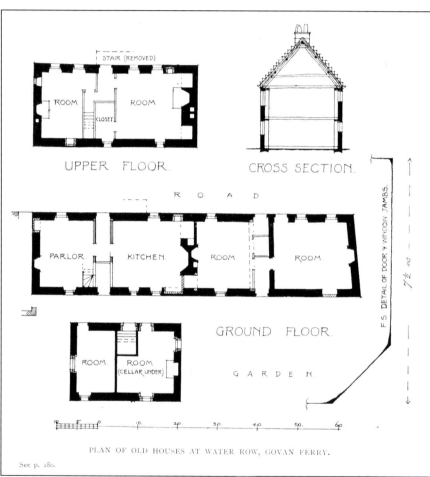

PLAN OF OLD HOUSES AT WATER ROW, GOVAN FERRY.

See p. 280.

FIGURE 4.7
Plans of the old houses
on the west side of Water
Row made in 1911, prior to
demolition. These include
the two thatched houses,
single- and two-storeyed,
in fig 4.6. The single-storey
building had been bisected
by a pend and was still two
'single end' houses. The two-
storey property on the left
(right in fig 4.6) formerly had
a forestair to the first floor
before becoming a public
house. The cellar may have
been a loom shop accessed
by a stair from outside
(*Transactions of the Glasgow
Archaeology Society* 1916)

By the 1850s, this too had been bypassed by a new turnpike, Dumbarton
Road to the north (see Dunlop 1893, 59–60). Old Dumbarton Road originally
crossed the Kelvin via a ford or stepping stones (**fig 4.4**; Fairbairn 1885, xxvi;
Matheson 2000, 188). A stone bridge was built or finished in 1577 at the foot
of what is now Benalder Street, and this survived in widened form until

demolition and replacement in 1896 (**fig 4.5**; Dunlop 1893, 59–60; Fairbairn 1885, XXVI; Matheson 2000, 188; Napier 1873, 60–3; Roger 1857, 215). It is worth remembering that navigation problems with the upper Clyde forced much of the traffic to Greenock and Port Glasgow onto the road, a situation that only changed with the deepening of the river in the mid-nineteenth century.

The unique nexus of transport routes at Govan, Partick, and Kelvinhaugh attracted the development of inns. Govan ale was commended by Bishop John Lesley in the late sixteenth century and there is a reference to the brewing and selling of ale in 1592 (Brotchie 1905, 39; Renwick 1894–1900, volume 10, no. 3315). By the late eighteenth century, there were numerous 'ale' or 'rather whisky houses' (Pollock 1973, 370). In the mid-nineteenth century, the minister for the parish thought that they were 'so numerous as to form a great moral nuisance' (Leishman 1845, 718). As late as the 1790s, the proliferation of inns was not matched by other services, with no baker, butcher or public market (Sinclair 1973, 371). But some retailing did go on, as recorded in the Govan kirk session minutes: there were shoemakers in both Govan and Partick (15 June 1757; 2 July 1811; 30 April 1815), and a seamstress in Govan (29 June 1813). By 1845, Govan had a branch of the National Security Savings Bank of Glasgow (Leishman 1845, 717).

A Ferry Inn existed on Water Row from at least the sixteenth century and remained until the later nineteenth (**fig 4.6**; Brotchie 1905, 31, 98; Smart 2002, 80). A survey of the west side of Water Row before demolition in 1911 recorded the inn as a seventeenth-century building, with a date stone of 1694 (**fig 4.7**; Whitelaw 1916, 280–1). A two-storey structure, with crow-stepped gables and a thatched roof, its ground floor had originally been of two compartments with a through passage. A second floor and a garret were reached from an outside stair. An outbuilding to the rear comprised two rooms and a cellar. On the opposite side of Water Row, another hostelry of more recent date was established to satisfy the demands of a growing population (see **fig 4.15**). Water Row also housed Moses Waddell's Inn, on the south-west corner of Manse (now Pearce) Lane (**fig 4.8**; Brown 1921, 86–7). This eighteenth-century structure was replaced by the YMCA in 1898.

On the opposite side of the river stood the Pointhouse tavern, on the site now adjacent to the Yorkhill Basin (**fig 4.9**). This appears on Roy's map and presumably existed before that time. A painting of 1815 shows it as the westernmost of a terrace of three buildings, of two storeys with a garret and thatched roof (MacGeorge 1893, 54–6). The symmetrical façade of the building and comparison with Ferry Inn suggests an eighteenth-century date,

FIGURE 4.8
View along Manse Lane (now Pearce Lane) by J P Main, 1870. The buildings on the left, including Moses Waddell's Inn on the corner, are angled to funnel traffic towards Govan Old. The gate in the distance leads through the manse gardens and then into the churchyard (Brotchie 1905)

FIGURE 4.9
View of Pointhouse and its
ferry slip from the east; the
sailing boat is standing in the
mouth of the Kelvin, 1815
(MacGeorge 1893)

FIGURE 4.10
Entrance to Govan
Shipbuilding yard and
Sheephead Inn looking
west along Govan Road
(Reproduced by permission
of the Mitchell Library,
Glasgow)

or late seventeenth-century at earliest. Later in the nineteenth century, the whole group of buildings was pulled down and replaced on the same site (Brotchie 1905, 101; MacGeorge 1893, 55).

Govan also had inns along the old Main Street and the new Turnpike road (Ferguson 1919, 17). The Sheephead and the Black Bull stood where the two roads met at the Cross, and the Stag stood at the east end of Main Street, near the Kelvinhaugh crossing (Houston 1922, 127; Smart 2002, 80, 82). The

FIGURE 4.11
The Bunhouse Inn by
Old Dumbarton Road in
Kelvinhaugh on the eastern
approach to the Partick
Bridge (*The Regality Club*
1889)

FIGURE 4.12
Fairfield farmhouse in Elder
Park is the oldest building
to survive in Govan. There
are plans to restore the park
(GUARD)

Sheephead was heightened from an earlier one-storey building sometime in the eighteenth century (**fig 4.10**; Brotchie 1921, 82–3). The Old Bridge Inn, a two-storey thatched and crow-stepped structure, stood near the bridge in Partick while the Bunhouse Inn stood by Old Dumbarton Road in Kelvinhaugh. The Bunhouse, which had a datestone of 1695, was probably on the site of what is now a car park beside the Kelvin Hall (**fig 4.11**; Dunlop 1889, 129–31; 1893, 58; Matheson 2000, 188).

The decline of agriculture and the rise of manufacturing

Alongside the eighteenth- and nineteenth-century extension of Govan as a major communications hub, with the building of new roads and the deepening of the Clyde, went significant changes in the character of the surrounding farmland for this was also the period of agricultural improvement. A number of farms surrounded the village well into the nineteenth century (Brown 1916, 21; Ferguson 1919, 15). Roy's map shows that the fields were already enclosed by hedges by *c* 1750, just as they were to be described in the 1790s and 1840s (**fig 2.6**; Leishman 1845, 669; Pollock 1973, 360–1). A significant survival representing this period of rural Govan is the Fairfield farmhouse, still standing in Elder Park (**fig 4.12**). By 1793, corn, peas, and barley were being grown. Jethro Tull's system of rotation having been tried, the regular rotation of crops was in

place, and threshing had been mechanised with the introduction of Meikle's threshing machine (Pollock 1973, 359–64). By 1845, potatoes, already a standard by 1793, had become a major crop (Leishman 1845, 695; Pollock 1973, 362). Fruit growing seems to have been limited: Partick orchard was replanted with crops in 1632 (Napier 1873, 30). Meadows and pasture are on record north of the Clyde in the sixteenth century, so the fact that relatively few sheep and cattle were kept by the 1790s may have been a recent trend (Murray 1924–32, volume 1, 62 n.3; Pollock 1973, 363; Renwick 1894–1900, volume 10, nos 3264, 3298). The Govan kirk session minutes record the payment of compensation on 15 April 1722 to a man, twelve of whose cattle had apparently been killed by a dog.

The inhabitants of the town maintained links to farming and fishing up to the nineteenth century. Govan's weavers cultivated their gardens for produce to be sold in Glasgow (Dreghorn 1919, 22), while many also fished in the Clyde in the summer months, salmon fishing on the Clyde and the Kelvin being mentioned in sources from the seventeenth to nineteenth centuries (Brown 1921, 87; Dreghorn 1919, 22; Fraser 1863, 44; Marwick and Renwick 1876–1916, volume 4, 383). A fisherman's hut on the Clyde shore near Water Row is shown in a print of *c* 1815, and this survived until *c* 1840 (**fig 4.13**; Brotchie 1905, 101). No doubt other such structures, presumably for storing the necessary gear, existed along the shore.

The townspeople had access to the town commons, which they used for pasturing cattle, cutting peat and turf, washing, and the bleaching and dyeing of clothes (Brotchie 1905, 177–9, 207–9; Ferguson 1919, 18). The commons are represented on Roy's map as pasture using broken diagonal lines in contrast to the rigs of cultivated fields. One of the commons lay at the east end of the town, on the site of the later Prince's Dock; another lay on the south side of Main Street, almost in the town centre. To the south of the town, the Langlands and Drumoyne Commons extended along Langlands Road while the Craigton Commons lay along the Common Loan. Harmony

Row Commons lay along the east side of that road. Further ground existed to the east at Middleton, between Whitefield and Cessnock Roads. From 1878, the commons were managed by the Burgh, which sold, exchanged, feued or leased them out. Doomster Hill also appears to be have been common land; it certainly was not tilled.

The existence of these commons explains the pattern of roads leading south from Govan, although the roads also served to allow farmers access to the river fords (Houston 1922, 130). Roy depicts an early incarnation of Langlands Road and also shows what appears to be a predecessor of Harmony Row. The latter extends much farther to the south than today, this southern stretch probably being the Common Loan leading to the Craigton Commons. The Common Loan, if we are correct in giving it that name, eventually led to Craigton Farm and lay east of the present Craigton Road. Roy also shows an earlier version of Whitefield Road, from which the Middleton Commons would have been accessed.

Despite these enduring connections to the surrounding countryside, the lives of the townspeople were also substantially changed by the increasing link between the Clyde and Britain's empire through the eighteenth and nineteenth centuries, particularly through the expansion of the textile industry.

By the early nineteenth century, handloom weavers had come to dominate Govan's population. The first half of the nineteenth century saw the number of weavers increase still further: between 1793 and 1845 their number rose from 279 to 340 (Leishman 1845, 694; Pollock 1973, 370), although much of this rise was probably in the first two decades of the century. Most would have worked in their own homes, though references to weavers' shops throughout the town also imply the existence of workshops (Brotchie 1905, 112; Brown 1916, 22; 1921, 87; Ferguson 1919, 16–17). Weaving, indeed, had become the principal source of employment: the vast majority of those whose occupations are mentioned in the kirk session minutes were weavers, and the Govan Weavers' Society was formed in 1756 (Brotchie 1905, 138).

This picture of increasing numbers employed in handloom weaving masks the frequent difficulties the industry experienced in this period. During the French Revolutionary and Napoleonic Wars, the kirk session minutes record a former weaver being employed in the coal industry (20 December 1798), an apprentice laid off for lack of work (18 June 1803), and petitions for help from weavers 'in need of assistance in the present state of cotton manufactures' and asking to be put on the poor roll (19 March 1811; 28 and 30 July 1816). The latter group had been looking for work in Glasgow, presumably in factories. In the late 1820s and the 1830s, the number of handlooms in Govan, as in Partick and Glasgow, fell, while weaving in burghs and villages in the wider Glasgow region increased (Murray 1978, 22).

By 1845, as reported in the *New Statistical Account*, the weavers were apparently in a depressed state (Leishman 1845, 694; Pollock 1973, 370); in

1844 it was possible to set up the first Roman Catholic school in the parish in a former weaving shop (Greenhorne 1914, 28). As elsewhere in Glasgow, the Govan handloom industry did continue through the mid-nineteenth century, despite the problems outlined above and the operation of powerloom factories locally (Leishman 1845, 698; Pollock 1973, 359; see Grosicki 1958, 241–3) but the industry did not long survive Govan's re-orientation to heavy industry from the 1830s and 1840s and appears to have come to an end by the 1860s.

The textile-finishing industry had expanded in the eighteenth century, though a mill for finishing cloth had existed on the Kelvin from at least 1508 (Marwick and Renwick 1894–1906, volume 1(1), 89, no. 586; Matheson 2000, 196; Napier 1873, 49, 55). Various bleachfields, tanyards and printfields, as well as lint steeping, are recorded and, although these concentrated to the north of the Clyde, there was at least one bleachfield at Govan (Leishman 1845, 698; Marvin 1958, 258–9; Napier 1873, 44, 64, 110; Pollock 1973, 358–9). This was located east of Water Row to utilise the stream and the common space around Doomster Hill. Bleachers are recorded in Govan and Kelvinhaugh in the Govan kirk session minutes of *c* 1800 (9 December 1798; 14 November 1802).

Early industry

Govan's earliest taste of industrialisation also emerged in the textile sector. Morris Pollok opened a silk-twisting mill a short distance to the west of the Parish Church in 1824 (Brotchie 1905, 103; Leishman 1845, 697; Smart 2002, 76, 82). This closed in 1873 and was demolished in 1901 when the Fairfield shipyard expanded onto the site. An engraving of the factory shows the five-storey mill and adjacent smaller buildings with a road leading down to the river's edge (**fig 4.14**).

Textile dyeing was a long-established occupation, and dyers are mentioned in documents of 1660 and 1722 (Marwick and Renwick 1876–1916, volume 2, 435; volume 5, 159). In the early nineteenth century, a dye works was erected by Alexander Reid just east of Water Row (**fig 4.15**) Brotchie 1905,

FIGURE 4.14
An engraving of the silk factory from the north shore by Swan *c* 1840, taken from the letterhead of Morris Pollok, silk throwster (Reproduced by permission of the Mitchell Library, Glasgow)

FIGURE 4.15
Buchanan's Waverley Tavern dominates the lower end of the east side of Water Row, with the ferry slip in the foreground and the dye works chimney in the rear (Reproduced by permission of the Mitchell Library, Glasgow)

FIGURE 4.16
The Bunhouse Mill on
the east side of the Kelvin
(Reproduced by permission
of the Mitchell Library,
Glasgow)

104; Leishman 1845, 697; Marvin 1958, 258–9; Smart 2002, 76, 81). This successor to the bleachfield is described in an advertisement appearing in the *Glasgow Herald* in 1822: it had recently been renovated and was to be let with its steam engine, madder-mill, coppers, tubs, stands and other utensils (Brotchie 1916). Thanks to Leishman's antiquarian interest we know that water supply came from a reservoir built into the top of Doomster Hill. The works were eventually removed to make way for a shipyard, but excavations have identified traces of the dye works (Driscoll, Will and Shearer 2008).

In Partick, the castle grounds were also given over to a dye works (Napier 1873, 46). Pointhouse saw early industrial activity with the Slit Mills (1738) of the Smithfield Iron Company, which made slit iron for the production of tools and nails (Dunlop 1893, 60–2; Marwick and Renwick 1876–1916, volume 5, 494; volume 6, 76, 102–3; Matheson 2000, 177). This was converted to a grain mill after 1780 and continued in use well into the nineteenth century, being reconstructed in 1815 (Napier 1873, 57).

Partick has a medieval heritage of flour milling. The Bunhouse Mill had been erected by the archbishop of Glasgow, and was granted out to a diverse group of individuals after the Reformation with all shares eventually falling to Glasgow's Incorporation of Bakers (**fig 4.16**; Dunlop 1889, 1320135; Fairbairn 1885, 26; Hume 1974, L46; Matheson 2000, 188). This mill was apparently rebuilt in 1569 (Marwick and Renwick 1894–1906, volume 1(1), p.dl), but it was destroyed by fire in 1886 and a new mill built on the site. The site was eventually acquired by the City and is now occupied by a car park for the Kelvin Hall.

The Bishop Mills also have medieval roots, as the Mill of Partick, being granted to Crawford of Jordanhill after the Reformation before falling to the City in 1608 (Hume 1974, L47; 1990, 86; Matheson 2000, 178, 195–6;

Williamson *et al* 1990, 374). A corn-drying kiln was added in 1653 (Marwick and Renwick 1876–1916, volume 2, 281–2). The original building was replaced in the eighteenth century and sold to the Slit Mills in 1809. The Mills were replaced again from the 1830s to the 1850s, finally being converted to flats in 1987 (**fig 4.17**).

By the late eighteenth century other industries in the area included: the first mill in the west of Scotland for chipping and rasping wood (1760s); mills for snuff and paper (by 1793); and a soapworks at Partick (by 1810) (Minutes of the Govan kirk session, 22 July 1822; Pollock 1973, 358–9). Coal extraction was also significant in the wider parish, and Jordanhill, Gartnavel and Bellahouston are singled out for mention in the *New Statistical Account* (Leishman 1845, 671–2). Though a pit was 'lately opened' in 1793, the majority had closed by 1816 (Brotchie 1905, 85; Pollock 1973, 359). There is reference in the Govan kirk session minutes to a coal-hewer living in the parish as early as 1714 (8 July 1714), but such men retained other interests: the cash book of the Govan Poor Fund records that in April 1713, a coal man was compensated for the loss of two acres of corn in a flood. There were two or three quarries (Napier 1873, 267; Marwick and Renwick 1876–1916, volume 9, 67; 1894–1906, volume 2, 30), and by 1845 ironstone and brick-clay were being extracted (Leishman 1845, 696). No early coal workings are known to fall within the Govan survey area, but the Langlands Brick Works became established at Drumoyne between publication of the first and second edition Ordnance Survey maps (ie sometime in the second half of the nineteenth century).

FIGURE 4.17
The Bishop Mills on the eastern approach to Partick Bridge in 1978 prior to restoration and development as flats (Reproduced by permission of the Mitchell Library, Glasgow)

The changing community

Though records are limited, assessments of pre-industrial Govan's population, social profile, and changing landholding structure are important in understanding the nature of the built character of the town in that period.

No estimate can be made of the population of Govan parish before the 1690s, when Hearth Tax returns for Lanarkshire become available. They can provide only an approximate total (Adamson 1981, 3): 728 paid, 148 deficient and 90 poor; following Adamson's method of multiplication by seven suggests a population of 6762 (*ibid*, 4, 103), a significant portion of whom will have lived outside the study area in the Gorbals and elsewhere in the parish. Webster's census of 1755, with its inexact figures and calculations (Flinn 1977, 250), gives a total of 4389, of whom 877 were fighting men, that is they were aged between 18 and 56 (Kyd 1975, 30). In 1771, Gorbals became a separate parish and so the population of 2518 reported in the Old Statistical Account (1793) gives a clearer indication of the population of Govan proper: there were nearly equal numbers of males and females and 532 children under the age of eight (Pollock 1973, 365). Chalmers disagreed with Webster, giving 2195 as the figure for 1755, but added the following figures: 3038 in 1801; 3542 in 1811, and 4325 in 1821 (Chalmers 1824, 759). In 1836 it was 6281, the increase ascribed to Govan's proximity to the commerce and manufactures of Glasgow (Leishman 1845, 693). None of these figures can be relied on as accurate population estimates, but they may be taken as a general indication of the size of the population and the trend of its growth.

If the study of population levels before the 1690s is difficult, then this is also true of the study of the occupational structure of even Scotland's larger towns (Lynch 1987, 2). After this, the only group of Govanites specified by occupation were the handloom weavers (Pollock 1973, 370; Leishman 1845, 694). Their importance in the community from at least the eighteenth century is reflected in the establishment of the Govan Weavers' Society in 1756 (see Brotchie 1905, 138–57). This was a friendly society or association set up to provide for destitute members, their widows or families. The Society continued despite attempts by some members to dissolve it in the 1850s and weaving coming to an end *c* 1863, surviving to celebrate its bicentenary in 1956.

The growth in numbers of handloom weavers was not only a part of the general changing population profile of Govan and area, but also a source of social tension – for those in established positions of power in particular. The radicalism of Scottish handloom weavers is recognised as a general feature of their history from a relatively early period through to the nineteenth century (Murray 1978, chapter 9), and Govan played its part in this history. Following the passing of the Corn Laws of 1815, which provided protection for the agricultural interest, Govan was amongst numerous weaving centres in the west of Scotland to stage protest meetings (*ibid*, 233–4). If there was open protest, there is also evidence that, by 1817, the influence of secret societies preaching a doctrine of radical reform had also spread to Govan and Partick (*ibid*, 217, 219). It may be significant that this evidence of radicalism in Govan comes from a period of notable economic strife for the weavers (see above).

If the weavers came to dominate the population of the town, there was also significant change amongst the landowning classes. In the medieval period, the major landholder was the church, although not all land was in their hands – even though David I granted most lands in the area to Glasgow Cathedral, part remained in royal hands, as is seen from the fact that, in 1452, James II granted a tack of the king's lands of Partick to Walter Stewart of Arthurlie (Fraser 1863, volume 1, 429). The first detailed evidence of landholding, apart from the muniments of the Maxwell family, is the archbishop's rental of the Barony of Glasgow, covering 1515–68 (Bain and Rogers 1875, volume 1, 72–194). This shows a variety of holdings, ranging from 5s to 25s, the commonest being 13s 4d (1 merk). These were largely inherited, son succeeding father or brother succeeding brother; a daughter might succeed or daughters jointly; widows enjoyed the property for life, but the heir was rentalled in his father's place (Sanderson 1982, 53–4, 57).

Change was soon to come, however, and a general feature of the history of landholding in sixteenth-century Scotland was the spread of the feu-ferme, which gave greater security of tenure (Whyte 1997, 29–30). As late as 1574, the lands mentioned above were still held of the archbishop as lord superior (Renwick 1894–1900, volume 7, 50, no. 2033), but in 1587 James VI granted the Regality of Glasgow in feu-ferme to Walter Stewart, the commendator of Blantyre (Marwick and Renwick 1894–1906, volume 1(1), cxliii–cxliv, 215–25, no. lxxviii). In 1596, the properties were confirmed to the feuars of Govan, dispensing them from the payment to renew their feus, since many were too poor to do so (Brotchie 1905, 44). This ran counter to the general trend, which was for inflation to erode the real value of feu duties in the later sixteenth century (Whyte 1997, 30); perhaps feuing in Govan was too recent for this effect to be felt.

It is possible to identify some of the individual changes from rentaller to feuar before 1596 (Sanderson 1982, 206–7; Bain and Rogers 1875, 189). When comparison with the earlier rental is possible, fifteen surnames recur. Some of the families named in the list were still residents in 1905 (Brotchie 1905, 44). By 1596, the 1 merk land had become rarer, and values ranged from 6s 3d to 25s. Feu duties were still paid in money and kind as late as 1845 (Leishman 1845, 686–7).

Thus in the sixteenth century, church lands in and around Govan were parcelled out in small lots to individuals. From the seventeenth century, larger estates were formed from the existing small portions and this process accelerated in the eighteenth and early nineteenth century as Glasgow's merchants sought country retreats in the area (Smart 2002, 75–6). Often they bought up a number of existing small portions and amalgamated them, building new country mansions situated at the core of designed landscapes. This process reflects a general trend in several areas of Scotland, where direct investment of urban capital in rural estates was unusual before the eighteenth century and where merchants had only a limited impact on the land market before 1740 (Lynch 1987, 23–4). Around Govan, as elsewhere, the eighteenth and nineteenth centuries thus saw a relatively new phenomenon: the colonisation of the countryside by the increasingly wealthy, urban, mercantile class.

Architectural traditions

Changes in the profile of the population and in the landholding structure were intimately connected to the character of Govan's domestic architecture in the pre-industrial period. The picture, in outline, is one of a rural village, with numerous craft workers, surrounded by country estates. Population profile and landholding structure, and the politics inherent in a changing rural community, are also factors evident in the character of the pre-industrial aspects of the churchyard of Govan Old Parish Church (see below).

Despite the lack of survival of pre-industrial village housing, late nineteenth- and early twentieth-century descriptions, illustrations and photographs, when examples remained or were known in living memory, allow a general appraisal (**figs 4.18 & 4.19**). Most people lived in single-storey, two-room, thatched cottages (Brotchie 1905, 94; Dreghorn 1919, 21–2; Ferguson 1919, 15–17; Young 1899, 99–101). One of these, on Water Row, survived until demolition in 1911 and was surveyed at that time (Whitelaw 1916, 280). Originally, it had two apartments with a through passage and had been built with rubble walls, crow-stepped gables and a thatched roof. A similar cottage on Main Street was described in the 1850s as having a room and a kitchen, with a bedroom in the garret above (Ferguson 1919, 16). Most cottages had a garden, once cultivated for food but almost exclusively for flowers by the later nineteenth century (Brotchie 1905, 126; Brown 1921, 87; Dreghorn 1919, 22; Houston 1922, 127; Young 1899, 99).

The Water Row cottage has been ascribed a late seventeenth-century date. This accords well with the general ascription of Govan's pre-industrial cottages to the period between the late sixteenth and early eighteenth centuries, with known date-stones falling between 1590 and 1730 (Roger 1857, 215). While there were undoubtedly also later eighteenth- and nineteenth-century examples, the broadly seventeenth-century date ascribed to many of the cottages still standing in Govan at the onset of industrialisation in the mid-nineteenth century is consistent with aspects of their architecture. In

FIGURE 4.18
Thatched cottage on
Govan Road at Shaw Street
opposite the entrance gates
to Govandale owned by the
silk throwster Morris Pollok,
1870 (Brotchie 1905)

FIGURE 4.19
Photograph of the same
seventeenth-century thatched
cottage on Main Street,
c 1900, before it was replaced
by the Lyceum Theatre
(Reproduced by permission
of the Mitchell Library,
Glasgow)

particular, the crow-stepped gable – a form with a wide currency, found also
in towns around the Baltic and in the Netherlands – became common on
merchants' houses in the larger Scottish burghs, like Glasgow or Edinburgh,
in the seventeenth century and was also adopted in smaller towns, like the
well-known centre of early industry at Culross in Fife (Glendinning, MacInnes
and MacKechnie 1996, 62–4).

Interspersed with the numerous one-storey cottages were occasional two-
storey examples, probably ranging in date between the seventeenth and
nineteenth centuries. The 1911 survey of Water Row recorded a two-storey
nineteenth-century building with a slate roof (Whitelaw 1916, 280–1). A two-
storey house with crow-stepped gables of likely seventeenth-century date

stood on Main Street (Brotchie 1905, 112). References to outside stairs suggest other examples (Brown 1921, 86).

The cottages tended to lie in short terraces, but by the mid-nineteenth century, at least, a number of larger, detached houses had been built with their own gardens. Where the occupants are known, these houses were home to Govan's early industrialists and other members of the middling classes. The Reids, who owned the dye works by the Cross, lived in Greenhaugh House before moving to Hillock House (Brown 1921, 87–9). Morris Pollok of the silk factory lived in Govandale (Smart 2002, 82), while John Elder and then William Pearce, shipyard owners, occupied Elm Park House (Brotchie 1905, 114, 116; MacLean 1922, 145). Southcroft House was occupied by the banker Thomas Baird and Dean Park was home to a Dr Hislop in the 1860s (Brotchie 1905, 112; Houston 1922, 127). It is unclear when larger houses such as these began to be built in Govan, though they may well be confined to the earlier nineteenth century and associated with the earliest industrialisation of the town.

The eighteenth and early nineteenth centuries saw the construction of numerous mansions in the countryside around Govan and Partick (**fig 4.20**).

FIGURE 4.20
The Ordnance Survey first edition map (1857) reveals a dense spread of grand houses in their own policies throughout Govan's rural hinterland. They give the names for many familiar Govan locations such as Fairfield shipyard and Harmony Row

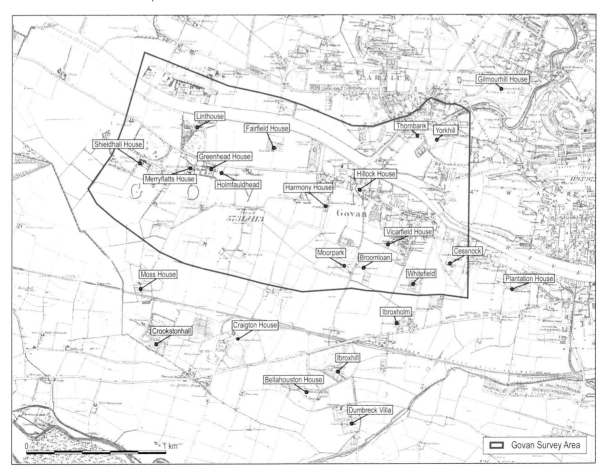

Fortunately, many were photographed and described in the late nineteenth century and the layout of their grounds can be seen on the first edition Ordnance Survey map of the 1850s. Most were built by Glasgow merchants, industrialists, and bankers, and only one or two by established local landowning families. Photographs show that many complied with the tenets of Georgian neo-classicism, with symmetrical façades bearing triangular pediments supported on classically inspired columns, for example, the fragment of the Linthouse mansion re-erected in Elder Park (see photographs in Annan 1878). Later houses do show some variation in style; a few examples suffice to illustrate the general process.

The Rowan family was established in Govan before the Reformation and owned the estate of Holmfauldhead from at least the seventeenth century (**fig 4.21**; Brotchie 1905, 44–6; Dalrymple Duncan 1899, 108–10). Stephen Rowan expanded the estate in the 1750s and was still in possession in 1795, by which date Richardson's map shows that a mansion had been built (**fig 2.7**; Dalrymple Duncan 1899, 112; Smart 2002, 75).

The adjacent estate of Linthouse, by way of contrast, was bought in the late eighteenth century by James Spreull, city chamberlain and son of a Glasgow magistrate, and a mansion house is shown on contemporary maps (**fig 4.22**; see Annan 1878, 163–4; Smart 2002, 96). Spreull sold the estate to Robert Watson, a Glasgow banker, who is said to have built a new house in 1820, though he probably only reworked the existing fabric. The house survived as offices within the Linthouse shipyard and, after final demolition, its Adam portico of 1791 was re-erected in Elder Park in 1921. The adjacent mansion of Fairfield, demolished in 1890, had some architectural similarities to Linthouse and was probably also built in the eighteenth century (see photograph in the *Transactions of the Old Govan Club* **3**(2), 1924).

Moore Park was built in the early nineteenth century by the Hagarts, a merchant family who owned a portion of the later Moore Park estate (**fig 4.23**; see Annan 1878, 181–2). The estate itself was formed from smaller fragments by Richard Alexander Oswald and was sold in 1821 to John Thomas Alston; both men were Glasgow merchants. In 1826 it passed to James Campbell, of a Glasgow/West India merchant dynasty, in 1841 it was sold to the tobacco merchant Alexander Kerr, and finally in 1852 it passed to John Mitchell, merchant and ship owner.

Richard Alexander Oswald of Moore Park was the son of Alexander Oswald of Shield Hall, but the Oswalds were not an old Govan family. The Shield Hall estate was first formed from smaller portions c 1720 by Bailie Hamilton, maltman in Glasgow, and the older part of Shield Hall House was probably built by him (see Annan 1878, 235–6). After several changes of ownership, the estate fell to John Wilson, Glasgow merchant, and then to Alexander Oswald, a Glasgow merchant, industrialist, and building speculator. Through

FIGURE 4.21
The entrance to
Holmfauldhead House,
photographed *c* 1900
(Reproduced by permission
of the Mitchell Library,
Glasgow)

FIGURE 4.22
Linthouse, photographed
c 1870 (Reproduced by
permission of the Mitchell
Library, Glasgow)

the nineteenth century it passed to a succession of Glasgow merchants before
being sold to the iron merchant Robert Cassells in 1875.

Examples could be multiplied: the mansions of Merryflats, Greenhead
and Broomloan were all built in the eighteenth century (Smart 2002, 76).
By the 1850s, Whitefield House, Vicarfield House, Ibroxholm and Harmony
House had been added (Smart 2002, 76). Craigton was built by the Ritchies,

FIGURE 4.23
Moore Park house seen
from its gardens *c* 1870
(Reproduced by permission
of the Mitchell Library,
Glasgow)

FIGURE 4.24
Thornbank *c* 1870
(Reproduced by permission
of the Mitchell Library,
Glasgow)

wealthy eighteenth-century tobacco merchants, and Cessnock by a Glasgow
manufacturer *c* 1800 (Annan 1878, 49–50, 67). Ibroxhill was built after 1801
by John Bennet, writer in Glasgow, and Plantation by John Robertson, a late
eighteenth-century Glasgow/West India merchant, which explains the name
of the estate (Annan 1878, 139, 203–4). To the north of the Clyde, houses
were erected by Glasgow merchants at Yorkhill in 1805 and Thornbank *c* 1775
(**fig 4.24**; Annan 1878, 243–8, 263–4; Fyfe 1907, 166).

Partick Castle continued in use into the eighteenth century, being described *c* 1710 as 'a well built and convenient house, well planted with barren timber, large gardens, inclosed with stone walls' (quoted in Leishman 1845, 692). The tower was unroofed and ruinous by the 1780s, when it was quarried for the building of an adjacent farmhouse (**fig 3.20**; Napier 1873, 22, 33–4). For some years it had been let to tenants, the last of these leaving around 1770, and it was finally demolished in the 1830s.

The post-Reformation Church

We know more about the fabric and day-to-day workings of the church in Govan for the post-Reformation period than for the medieval period, owing to an increased number and variety of documentary sources and the survival of elements of the post-Reformation churchyard. Along with illustrations of the church itself and some of the other parish institutions, like the school, these sources show that the parish was integral to the daily management of society. This was a role that continued, in a transformed state, through industrialisation, but was to be increasingly eroded with the growth of secular civic and philanthropic institutions (see Chapter 5).

The medieval parish church building was replaced in 1762 (Brotchie 1905, 159–60; Leishman 1921, 70; Pollock 1973). As depicted on a survey of the graveyard of 1809, the new church lay on the site of the southern part of the present nave. In plan, it was a simple rectangle, oriented east–west, with projections to the east, west and south – probably two loft-stairs and a porch. The spire, although part of the original design, remained unfinished in the 1790s.

By the 1820s, the fabric of the church had apparently deteriorated: 'the roof is gone; the back wall falling, and ... the side walls ought to be rebuilt' (quoted in Leishman 1921, 70–1) and it was replaced in 1826 (**fig 4.25**; Davidson Kelly 1994a, 12; Murray 1996, 7; Leishman 1845, 711; Leishman 1921, 71). Designed by James Smith of Jordanhill, the 1826 structure was a 'simple Gothic structure, with lancet windows and battlements' (Leishman 1845, 711). The design of its tower and spire was apparently taken from the church of Stratford-upon-Avon. A later plan shows that it lay on the site of its 1762 predecessor (Davidson Kelly 1994a, 12). By the 1880s, this 1826 church was considered inadequate in size and unfit for the new style of worship favoured by the then-incumbent John Macleod (McKinstry 1992, 5) so in 1885 it was removed and rebuilt in Golspie Street as the Elder Park Church, which has since been demolished (Murray 1996, 7; Young 1899, 97).

The graveyard also saw continued and changing use. The burial monuments in the churchyard span the fifteenth to twentieth centuries and form a significant historical resource, with documentation on the use of the cemetery only surviving from 1855 (Cutmore 1997, 8). A recent survey of the monuments, building on previous surveys of 1809 and 1936, has established that apart from the early medieval 'Govan School' sculpture discussed above, the oldest monument is a simple, undecorated recumbent of the fifteenth century (see Cutmore 1996; 1997; 1998; see also Willsher 1992). Fourteen monuments date from the seventeenth century, 83 from the eighteenth, 6 date to the nineteenth century before 1809, 132 date to the remainder of the nineteenth century, and 1 to the twentieth century.

The profile of the burial population pre-1809 was mixed. Almost half the lairs contain monuments to the prominent local landowning families of Rowan and Steven. In the seventeenth century, the use of burial monuments was confined to the landowning class. In the eighteenth century, a significant change occurred as local artisans began to be represented, and many of the stones from this period carry trade symbols. This was also a time when Glasgow's merchants were creating country estates around Govan and, with Govan and Partick, Glasgow is a common place of residence recorded on the stones.

The churchyard did not simply come to be used by a more varied population, but also became a significant resource for these different groups as they sought to establish or defend their position within the social hierarchy. The artisans seem to have sought to develop some form of solidarity through common adherence to a preferred monument type, the headstone. This was a relatively new form, but it appears to have been in use by the early eighteenth century at least. The kirk session minutes for 22 January 1723 record the decision to fine those, other than heritors, who had brought large gravestones or headstones to the churchyard – the fines were to be £6 Scots for large stones and £3 Scots for a headstone. Most earlier memorials had been of the flat grave slab type, and this form continued to be preferred by established landowners.

These landowners also reused the early medieval monuments in the churchyard, to which they added their own inscriptions. An 1899 plan of these, before their removal into the church, shows them lying exclusively in the lairs of established landowning families (Stirling Maxwell 1899). Some were re-inscribed in the seventeenth century, at a time when many of these families were aggrandising themselves through the formation of larger estates. Others were re-inscribed in the eighteenth and early nineteenth centuries, when the position of these families was under challenge from incoming merchant landowners and emerging artisan and other groups.

The established landowning class did not have the last say, however. A 1936 survey of the graveyard shows weavers to have been the most common group commemorated, suggesting their increased prominence through the earlier nineteenth century; the number of farmers memorialised also rose.

FIGURE 4.25
The spire of the 1826 Govan Old Church designed by James Smith of Jordanhill, modelled on Stratford-upon-Avon, was a familiar landmark in many of the nineteenth-century images of Govan. This moonlit view comes from an 1879 calendar of William Barr and Son, Warehousemen (general outfitters), Great Western Buildings, Govan (Reproduced by permission of the Mitchell Library, Glasgow)

The ongoing anxiety of the heritors is perhaps reflected in their patronage of new churches in 1762, only a few years after the foundation of the Govan Weavers' Society, and again in 1826. The Gothic style of the latter, like the reused carved stones, referred back to a medieval past.

The church was further embedded in society through its social functions, in relation to care of the poor, the provision of education and the policing of morals, amongst other things. Many of these functions are not explicitly discernable in the built environment: for instance, charity for the poor did not involve the construction of a poorhouse, as later, but took place in the home.

The Reformation emphasised discipline (Donaldson 1971, 141), and this issue was a significant concern for the Govan kirk session, which undertook to denounce moral lapses such as adultery, fornication, irregular marriages and drunkenness. The guilty could be excluded from the sacrament and fined. It was accepted that 'the mass of society should be closely controlled in their daily lives' (Mitchison 1983, 143).

The poor and infirm were put on the parish poor roll and paid monthly, an arrangement which kept them in their own homes, though they had to bequeath their possessions to the parish for the benefit of the poor (eg Govan kirk session minutes, 8 July 1744). In the early eighteenth century, there are instances of help for people outside the parish, but by the end of the century it was necessary to have been resident for three years (Govan kirk session minutes, 4 June 1809; 15 April 1815). In 1724, the heritors and the session resolved that poor strangers were not to be a burden on the session (Govan kirk session minutes, 20 February 1724). In 1751, the sheriff-depute ordered all vagrants and beggars to go to their own parishes (Govan kirk session minute,s 13 October 1751).

There is more material on the care of the poor, orphans and abandoned children for the late eighteenth and early nineteenth centuries. This is perhaps a reflection of the charitable interests of the Reverend John Pollock (minister 1791–1820), who kept a list of needy parishioners who were not on the official roll, but to whom regular disbursements were made each January. In his time, there were twice-yearly meetings of the session to consider the state of the poor. It was necessary to board out the orphaned and abandoned children, sometimes to find a wet-nurse, and to place older boys as apprentices, all at the expense of the parish. The desire to pay as little as possible, a recurring anxiety, was not parsimony but the result of fear that the funds would run out: on one occasion the Reverend Pollock himself was out of pocket (Govan kirk session minutes, 7 April 1801).

The most obvious physical manifestation of the social role of the parish was the parish school that once stood at Govan Cross (**fig 4.26**). A series of Acts of Parliament (1633–96) aimed to make the heritors of every parish contribute to the building of a school and to the salary of the schoolmaster (Donaldson 1971, 264). Since they paid for it, heritors tended to regard education as

FIGURE 4.26
Photograph *c* 1910 of the
first parish school, which
stood on the north side of
Govan Cross (Reproduced by
permission of the Mitchell
Library, Glasgow)

existing to support the current social system (Mitchison 1983, 146). The first
post-Reformation school in Govan is mentioned in 1652 (Brotchie 1905, 65),
and repairs to the schoolhouse were mooted in 1713 (Govan kirk session
minutes, 15 October 1713). In 1715, there was a general collection in Partick
towards building a school and schoolhouse there, though by 1747 the salary
had to be increased in order to attract a qualified schoolmaster (Govan kirk
session minutes, 11 November 1714; 1 and 8 March 1747).

In 1726, the presbytery of Glasgow ordered the heritors and others to
provide an annual salary for the schoolmaster of Govan, but a meeting of
heritors and session members delayed reaching a decision, which would
have involved assessing the heritors (Govan kirk session minutes, 23 October
and 3 November 1726). By 1751, the schoolmaster still had no salary; his
income came from the office of session clerk, interest on money mortified
(bequeathed) to the schoolmaster, and £20 Scots paid by the University of
Glasgow (Govan kirk session minutes, 14 April 1751; 11 August 1754). Some
result must have come from action by the presbytery, for in 1756 the new
schoolmaster was paid 1s 6d for English, 2s for writing, and 2s 6d for Latin
per quarter (Govan kirk session minutes, 10 September 1756).

The schoolhouse at Govan Cross was built anew in 1800, originally housing
the schoolmaster on the first floor and the schoolroom on the ground floor
(Brotchie 1905, 234; Marwick and Renwick 1876–1916, volume 9, 133).
Later, the upper flat was also used as a classroom. Schooling provision rose
dramatically in the early nineteenth century; in the 1790s, there were only
five schools in the whole parish, including the Govan parish school (Pollock
1973, 367, but by the 1840s, there were three schools in the village of Govan

FIGURE 4.27
Photograph of Govan
Manse, 1858, from the south
(*Transactions of the Old Govan
Club* 1923)

and three in Partick (Leishman 1845, 715). The old parish school became vested in the Govan School Board in 1873, and was replaced by the Hill's Trust School on Golspie Street in 1875 (Brotchie 1905, 234).

In the 1790s, just prior to the building of the new school, a new manse with a court of offices was built to the east of the church, apparently on the site of its predecessor and possibly incorporating elements of the earlier fabric (**fig 4.27**; Brotchie 1905, 159–62; Leishman 1923, 9–10; MacFarlane 1965, 81; Pollock 1973, 367; Sillars 1924; Young 1899, 97; see Chapter 3). The new manse was occupied until 1858, when encroaching industrialisation encouraged a removal to Paisley Road West (Leishman 1921, 178–80; MacFarlane 1965, 81; Young 1899, 97 n.1). The building was then let in single rooms until demolition, to be replaced by tenements. The site was eventually colonised by the shipyards, and excavations have suggested that it was heavily truncated and levelled at that time (Driscoll and Will 1996, 13–15; Driscoll, Will and Shearer 2008). The manse is thought to have been constructed on a slight knoll, and most traces of it may have been removed, although there may be pockets of archaeological survival remaining (see Chapter 3).

Discussion

Valuable sources exist for the history of Govan and its surrounding area in the early modern and pre-industrial eras: architecture, burial monuments, documents, and maps. To these we should add the potential resource of below-ground archaeology, which has yet to be fully appraised and investigated.

Although there is much still to learn about this period, the currently available sources allow an outline reassessment of the received narrative that Govan was a sleepy, slow-moving, and almost unchanging backwater before the advent of industry. These sources show, rather, the ongoing development of a dynamic community.

The Reformation had a significant, if not straightforward, connection to this community's development. Particularly through the kirk session records, we see the extent of church involvement in the daily lives of the population, ranging from policing functions (particularly in relation to moral offences) through education to provision for the poor. The landholding dominance of the medieval Cathedral of Glasgow was also broken, and many people who had previously rented land from the church now became owners, or feuars. From these initially small lots of land, larger estates were eventually formed.

Such estates were sometimes owned by families which were already established in the Govan area, but many were created by incoming Glasgow merchants using the substantial capital they had accumulated through colonial trade – particularly from tobacco and sugar. The creation of colonial fortunes was intimately tied to the transformation of Glasgow's transport network, most prominently through the 'improvement' of the Clyde. It also relied in part, in this locality, on the processing of colonial produce. While there appears to have been some tension between established and incoming landowners, social tension was heightened far more by a substantial artisan class emerging from Govan and Glasgow's new-found colonial connections, and this class was above all dominated by the handloom weaver. The churchyard of Govan Old Parish Church is an arena where these tensions were played out in physical form, and so is central to Govan's heritage.

If the outline character of the Govan community is known, many questions remain to be answered, and even to be asked. We can give an impression of the built environment of the town, with its one-storey cottages and two-storey houses and surrounding farms, mansions, and estates. What we cannot yet do is enter in detail into the lives of the population, their everyday routines and practices. This is an area where future documentary research may yield results, but it is also an area where archaeology has a fundamental role to play. Should relevant archaeological remains survive, we can start to investigate the working life of Govan's artisans in more detail, we can begin to piece together the changing character of society at its day-to-day level, and we can go beyond to ask wider questions. Just how, for example, did changes in the lives of the inhabitants of this small but dynamic Clyde town relate to the wider economic and social changes bound up with a pre-industrial global network connecting Govan and Glasgow to the other side of the Atlantic?

The history of pre-industrial Govan, its changing community and its wider connections, has been a neglected subject. This neglect stems, in no small part, from the previous assumption that Govan was an isolated and unchanging rural village. If this assumption is accepted, as it has been, no room is left for questions about the complex and changing nature of the Govan community. It is through the evidence of the built heritage, both as visible remains and those yet to be found below ground, in combination with an important archival resource, that we can begin fully to address the complexity of early modern and industrial Govan.

5   The Burgh of Govan (c 1850–1912)

Introduction

Govan's industrialisation prompted a contemporary rush of antiquarian interest in the history of the town and its changing character. Brotchie's *The History of Govan* (1905) is the most in-depth example, but numerous other works were published in journals like the *Transactions of the Old Govan Club*, the *Transactions of the Old Glasgow Club* and *The Regality Club*.

Common themes run through these works: many present romanticised descriptions of the pre-industrial village, lamenting the loss of a rural idyll (eg Brown 1921; Davidson 1923; Dreghorn 1919; Fairbairn 1885; Ferguson 1919; MacLean 1922; MacFadyen *et al* 1926; Park 1916; 1920; Sillars 1924; Young 1899). This is set in contrast to a rather ambiguous view of the changes accompanying industrialisation. On the one hand, industry brought wealth, progress and fame, and individual industrialists (especially shipbuilders) were often eulogised (eg Hillhouse 1925; Napier 1924). On the other hand, it also brought increasingly unsatisfactory living conditions and ill-health. The role of burgh councillors and private philanthropists in addressing the problems of the industrial town is particularly praised. Indeed, another subtext to the production of a distinct historical image for Govan was the ongoing annexation battle between the burgh and Glasgow, and the threat to Govan's separate identity posed by eventual annexation in 1912 (see foreword to Brotchie 1905).

Thus, an 'official' version of Govan's history emerged, aiming to establish Govan's antiquity, to naturalise its independence, and to justify its new-found position and the actions of the industrial and civic elite. A similar process was simultaneously underway in Glasgow (Nenadic 1996). This version of Govan's history took material form in the changing town plan. Most of the present street names post-date the 1912 annexation to Glasgow; of those that pre-date 1912 many, like Broomloan Road, Craigton Road or Harmony Row, perpetuate the names of estates, farms or other aspects of the pre-industrial history and rural hinterland of the town. Other pre-1912 names, however, memorialise Govan's industrialists and civic authorities: Barnwell Terrace (a partner in the Fairfield yard); Elder Street (John Elder, shipbuilder), and McKechnie Street (John McKechnie, early burgh commissioner). National and imperial history are also remembered in names given both before and after 1912: Mafeking Street is named after the famous Boer War siege and Aboukir Street and Cressy Street tie into Govan's shipbuilding identity, both being cruisers sunk by U-boats in 1914. Neptune Street, named after a steamer launched from Napier's Yard in 1861 that ran the Yankee blockade during the American Civil War, had earlier been Victoria Street, then Queen Street.

There is a need to reassess Govan's heritage of the industrial era, and this chapter aims to begin that process. Govan's built environment, large portions of which date from the nineteenth- and early twentieth-century, forms a significant resource from which to derive a new understanding of the development of the modern town. Elements of the established story, which give prominence to the shipbuilding industry, burgh government and philanthropic works, will retain their significance. The international context of Govan's development must also still be recognised.

But these established elements of the story must be recast to give a fuller understanding of those other sections of the population whose lives and actions were just as integral to the creation of modern Govan. Alongside a reinterpretation of Govan's accepted heritage – its industries, statues, and institutions – a recognition of the importance of the domestic aspect of the burgh's heritage will be particularly relevant.

Despite many losses, Govan's later nineteenth- and early twentieth-century heritage forms a significant historical, archaeological, and cultural resource. The value of individual buildings, statues, sites and other features is enhanced by the fact that the relationships between various strands of the story – industry and transport, population and housing, public institutions, and their social and religious environment – are still legible in the townscape.

Industrialisation

Brotchie's (1905, 243) dictum 'Shipbuilding made Govan and Govan made shipbuilding' sums up the primary role of the shipyards in Govan's industrialisation. While other industries did develop back from the river, most were tied to shipbuilding in one way or another. Notable exceptions were a continued focus on textiles and victuals (**fig 5.1**).

From the late eighteenth century, a flourishing wooden-shipbuilding industry emerged on the lower Clyde (see Moss and Hume 1977, 87–112 on this and what follows; see also Lavery 2001, 81–98; Walker 2001). Glasgow developed an early specialism in marine engineering and, from the 1830s and 1840s, moved firmly into shipbuilding itself. The neighbouring districts of Govan, Kelvinhaugh, Partick, and Whiteinch became a particular focus as city-centre land values rose and firms moved downstream (Hume 1990, 90; Lavery 2001, 86).

Clyde-built iron passenger liners saw particular success and the Clyde yards, prominently those in Govan, became renowned for their engineering expertise. From the 1860s, cost advantages encouraged the relocation of established firms to the Clyde and significant investment led towards eventual global domination of the industry. This position was undermined from the

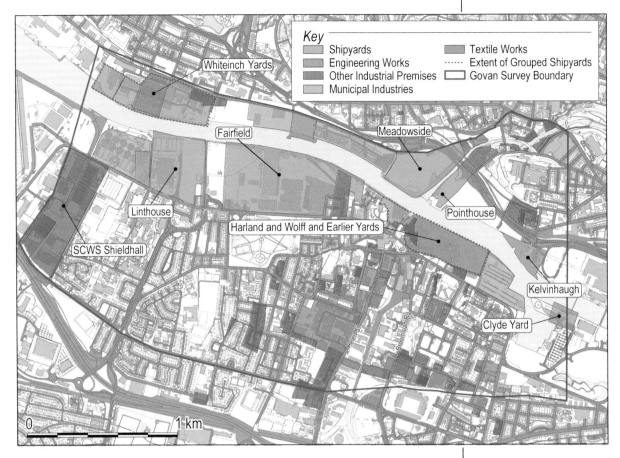

FIGURE 5.1
This map showing the location of industry in Govan illustrates how virtually the entire waterfront was given over to shipbuilding and many of the premises away from the river produced objects used in the shipyards

Key

- Shipyards
- Engineering Works
- Other Industrial Premises
- Municipal Industries
- Textile Works
- ······ Extent of Grouped Shipyards
- Govan Survey Boundary

Whiteinch Yards

Fairfield

Meadowside

Linthouse

Harland and Wolff and Earlier Yards

Pointhouse

SCWS Shieldhall

Kelvinhaugh

Clyde Yard

0   1 km

early twentieth century by a number of factors. Lacking incentive, innovation in engineering receded, and so did demand for ships of larger capacity given the physical limitations of many of the upper Clyde yards, Govan included. Many firms closed in the 1920s and 1930s and, although final collapse was stayed by the Second World War and a relative period of prosperity in the 1950s, the 1960s saw severe and nearly final contraction.

The yards in the Govan survey area can be divided into three main groups: those around the Kelvin; those at Whiteinch, and those in Govan itself.

Three main yards emerged by the Kelvin at Kelvinhaugh, Meadowside, and Pointhouse (Hume 1974, 82–4, 126, K4, L28, L36; Moss and Hume 1977, 97; Osborne *et al* 1996, 71; Walker 2001, 160–5; Williamson *et al* 1990, 374). Kelvinhaugh was the earliest, building wooden ships from the 1830s, but was redeveloped from the 1860s as Yorkhill Quay.

Meadowside (**fig 5.2**) was founded in 1847 by Tod and MacGregor, who had earlier founded Glasgow's iron shipbuilding industry at Mavisbank. Shipbuilding there ceased in 1935, though repair work continued under Harland and Wolff until 1962 (on Harland and Wolff see Moss and Hume 1986). An 1895 office and drawing block survives, Scotway House (**fig 5.3**), as does a large brick shed that appears on maps of the 1890s. Elements

FIGURE 5.2
Meadowside Yard, 1912,
looking north from the
Govan side (Reproduced by
permission of the Mitchell
Library, Glasgow)

FIGURE 5.3
Scotway House, former
offices of Meadowside yard
(Source: GUARD)

of the yard riverfront remain, notably the Kelvin entrance to the graving dock, which dates back to the original development of the site in the mid-nineteenth century. This graving dock, Glasgow's oldest, has significant archaeological potential.

Pointhouse was founded in 1862, was acquired by Harland and Wolff in 1919, and closed in 1962. No upstanding buildings remain, the site having been taken over by the expanding Yorkhill Quay and Basin, but traces of the main slipway into the Kelvin were still discernible until recently.

The Whiteinch yards – Whiteinch Jordanvale, East Whiteinch, Park and Clydeholm – developed from early foundations and continued in use beyond the First World War (Hume 1974, M90, M93; 1990, 98; Moss and Hume 1977, 110; Walker 2001, 159–60, 165; Williamson *et al* 1990, 387). Whiteinch Jordanvale began operating in 1826 and Park in 1854. The latter closed in 1922 and the former was acquired by Barclay Curle and Co in 1923. Barclay Curle had moved to Clydeholm in 1855, and its 1923 expansion also took in the 1848 East Whiteinch yard; the expanded Barclay Curle yard closed in 1965.

Barclay Curle underwent modernisation in the 1950s but there is an office block of 1883. Two features are of particular note: the main shop of the North British Diesel Engine Works (1912–13), and an associated Titan cantilever crane by Sir William Arrol and Co of similar type to the better known but later Finnieston crane (**fig 5.4**). Despite some later modification, the Engine Works is architecturally distinctive, strongly resembling Peter Behrens' pioneering 1908–09 AEG turbine factory in Berlin.

Govan's yards lay in three main groups: the Clyde yard isolated at the eastern edge of the town; a group around Water Row and Govan Cross; and the Fairfield and Linthouse yards to the west (Arrol 1909, 164–6; Brotchie 1905, 248–54, 256, 261–70; Hay and Stell 1986, 121–8; Hume 1974, 78, 82–4, 269, K1, K15, L12; McKenzie 2002, 187–8; Moss and Hume 1977, 113–44; Osborne *et al* 1996, 57–8, 64–8, 71–3; Walker 2001, 169–80; Williamson *et al* 1990, 596). Little is known about the mid-nineteenth-century Clyde yard, the site being redeveloped as the Cessnock (Prince's) Dock in the 1890s. Similarly, little is known of the later nineteenth-century Water Row yard.

The other yards around Water Row were the early hub of Govan's shipbuilding industry and were all later absorbed by the massive Harland and Wolff yard, operating between 1912 and 1962 (Hume 1974, K15; Osborne *et al* 1996, 57–9; Walker 2001, 171–2). The earliest of the group was the Old Govan yard (**figs 5.5 & 5.6**). This opened in 1839, but owes its chief fame to its operation under Robert Napier from 1841 and Randolph and Elder from 1860 to 1863. Napier has been dubbed the 'Father of Clyde Shipbuilding' for his role in the early development of the industry and for his tutelage of many of the industry's prominent figures in the 'kindergarten of Clyde shipbuilders' (Moss and Hume 1977, 88; Walker 2001, 168). John Elder, co-founder of Govan's Fairfield yard, was Napier's chief draughtsman and William Pearce, who later took over at Fairfield, was his general manager (Moss and Hume 1977, 88–9; see Hillhouse 1925 and Slaven 1986 for biographies).

Napier expanded into the established Govan East yard in 1850. This operated in conjunction with the Old Yard for a time and on Napier's death it passed to Dr A C Kirk, noted for his introduction of the redesigned triple-expansion engine in 1886 (Moss and Hume 1977, 93). Lying between these was the Middleton Yard (1842), which expanded after 1864.

These yards were extensively redeveloped under Harland and Wolff until closure in 1962 (**fig 5.7**). A 1970s corporation housing development now occupies much of the site and, to the west, an open space is used for car parking (see **fig 2.1**). A wet basin, the former slipways on the Clyde riverfront, and the 'Big Shed' on Govan Road survive from the Harland and Wolff period.

In contrast, Fairfield and, to a limited extent, Linthouse retain important early survivals. The Fairfield Shipbuilding Yard and Engine Works in particular is notable for its individual historic buildings and structures, its continuing

FIGURE 5.5
Mackie and Thomson's Old
Govan Yard, also known
as the Govan Shipbuilding
Yard, 1891 (Reproduced by
permission of the Mitchell
Library, Glasgow)

coherence as an entity, and the level of interest it has attracted from historians. Particular value derives from the survival of structures from several periods in a setting that allows their continued appreciation as a group. Fairfield is also of wider significance in Govan, as its managers and their families, especially the Elders and Pearces, were noted philanthropists and church patrons (see below).

In 1863 Randolph, Elder and Co (later John Elder and Co) formed the yard from a portion of the Fairfield estate. William Pearce became sole partner in 1878, and before his death in 1888 he initiated an era of expansion that saw Fairfield assume special prominence (**fig 5.8**). The twentieth century saw

FIGURE 5.6
Advertisement for Mackie
and Thomson Shipbuilders,
Scotland's Industrial Souvenir,
1905 (Courtesy of K Sertis)

FIGURE 5.7
Aerial view of the Harland and Wolff yard, *c* 1930, which dominated the Water Row area from 1911 to the 1960s. The Framing Shop (top) ran from the west side of Water Row to Govan Old and the Platers' shop occupied the site of the Old Govan Yard on the other side of Water Row (Reproduced by permission of the Mitchell Library, Glasgow)

various phases of management, famously under Upper Clyde Shipbuilders, and the yard still operates under BVT surface fleet.

The former engine works dates to between 1869 and 1871 (**fig 5.9**), and was designed as a series of tall naves and intervening galleries. The 50-foot clear (*c* 15m) height was to allow the erection of the inverted vertical triple expansion engines patented by John Elder. A small version of this archetypal marine engine is shown in the statue to John Elder that stands in front of the Engine Shop in Elder Park, with a hyperbolic inscription placing him second only to James Watt as a steam-engine maker. This is Scotland's largest cast-iron framed building and is of considerable archaeological potential (Hay and Stell 1986, 124–8). The boardroom and drawing office block survives on Govan Road (1889, extended in the 1950s) (**fig 5.10**) and so did a drawing office and mould loft (in which full-scale patterns were traced on paper of what was to be cut from sheet steel) on Elder Street (1903). An Art Deco block (1940) stands back from the Elder Street offices. A Titan cantilever crane by Sir William Arrol (1911) stood to the east of the fitting-out basin and was used for the installation of engines and boilers, previously done by sheerlegs (**figs 5.11 & 5.12**). There are similar Arrol cranes in Greenock, Whiteinch and Clydebank. Arrol also built additions to the engine and boiler shop. The south end of the basin is lined by the nineteenth-century pipe-shop. The fabrication shops were reconstructed between the 1960s and 1990s, so that ever-larger parts of ships could be built under cover.

The Linthouse Engine Works and Shipyard also has surviving historic elements, though these are scattered. Alexander and Sons formed the yard from the Linthouse estate from 1869 and the yard eventually closed in 1968. The *in situ* surviving element of the complex is a reinforced concrete and brick office block of 1914 on Holmfauld Road (**fig 5.13**). The iron- and timber-framed engine works (1872) was removed in 1986–90 to the Scottish

FIGURE 5.8
Aerial view of Fairfield
shipyard and Govan Road
c 1930 before enlargement
of Meadowside Granary,
opposite, in 1938
(Reproduced by permission
of the Mitchell Library,
Glasgow)

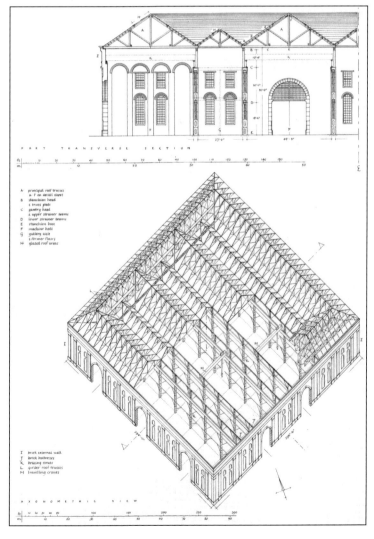

FIGURE 5.9
Survey drawing by Geoffrey
Hay (1980) of the Fairfield
Yard engine works of 1869
(Crown copyright: Royal
Commission on the Ancient
and Historical Monuments
of Scotland)

FIGURE 5.10

Clocking off at Fairfield Yard: the main entrance is between the drawing office and the mould loft (Reproduced by permission of the Mitchell Library, Glasgow)

FIGURE 5.11

Fairfield's fitting-out basin, showing the sheerlegs that were to be replaced by a Titan crane in 1911 (Reproduced by permission of the Mitchell Library, Glasgow)

FIGURE 5.12

(left) The Titan cantilever crane was built in Fairfield's fitting-out basin in 1911 and demolished in 2005 (Crown copyright: Royal Commission on the Ancient and Historical Monuments of Scotland)

FIGURE 5.13

(bottom left) The office block of the Linthouse Yard, built 1914, now occupied by Govan Workspace and others (GUARD)

FIGURE 5.14

(below) The Linthouse engine shop which was dismantled in 1987 and re-erected at the Scottish Maritime Museum in Irvine

Maritime Museum in Irvine (**fig 5.14**), the largest historic building to have been relocated in Scotland (Hay and Stell 1986, 121–4). Parts of the site have seen recent redevelopment by Barr and Stroud/Thalys. A notable related survival is part of the Linthouse Buildings tenement block, which housed workers from the yard (see below).

Linthouse, Fairfield, and Barclay Curle were the only yards to have their own on-site engine shops (**fig 5.15**); the other yards relied on off-site engine production, and all yards were served by the related industries that grew up away from the river. Concentrated on Helen Street and Broomloan Road, these industries emerged along a corridor bordering the Glasgow and Paisley Joint Railway of the 1860s. A second corridor followed an eastward branch of the railway leading to Prince's Dock. Not all of the secondary industries related solely to shipbuilding, as some were also essential to locomotive manufacture, but they are discussed here as a group.

Marine engineering was a Glasgow speciality from the early nineteenth century (Hume 1990, 90; see Hume 1974, 77–8). Many of the early Glasgow shipyards had separate engineering sites in districts like Anderston, Lancefield, and Finnieston but a group of other firms emerged in Govan and Partick from the 1870s. Of these, an isolated survival is the Helen Street works of British Polar Engines, dating between 1884 and 1905 with a later Art Deco office block (Hume 1990, 92; Williamson *et al* 1990, 598).

Around the core engineering and shipbuilding concerns, a variety of firms emerged supplying components and tools. Some shipyards had their own boiler shops, as at Fairfield and Pointhouse, now demolished (Hume 1974, L35, H1), but independent boilermakers existed too, like the now-demolished Moorepark Boiler Works on Helen Street (*ibid*, K50). Often, engine and boiler works were combined under one roof, as at the Clydeside Engine and Boiler Works and the Whitefield Works, both on Carmichael Street. The main block at Whitefield was demolished in 1969, but historic elements may survive amongst the present buildings on both sites (*ibid*, K27).

Various iron foundries were also established around this time, and from the 1860s Govan and its environs had its share of such concerns (*ibid*, 64–5, K51, L29). All are now gone, the chief survivor of Glasgow's iron founding industry lying in Anderston (Hume 1990, 91). Tube works, producing welded iron tubes for gas, steam and water, emerged on Helen Street and Broomloan Road from the 1870s (Hume 1974, K46, K61).

Steel founding was a more specialised trade and, as a result, there were few steel foundries in Glasgow (Hume 1974, 67). Exceptions were the 1881–82 Govan Steel Works and the 1893 Caledonian Steel Foundry, both in Helen Street and both since demolished (*ibid*, K56, K58).

Several brass foundries were located in and around Govan. The 'heavy end' of the trade was represented at the surviving Steven and Struthers foundry on Eastvale Place in Yorkhill (1897), which specialised in bells and propellers (Hume 1974, 68, K7; 1990, 91). Carmichael Street in Govan housed the Whitefield Brass Works, and elements of this may survive amongst the buildings presently on the site.

In general, coppersmiths were less numerous. Of the five now or recently extant examples in Glasgow, two were on Govan's Woodville Street (Hume 1974, K38, K40). One of these is instantly recognisable by its Flemish gable and the curved pediments of its dormer windows (Williamson *et al* 1990, 599).

Wireworks manufacturing wire ropes were indispensable in producing ship and crane rigging amongst other things (Hume 1974, 70–1). An earlier hemp ropeworks at Kelvinhaugh (since demolished) was established by the mid-nineteenth century. The 1890 Govan Ropeworks on Helen Street, which may have produced hemp and canvas as well as wire rope, was demolished

FIGURE 5.15
Aerial photograph of Govan and Partick taken by the Luftwaffe in 1939 and marked with targets. F is Stephen's Linthouse Shipyard (Crown copyright: Royal Commission on the Ancient and Historical Monuments of Scotland)

in 1969 (*ibid*, K49), but elements of the Ladywell Wire Works of 1907–08 on Broomloan Road still survive (*ibid*, K48).

Machine tool manufacture was, at first, a branch of general engineering, but specialists in heavy tools for plate-working in boilermaking, shipbuilding, and structural engineering soon appeared (Hume 1974, 74). Examples once existed at the Artizan Machine Tool Works (*c* 1882) on Old Dumbarton Road and the Albion Works on Govan's Woodville Street (1880) (*ibid*, 74, K43, L48).

Despite the prominence of heavy industry, the area did not lose touch with its textile heritage. Pollok's silk factory continued in use to *c* 1900, eventually falling under the expanding Fairfield shipyard (Brotchie 1905, 103). Maps of the 1890s show a second silk works on Dunsmuir Street. Cotton factories were operating on Castlebank Street and in Kelvinhaugh by the mid-nineteenth century (see Hume 1974, 29, K9 on the latter) and by the later nineteenth century, weaving factories were operating in Broomloan and on Helen Street (see Hume 1974, 33, K60 on the latter). These textile production firms were complemented by print works in Govan, Ibrox and Kelvinhaugh, and bleach works in Kelvinhaugh and on Castlebank Street.

There was also expansion and transformation of the victualling trade to provide for the subsistence of the growing population. The tradition of milling on the Kelvin was continued in the Scotstoun Flour Mills (1877 onwards), Scotstounmill Road, which continue in operation (Hume 1974, 4, 5, 7, L41; Williamson 1990, 374). The Bishop Mills were rebuilt from the 1830s (Hume 1974, L47; Williamson *et al* 1990, 374) while the Bunhouse Mill was replaced by the Regent Flour Mills in 1887–90, and the premises acquired by the Scottish Co-operative Wholesale Society in 1903 (Hume 1974, 4, 5, 7, L46, M86).

Bakeries were constructed on Copland and Craigton Roads in the 1900s (Hume 1974, K33, K36, K67) and there was an aerated water works on Helen Street from *c* 1900 (*ibid*, K55). Mention should be made of several other notable commercial buildings: the Carmichael Works (chemical) on Carmichael Street; the elaborate brush factory of 1897 at 140 Copland Road (*ibid*, K37); the former Govan Press Buildings of 1888–89 off Govan Road (*ibid*, K22; Murphy 1920); the former Savings Bank on Govan Road (Williamson *et al* 1990, 597–8); and the former British Linen Bank which dominates the corner of Govan Road and Water Row (*ibid*, 595–6).

Towards the end of the nineteenth century, consumer demand was booming and individuals such as Sir Thomas Lipton began to provide staple fare for working-class consumers (Maver 2000, 128–30). A number of other grocery and provision concerns emerged in the 1870s and 1880s, most with a consumer base in working-class districts (*ibid*, 130).

In this climate, the Scottish Co-operative Wholesale Society (SCWS) was established in 1868 and branches of retail co-operative societies began to appear in Glasgow in the 1870s (Maver 2000, 130–1). The earlier Govan Victualling Society, founded in 1800, had been a pioneering example of an

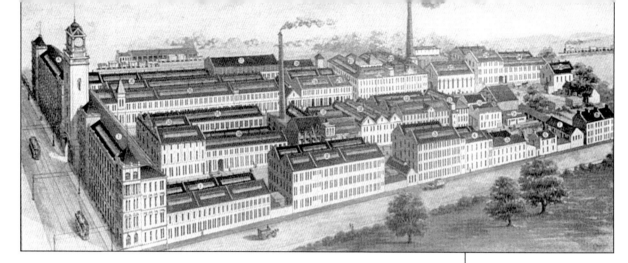

FIGURE 5.16
Aerial view of the Scottish
Co-operative Wholesale
Society works at Shieldhall,
1913

FIGURE 5.17
The cabinet factory within
the Scottish Co-operative
Wholesale Society works at
Shieldhall (Crown copyright:
Royal Commission on the
Ancient and Historical
Monuments of Scotland)

organised consumer co-operative society, and as the century progressed more retail societies emerged in Scotland (Brotchie 1905, 275–6). Co-operation appealed to the working-class shopper not only because prices were cheap, but because of the regular returns from the 'dividend', based on the quantity of purchases. The success of co-operation provoked a hostile reaction from independent traders, who claimed that it was undermining free competition and private enterprise.

The SCWS was founded as a cost-effective way to supply retailers, and proved to be a highly successful enterprise (Kinloch and Butt 1981, 36–9), supplying a range of goods. The Society's first premises were in central Glasgow, but in 1885 a 5 ha site at Shieldhall was identified as suitable for expansion, and production soon came to be concentrated there, with construction commencing in 1887 (Hume 1974, 264; see below). Sir William Maxwell, SCWS chairman, was the driving force behind the development, and

FIGURE 5.18
The Luma Lamp Factory
is the only surviving major
element of the SCWS
Shieldhall works, 1939,
shown here soon after
completion. It has now
been converted into flats
(Reproduced by permission
of the Mitchell Library,
Glasgow)

he oversaw the construction of the first factories, for footwear manufacture (Slaven and Checkland 1990, 379–81). Maxwell and his fellow directors looked to the massive new Singer sewing machine factory at Kilbowie, Clydebank, for stylistic inspiration for Shieldhall.

The various premises of the SCWS have been described as the 'crowning glories of co-operative architecture and enterprise' (Hume 1974, 102). Built from 1887, the SCWS works at Shieldhall comprised a massive complex of one-, two-, three-, four- and six-storey buildings, mainly in red and white brick with some sandstone construction (**figs 5.16 & 5.17**; Hume 1974, 284, M88; Spalding 1994, 17–19). This was one of the largest industrial sites in Glasgow, built to answer a growing demand for SCWS products. By 1918 there were seventeen different departments, producing a wide range of food, clothing and manufactured goods, and providing employment for some 4000 people. The SCWS sought to provide model conditions for their workers and the factory was originally to be accompanied by a model village, but the opening of an electric tramway in the area rendered it unnecessary to build houses locally. Despite the undeniable significance of the SCWS Shieldhall complex, the only surviving visible element is the Luma Lamp Factory, erected in 1939 by the SCWS in co-operation with the Swedish Co-operative Society and dominated by its lamp-testing tower (Watson 2000; **fig 5.18**).

Port and transport infrastructure

Govan's industrialisation required continued changes to the nature of transport. Alterations to the Clyde entered a new phase in 1824, with the initiation of substantial dredging, straightening and widening programmes (Riddell 1979, 84–7, 89 and *passim*). These river alterations allowed increasingly larger ships to navigate to Glasgow, facilitating exports and the movement of industrial raw materials. In Govan, they were a significant factor in the development of shipbuilding. The bed of the Clyde at its confluence with the Kelvin was lowered by approximately 25 feet (*c* 7.5m) between the 1820s and 1940s (Galbraith 1958, fig 25).

The concentration of shipyards at Govan severely restricted the westward expansion of Glasgow's harbour facilities (Riddell 1979, 133). Notable quay expansion took place from the 1840s, but the construction of off-river docks became a necessity from the 1860s (Hume 1974, 125–6). Queen's Dock, now the site of the SECC, was opened in 1877 and its former hydraulic pumping station survives (**fig 5.19**; Hume 1974, 126; Osborne *et al* 1996, 40–6). Dock development then ceased for fifteen years, to be resumed with the Cessnock (Prince's) Dock of the 1890s (**fig 5.20**), and continued with Yorkhill Quay's new basin of 1908 and the King George V Dock of 1931 (Hume 1974, 126). Prince's Dock became the site of the Glasgow Garden Festival in 1988 and is now home to the Glasgow Science Centre, though it retains its main hydraulic power station and auxiliary accumulator tower (**fig 5.21**). The long, single-storey Anchor Line transit sheds at Yorkhill were, until recently, a rare survival (Williamson *et al* 1990, 296), but have now made way for the new Museum of Transport.

The other major monument to shipbuilding and repairing is the Govan Graving Docks at the entrance to Prince's Dock (**figs 5.22 & 5.23**; Hume 1974, 126-127, K14; Osborne *et al* 1996, 56; Riddell 1979, 136, 137, 222, 329; Williamson *et al* 1990, 99, 595, 598). These dry docks were built between 1869 and 1898 for the Clyde Navigation Trust, providing ship-repairing facilities for Glasgow's harbour. They were each the largest in Scotland when built, and No. 3 dock (880 feet long (*c* 268m), which could be split into two by a caisson) was briefly the longest in the world until overtaken by Canada Dock, Liverpool, and only 7 feet (*c* 2m) shorter than Thomson's Dock in Belfast after the latter was extended for the Titanic (*Encyclopedia Britannica* 1911). The hydraulic power station for No. 1 Dock still stands, other surface buildings having been cleared in 2003, leaving in place the archaeology of the hydraulic systems below ground level (especially as relates to the engines for No. 3 Dock).

FIGURE 5.19
Queen's Dock in 1936, showing a fixed steam crane on the left and the new Finnieston electric cantilever crane on the right (Reproduced by permission of the Mitchell Library, Glasgow)

FIGURE 5.20
Cessnock (Prince's) Dock,
c 1965 (Reproduced by
permission of the Mitchell
Library, Glasgow)

FIGURE 5.21
Aerial view of eastern Govan
looking east (2005). In the
distance are the Science
Centre and BBC built on
Prince's Dock. The three
graving docks are the most
conspicuous remains of
the shipbuilding industry in
this part of Govan (Crown
copyright: Royal Commission
on the Ancient and Historical
Monuments of Scotland)

Lairages for the landing of live cattle were built at Shieldhall in the later nineteenth century and at Merklands from 1907 (**fig 5.24**), and grain imports to the city came to be concentrated at Meadowside Quay, where an enormous granary was constructed in 1911 (**fig 5.25**); the granary was extended in 1938 and 1970 but has since been demolished (see Hume 1974, 126).

Govan's ferries remained the only way to cross the Clyde at this point until the construction of the Finnieston harbour tunnel in the 1890s, then the largest such tunnel in the UK (Hume 1974, 107, H119, K5, K13, L11; 1976, 166; Osborne *et al* 1996, 38–9, 57, 70–1; Riddell 1979, 140–1). The Govan

FIGURE 5.22
Three paddle steamers in
No. 3 Dry Dock, Govan
Graving Docks, *c* 1910. Built
in 1898 it is 880 feet long
(*c* 268m) (Reproduced by
permission of the Mitchell
Library, Glasgow)

FIGURE 5.23
Aerial view of the Govan
Graving Docks in their
current abandoned state,
opposite the *Glenlee* and the
Anchor Line transit sheds
(Crown copyright: Royal
Commission on the Ancient
and Historical Monuments
of Scotland)

Ferry was taken over by the Clyde Navigation Trust in 1857 and continued in use until the mid-1960s (**fig 5.26**). The Kelvinhaugh to Govan passenger ferry continued in use as late as the 1980s. Govan Ferry West, running from Meadowside to near the Old Parish Church, was in operation by the later nineteenth century and would have carried passenger traffic. A second vehicular ferry and another passenger ferry ran from Whiteinch to Linthouse from the later nineteenth and early twentieth centuries; the route closed in 1963.

Following the introduction of variable-level vehicular ferries, existing

FIGURE 5.24
Merklands Lairage, *c* 1930
(Reproduced by permission
of the Mitchell Library,
Glasgow)

FIGURE 5.25
Meadowside Granary
c 1970, reputedly the largest
brick building in Europe in
1955, was demolished for
housing development in 2004
(Reproduced by permission
of the Mitchell Library,
Glasgow)

FIGURE 5.26
Govan Ferry, *c* 1890
(Reproduced by permission
of the Mitchell Library,
Glasgow)

FIGURE 5.27
The variable-level vehicular
ferry to Govan (Reproduced
by permission of the
Mitchell Library, Glasgow)

slipways were replaced with small, gated docking bays (**fig 5.27**). The most recent fixed provision for the passenger ferries consisted of stairways set into quays or projecting from the riverbanks. Terminals survive at Yorkhill Quay, by the Govan Graving Docks, at Water Row, Pointhouse, and on the north bank at Govan Ferry West.

Linked with the development of the river and with passenger transport was the introduction of the railways. The 1830s and 1840s saw the first 'railway mania', with the construction of major trunk lines heralding a new era of expansion (Butt 1967, 180–1; Hume 1976, 37–40). Three main lines fall within the survey area in Govan: running south from Govan Cross was the Glasgow and Paisley Joint Railway, with a station (since removed) and goods yard built near the Cross in 1868 (Hume 1974, K20; Smart 2002, 91). The line from Glasgow to Helensburgh, which passes through Stobcross and Partick, was completed in 1858 (Galbraith 1958, 317; Hume 1974, 120, I34) and, joining this line, the Lanarkshire and Dumbartonshire Railway opened in 1896 (Johnston and Hume 1979, 108). This runs along South Street before crossing the Kelvin and passing underground.

In competition with the railway passenger services, the first street tramways were opened in the 1870s (Butt 1967, 184; Hume 1974, 109–10, L42; Hume 1976, 36–41; Johnston and Hume 1979, 109). From an early period, tramways in the burghs adjoining Glasgow were integrated with the Glasgow system. The Vale of Clyde Company ran a horse, and later steam, tram to Govan until 1893, and a depot was situated just south of the present subway station at the Cross. Electrification of the system began in 1898 and was complete by 1901. No features of the Vale service to Govan survive, but parts of a depot and stables of the Glasgow Tramways Company (*c* 1883) have been incorporated into a building on Thurso Street in Partick.

Increasing congestion was targeted by the Glasgow subway system (Hume 1974, 125, K21; Johnston and Hume 1979, 125–31), which was completed in 1896. Bought by the Glasgow corporation in 1922, the system retained most of its Victorian character until modernisation in 1976, although the cable traction system was replaced with the completion of electrification in 1935. Two stations, at Govan Cross (formerly entered through a public house) and Ibrox (Copland Road), fall within the Govan survey area (**figs 5.28 & 5.29**), and Govan also housed the stock-maintenance workshops for the whole system. Both the Govan and Copland Road stations were modernised in the 1970s. The subway workshops on Broomloan Road are still in use as such.

FIGURE 5.28
Govan Cross subway station was entered through a public house (Reproduced by permission of the Mitchell Library, Glasgow)

FIGURE 5.29
Copland Road subway station (Reproduced by permission of the Mitchell Library, Glasgow)

Population and housing

As observed in Chapter 4, the population of Govan parish in the 1790s was around 2500 and this had grown to over 4000 by the 1820s. From the 1830s, the developing industries, especially the shipyards, attracted an influx of workers from both urban and rural areas (Maver 2000, 98). In 1864, when the police burgh of Govan was inaugurated, the population of the new community was estimated to be around 9500 (Glasgow Boundaries Commission 1888, 88). By 1901, according to census returns, there were 82,174 inhabitants, and Govan was Scotland's seventh most populous town, exceeding Greenock and with over twice the number of inhabitants of Perth. Given its limited territory, covering 534 ha by the 1900s, it was also one of the most congested communities in Scotland. The burgh's later rate of growth was relatively constrained compared with Lanarkshire steel towns like Coatbridge, Motherwell, and Rutherglen, but by 1911, on the eve of annexation by Glasgow, Govan still retained significant demographic status with a population of 89,725. Initially relatively diverse, through the later nineteenth century the population became increasingly proletarian.

It was the social and environmental problems attendant on population growth that led to the creation of the police burgh (see below). Iron shipbuilding was taking off at this time and the industry was moving from central Glasgow to less congested sites downriver. The success of shipbuilding was reflected in the continuing rise of Govan's population. Between 1871 and 1881 the number of inhabitants expanded from almost 20,000 to 50,000. While the incomers came overwhelmingly from Scotland, both Highlands and Lowlands, there was also a substantial Irish presence in Govan. The Highlanders and Irish tended to settle close to the Clyde Trust graving docks, to the east of the burgh, and near to Plantation Quay. Sir William Pearce, the Kent-born proprietor of Fairfield's Shipyard, showed that shipbuilding could also attract English migrants.

In the late nineteenth century, shipbuilding was increasingly susceptible to economic downswings, partly attributable to fluctuations in global demand and partly to local circumstances. Govan was hit hard after the 1878 collapse of the City of Glasgow Bank, which prompted a crisis of financial confidence throughout the west of Scotland. By 1884, according to one commentator, rising unemployment meant that 'the clangour along our river-side has become ominously faint' (Nicol 1885, 81). The depression helped to deter job seekers from moving to Govan, and for all that population growth

FIGURE 5.30
The concentration of housing in the nineteenth century shows the strong zoning between residential areas and those occupied by manufacturing sites. Although the settlement builds upon earlier areas of settlement, it is clear that much of this has been fitted around the various works

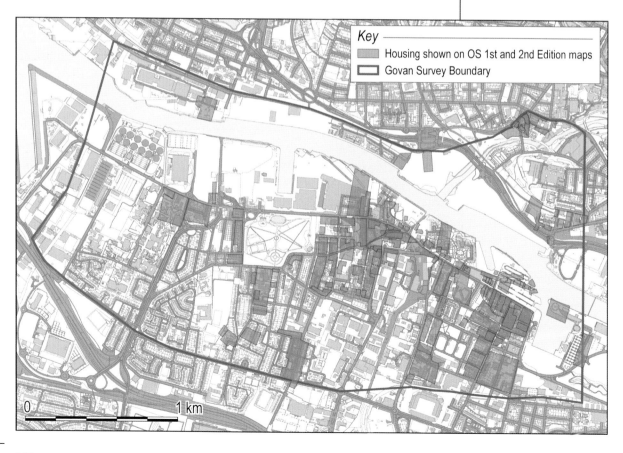

Key
Housing shown on OS 1st and 2nd Edition maps
Govan Survey Boundary

0   1 km

continued during the 1880s, the pace was much less marked than previously. Yet there was a minor demographic boost when the burgh boundaries were extended in 1901. At that time, the burgh absorbed the Linthouse district and territory near to the SCWS factories at Shieldhall, which added 5600 to the population.

The arrival of heavy industry, the growth of Govan's industrial population, and the changing social profile were intimately tied to changes in the character of housing (Horsey 1990, 3). As throughout Glasgow, the bulk of the pre-1914 housing stock was built by the private sector for rent (see, for example, Horsey 1990, chapter 1; Rodger 1989a). Govan's industrial era housing can be divided into four categories: tenements, terraced houses, villas and lodging houses (**fig 5.30**). The mix of types indicates the initially diverse profile of the industrial population, while the eventual predominance of the tenement is symptomatic of increasing social polarisation. By the later nineteenth century, Glasgow's middle classes were increasingly suburbanised, leaving central urban areas to business, industry, and the working classes (Fraser and Maver 1996bc 419), although sizeable tenements existed for them in the West End and some other districts.

The tenement is essentially a multiple-occupancy block (Gibb 1983, 137). Typically of four storeys, it has a common entrance and stair (the 'close') leading to individual houses inside (Williamson 1990, 48–51). The smallest flat was the one-room 'single end'. Two-room flats were common and larger flats could extend to four or more rooms. This size difference reflects the diverse make-up of the tenement population, ranging from the unemployed to the professional middle classes. Tenements along main roads and at important junctions often received additional exterior elaboration.

Govan's first tenements of this type had emerged by the 1850s (see Brotchie 1905, 130–1; Davidson 1923, 13; Houston 1922, 127–31). At that time, though, the town retained its village character and tenements were spread thinly. Many of these earliest blocks housed the better-off members of the working population, such as shipyard foremen (Brotchie 1905, 131; Ferguson 1919, 16; Smart 2002, 84; Williamson *et al* 1990, 585). From the 1860s, tenement building expanded exponentially, many being built specifically to house the new shipyard workers, as at Linthouse (Smart 2002, 83, 86; Williamson *et al* 1990, 585, 596; Worsdall 1989, 99–100). Single-end and two-apartment flats predominated: by 1891, 86% of families in Govan were living in one- or two-room properties (Foster 1997, 26).

Amongst the earliest blocks were those east of Govan Cross, particularly on Govan Road (**fig 5.31**). Most have now gone and the only surviving one that is shown on the first edition Ordnance Survey map of the 1850s is Buckingham Square, between Copland Place and Summertown Road. The three other surviving blocks in this area – on Southcroft and Clynder Streets and beside Ibrox underground station – all date from the 1890s or 1900s.

A further group of survivals clusters in central Govan. The earliest here is part of the block on Burleigh Street, which is evident on the first edition Ordnance Survey map. The other blocks date from the 1890s and 1900s. Groups lie on either side of Govan Road on Langlands Road (**fig 5.32**), Shaw, Rosneath, Howat, Elder, Luath, Taransay, and Rathlin Streets. Here in the 1960s, Assist Architects pioneered the renovation of tenements, including the installation of plumbing and improvement of back courts that enabled a halt to be called to the total destruction of existing communities seen in other parts of Glasgow.

To the west of Elder Park, the surviving part of Linthouse Buildings on the north side of Govan Road was in place by the 1890s and the blocks on Drive Road; Hutton, Kennedra, Peninver, and Clachan Drives; on Cressy and Aboukir Streets; and Burghead Place largely date to the 1890s and 1900s (**figs 5.33 & 5.34**). Finally, to the south of the park are seven blocks on Langlands, Crossloan, and Craigton Roads, and on Uist and Elderpark Streets. The Langlands Road block was built prior to the 1890s, but all the others belong to the 1890s or 1900s.

From the 1850s, Glasgow also saw the construction of numerous middle-class enclaves of terraced houses, cottages, and villas (Williamson 1990, 51–2). Govan has two main suburbs of such houses: the earliest, already present by the time of the first edition Ordnance Survey map of the 1850s, lay in and around Merryland and Vicarfield Streets (Smart 2002, 84; Williamson *et al* 1990, 598), with examples surviving in Merryland Street. Further terraces were later erected to the south on Copland Road, Copland Place, Brighton Place and Woodville Street.

A second suburb was completed to the west and south of Elder Park c 1900 (Williamson et al 1990, 596). This group of terraces and semi-detached villas survives virtually complete: along Craigton Road from Edmiston Drive to Luss Road and Arthurlic Street; at Barnwell Terrace and on the corner of Drumoyne Road and Nimmo Drive; on Drumoyne Drive and Avenue, and on Langlands Road, St Kenneth and Holmfauldhead Drives, and Drive Road (**fig 5.35**).

Alongside the above, a notable isolated example of its type is Napier House, a model lodging house of 1898–99 between Govan Road and Clydebrae Street (**fig 5.36**; see Williamson *et al* 1990, 598). Common lodging houses had provided for the thousands of single, itinerant men taking work in the city. Many of these became notorious 'flea barracks' and 'fever dens', prompting the construction of improved 'model' accommodation from the 1870s (Fraser and Maver 1996b, 375). This one is built in part of mass concrete.

The Burgh of Govan

In 1864, c 450 ha of Govan parish, centred on the old village of Meikle Govan, became a self-governing police burgh by authority of the Sheriff of Lanarkshire (Glasgow Boundaries Commission 1888, 87). Before this time, problems of effective law enforcement had become glaringly apparent, to the alarm of local property owners. There was cause for concern not only about the turbulent behaviour of the industrial workforce, but also about the inadequate state of road maintenance, street lighting, drainage, and cleansing. The spectre of fever and disease, more readily associated with the wynds and closes of central Glasgow, seemed to be threatening the village, and contemporaries attributed the deteriorating environment to the living conditions of incoming migrants. At the police burgh's inaugural meeting of householders, in May 1864, one speaker pointedly referred to levels of overcrowding, claiming that 'it was by no means uncommon to find in a very small apartment a man and his wife and six lodgers' (quoted in Brotchie 1905, 172).

Twenty-two proprietors in Govan village had signed the original petition to create the burgh, under the terms of the General Police and Improvement (Scotland) Act of 1862. Commonly known as the 'Lindsay Act', it consolidated and extended previous legislation which allowed for more efficient local government in hitherto unrepresented populous places (Maver 2000, 98–100). Police burghs afforded an administrative mechanism that was deemed vitally important for providing community cohesion amidst the unprecedented expansion of Scotland's mid-Victorian industrial communities. The Lindsay Act specified a minimum threshold of 700 inhabitants for the formation of a burgh; with *c* 9500 residents Govan well exceeded the definition of a populous place (Urquhart 1991, 36). There was consequently no difficulty in receiving the sanction of Sheriff Archibald Alison, an old-style Tory who thoroughly approved of any moves to tighten police controls and protect public order.

Govan's new administration was more modest and functional than that of neighbouring Glasgow, which as a royal burgh had distinguished municipal origins stretching back to the twelfth century. Indeed, until 1900, Scotland's police burghs were not permitted the civic paraphernalia afforded to traditional town councils; the elected representatives were designated as commissioners rather than councillors and there was a chief magistrate rather than a provost (Atkinson 1904, 80). Yet whatever the legal status of Govan's chief magistrate in 1864, civic pride was steadily evolving in the community and he soon acquired the courtesy title of provost. Predatory Glaswegian intentions towards the burgh, manifested in an abortive attempt at annexation during the late 1860s, helped to reinforce this distinctive sense of separate identity (Fraser and Maver 1996a, 464).

The burgh had a ratepayer (or taxpayer) franchise, with male electors initially returning twelve commissioners, including three magistrates. Population growth and boundary extension increased this number to 21 commissioners and 6 magistrates by 1912. Women ratepayers could vote for the commissioners from 1882. Contested elections were relatively infrequent in the burgh's early years, but the more volatile politics of the 1900s eventually gave a competitive edge to municipal affairs.

Throughout the burgh's existence, the commissioners had been confronted with the conundrum of how to match public services with population growth. Policing provision remained relatively consistent, with 12 officers in 1864, 75 during the 1880s, and 119 by the 1900s (Glasgow Boundaries

Commission 1888, 88–9; Brotchie 1905, 186, 293). There were three police stations in the burgh. Fire fighting was another important responsibility, and the commissioners worked in tandem with the leading shipbuilders to prevent major conflagration. Steam fire engines and other apparatus were permanently based in the shipyards. The pivotal role of police and fire fighters showed how closely local government was bound up with protecting Govan's economic interests. The tight relationship between commissioners and employers in operating community control was one reason why the Independent Labour Party (ILP) began to make electoral gains in the 1900s.

Public health was a key issue for Victorian reformers, and a distinguished medical practitioner, Dr John Aitken, became the burgh's first medical officer of health, to be succeeded in 1880 by Dr James Barras. By 1911 Govan's death rate was 15.3 per 1000 of the population, lower than that of Glasgow (17.7), Dundee (17.6), and Edinburgh (16) (Glasgow corporation 1911, 6). In due course, however, health became a matter of close liaison between Govan and Glasgow and encouraged pro-annexationists to campaign for a joint improvement strategy to initiate integrated housing and town planning projects. In 1900, the outbreak of bubonic plague in Govan became a particularly notorious example of the need for collaboration, if only to dispel lurid rumours that infected Glasgow rats had migrated to the burgh by scurrying along the telegraph wires (Macgregor 1967, 6–7). By 1912, Glasgow Corporation was attacking Govan's financial capacity to provide health services (Lindsay 1912, 97–8). Govan Combination Hospital, run jointly by representatives from the police burgh and Govan parish council, came under criticism not because of the quality of its medical staff, but because there were insufficient beds to treat infectious diseases.

Despite renewed pressure during the 1880s, the Govan commissioners had doggedly refused to become part of 'Greater Glasgow', and they celebrated their continuing autonomy by constructing an elaborate town hall in Govan Road, opened in 1901. This did not stop repeated overtures from the city, however, nor, for all the rhetoric and display of the burgh commissioners, were Govanites necessarily opposed to annexation. There were areas, notably in the populous Plantation district, where the ILP was gaining electoral strength (Lindsay 1912, 102–3). The politicisation of burgh affairs during the 1900s began to swing working-class opinion around to supporting a Glasgow connection, not least because it was shown that Govan's less wealthy inhabitants would save money in rates. The financial factor eventually decided the issue in 1912, when richer ratepayers were assured favourable tax concessions over a ten-year period. Material benefits were also promised, including substantial policing and environmental improvements, and these were implemented after the First World War.

In 1866–67, soon after the foundation of the burgh, the first municipal buildings were constructed in Orkney Street, where they remain (**fig 5.37**;

Brotchie 1905, 175, 185; Williamson *et al* 1990, 591). In 1899, these were extended to the south with new buildings for the burgh police and fire services, both of which had been housed in Orkney Street from the outset. The extension occurred as a new town hall was being built at the east end of the town on Govan Road (**fig 5.38**). Built between 1897 and 1901, this contained a new council chamber, offices for the various burgh departments, committee rooms, and a theatre and concert hall, amongst other things (McKenzie 2002, 180–2; Williamson *et al* 1990, 591; see also *Building News* 21 May 1897, p 739, and 28 May 1897, p 775). It is perhaps no coincidence that the new, massively enlarged municipal buildings were erected shortly after the culmination of a series of annexation battles with the City of Glasgow in 1891. The new buildings might be seen as both an expression of Govan's triumph in that process and of ongoing concerns over its independence.

Manifestations of the burgh's social functions are still clearly seen. The Govan Combination Hospital, now the Southern General, was originally operated by a board comprising members of the Govan and Kinning Park burgh councils and the Govan parochial board (**fig 5.39**; Brotchie 1905, 232). Extant buildings include the 1867–72 Govan Combination Poorhouse and the original asylum (Williamson *et al* 1990, 594). Various other buildings and extensions survive from the 1880s, 1890s, and 1900s, including hospital blocks, a nurses' home and a children's home.

Early in the twentieth century, private benefactors sought to complement the work of the Combination Hospital. Isabella Elder's Elder Cottage Hospital on Drumoyne Road was built in 1910–12, and a contemporary nurses' home lies opposite (**figs 5.40 & 5.41**; McAlpine 1997, 170–3; Williamson *et al* 1990, 593–4). The architecture of each has a domestic theme, and the hospital was originally intended as a maternity home. It opened as a general hospital, however, with medical and surgical beds and an operating theatre. More recently, until final closure in 1987, it was used for convalescing patients from the Southern General.

FIGURE 5.37
(above left) Govan municipal buildings of 1868 (Brotchie 1905)

FIGURE 5.38
(left) Govan Town Hall (Reproduced by permission of the Mitchell Library, Glasgow)

Several existing villas in Merryland Street were converted to a nursing home from 1909, though much of the work dates to the 1930s (Williamson *et al* 1990, 598). The domestic theme was also taken up in the David Elder Infirmary of 1924–27 on Langlands Road (McAlpine 1997, 178; Williamson *et al* 1990, 593). Founded from a bequest by John Elder's brother, Alexander, this hospital was built to care for charity cases, especially sick and injured workers, and was also later used for convalescent patients.

As such institutions attempted to deal with the effects of urban and industrial illness, Glasgow's municipal authorities sought to tackle one of the root causes of disease by introducing a new, city-wide sewage system. From the 1880s, a programme of works was instigated to replace the existing system, whereby sewers discharged into rivers and streams, and ultimately the Clyde (Hume 1974, 136–7, L43, M89; Williamson *et al* 1990, 373, 594).

FIGURE 5.39
Southern General Hospital (formerly Govan Combination Hospital) (Reproduced by permission of the Mitchell Library, Glasgow)

FIGURE 5.40
Elder Cottage Hospital

FIGURE 5.41
Elder Cottage Hospital nurses' home

FIGURE 5.42
Aerial view of the Shieldhall
sewage works, *c* 1930, from
the south (Reproduced by
permission of the Mitchell
Library, Glasgow)

The first sewage purification works were at Dalmarnock and Dalmuir. The main sewer serving the latter could not be arranged with adequate fall, and so a pumping station was built on Dumbarton Road in 1904. A third works was completed at Shieldhall, on Renfrew Road, in 1910 (**fig 5.42**). The precipitation technique used in these treatment works produced quantities of sludge, and this was shipped from Shieldhall to a deep-water dumping ground in the Clyde estuary. The Shieldhall works still operate, though most of the facility now dates from *c* 1980; one older brick building survives on Renfrew Road. While Glasgow took the strategic initiative in hygiene improvement, local efforts to tackle cleansing, drainage, overcrowding, and other sanitation and health matters fell to the burgh of Govan (Brotchie 1905, chapters 14 and 15).

Schooling was managed from 1873 to 1918 by an elected school board that included some of Govan's noted industrialists alongside members of the ecclesiastical establishment (Brotchie 1905, chapter 19). It was the third largest board in Scotland, after Glasgow and Edinburgh. The board's territorial remit extended across the parish and included the districts of Govanhill, Kinning Park, and Pollokshields, as well as Hillhead, Kelvinside, and Partick to the north of the River Clyde (Stothers 1911, 214–15). A major programme of school building commenced in the 1870s, and by 1912 33 schools had been erected, serving 40,000 scholars and with a teaching staff of 850. From 1872 the minimum school leaving age in Scotland was thirteen years, rising to fourteen from 1901, which meant that the majority of board schools provided elementary education. However, the board also had charge of six higher-grade institutions, and there were some prestigious secondary schools in the Govan area. Bellahouston Academy, originally a private, semi-boarding institution, was taken over by the board in 1885, while Govan High School was opened under board auspices in 1910.

FIGURE 5.43 (above)
Hill's Trust School, c 1964 (Reproduced by permission of the
Mitchell Library, Glasgow)

FIGURE 5.44 (above right)
Greenfield Street School, c 1964 (Reproduced by permission of
the Mitchell Library, Glasgow)

FIGURE 5.45 (right)
Gilbert Street drill hall

In 1874, the existing parish school at Govan Cross was replaced with a new building in Golspie Street (**fig 5.43**; Smart 2002, 92; Spalding 1994, 22; Williamson *et al* 1990, 592). Known as Hill's Trust School, it was funded from a mid-eighteenth-century bequest by Abraham Hill, a Govanite whose wealth stemmed from a successful career as a merchant.

Another Govan board school stands in Broomloan Road. This was built in 1875, with a second building being added to it in 1894 (Williamson *et al* 1990, 593). Subsequently, in 1910, a new High School was built on Langlands Road, but this has since been destroyed by fire (Smart 2002, 92; Spalding 1994, 23). Kelvinhaugh Primary School, on Gilbert Street, also falls within the survey area and is a board school of 1886, although not one of Govan's (Williamson *et al* 1990, 296). One final surviving pre-1912 building is the Greenfield Street School on Uist Street and Nimmo Drive (**fig 5.44**).

To the complex of burgh and city, parish, and privately bequeathed institutions we might add several buildings associated with the state, particularly the armed forces. Govan's Whitefield Road has the 1905–06 drill hall of the Royal Naval Reserve, while Gilbert Street in Yorkhill retains that of the former Gilbert Street Volunteer Headquarters of the 6th Battalion Highland Light Infantry, dating from 1900–01 (**fig 5.45**; Williamson *et al* 1990, 296, 591).

The social environment

Social politics, labour relations, and philanthropy

Shipbuilders had first come to Govan because of the availability of undeveloped sites, which gave unencumbered access to the River Clyde. The attraction for John Elder, who acquired Fairfield in 1863, was that he could construct vessels to his own specifications, wholly on his own property (Murphy 1901, 87). Control and cost-effectiveness also related to the labour force. The west of Scotland had long been recognised as a low-wage region, and in 1872 one journalist referred specifically to the Clyde's advantage over the Thames, previously a main centre of British shipbuilding, because of the cheaper labour costs (Jeans 1872, 143–4). Significantly, Sir William Pearce, who came to work for Robert Napier's Govan yard in 1864, was London-trained. His arrival symbolised the decisive shift of economic emphasis from the English yards to Clydeside.

Between the 1860s and 1880s Govan's shipyard owners were characterised by their paternalistic outlook, and Elder particularly embodied this approach. For instance, with a workforce of around 4000 by 1869, he saw the need to establish an accident fund to cover costs arising from industrial injury; both the employer and workers contributed. His widow, Isabella Elder, was an enthusiastic philanthropist, and one of her innovations was the establishment of cookery classes for the wives and daughters of shipyard workers, some 200 Govan families being involved in the project. Martha Gordon, the cookery teacher, made clear that the Victorian values of morality and self-improvement provided the rationale for the classes, noting in 1888 that the gain to the women in 'personal neatness, in manners, speech and general tone' had been striking (quoted in Craig 1891, 197). Like the Elders, Alexander Stephen, the owner of the Linthouse yard, was committed to educational progress and served for twelve years as the first chairman of Govan school board (Carvel 1950, 88)

Stephen also became president of the Clyde Shipbuilders' Association (CSA) on its formation in 1889. Societies for mutual protection among shipbuilding and engineering employers had their roots in the 1860s, at a time when there was concern about the growth of worker organisation (Johnston 2000, 22). The emergence of the CSA, and later the national Shipbuilding Employers' Federation, indicated the move away from paternalism and towards more scientific management in industrial relations. Mechanisation and deskilling formed part of this process. In the face of heightened international competition, especially from Germany, the aim was to keep labour costs low by restructuring working patterns. In response, trade unionism grew on the Clyde, but initially made patchy progress; in 1892 Sidney and Beatrice Webb referred to the area as 'the home of piecework and contract work, of poverty, drunkenness, cupidity and competition' (quoted in Fraser and Maver 1996a, 333). Nevertheless, in the close-knit Govan community the labour movement began to make an impact from the 1880s, much to the discomfort of employers like Stephen.

During this decade, the Clyde economy was volatile, creating considerable job insecurity for shipyard workers, especially the unskilled. This contrasted with incidences of militant industrial action in specialist areas; for instance, the riveters were particularly vociferous about wages and conditions at a time of growing demand for their services in steel shipbuilding (Nicol 1885, 82–3). Over time, trade unionism came to cater for both skilled and unskilled workers, and the combined voice of organised labour in Govan was the Trades' Council, inaugurated in 1890 (Fraser 1978, 6). It acted as a forum for the various unions to pool their experience and resources on campaigning issues. In 1892, Govan Trades' Council also affiliated to a new political organisation, the Scottish United Trades' Council Independent Labour Party (STCLP), which gave financial backing to electoral candidates promoting issues such as the legal eight-hour day, full adult suffrage, and nationalisation, especially of land, mines, and railways. The STCLP was superseded by the ILP, formed on a British-wide basis in 1893. As a counter to employer control in so many aspects of Govan society, the ILP became a considerable force in local politics, supported both by the Trades' Council and the SCWS in Shieldhall.

Govan formed part of the North Lanark parliamentary constituency until 1885 when, after electoral reform, it was given its own MP. Political representation veered between the Liberals and Conservatives, with Sir William Pearce taking the seat for the latter party in 1885. After Pearce's sudden death in December 1888, the Govan constituency consistently returned a Liberal MP, with the notable exception of the 1906 general election. Confounding the nationwide Liberal landslide, Robert Duncan took the seat for the Conservatives and Unionists. The strong showing of an ILP candidate had divided Govan's left-wing vote, and consequently the ILP did not stand in 1910, when a Liberal was re-elected. Govan's support for socialist politics was confirmed in 1918, however, under post-war franchise rearrangements which allowed women to vote in parliamentary elections for the first time. Neil Maclean, a full-time organiser with the SCWS, won the seat for Labour with a majority of 815. He soon established a reputation as one the most radical and enduring members of the House of Commons (Knox 1984, 192–4).

We have seen that symbols of municipal government are prominent in Govan's built heritage. This point is neatly made by the 1884 memorial fountain to Dr John Aitken, the first Govan burgh medical officer and police surgeon, erected at Govan Cross (**figs 5.46 & 6.6**; Brotchie 1905, 196; McKenzie 2002, 450; Spalding 1994, 26; Williamson *et al* 1990, 595). But if this serves to remind us of the social role of the burgh, then the statue

FIGURE 5.46
Govan Cross from the west
facing Govan New Church
(St Mary's) showing the
spire, which is no longer
extant; behind the railings for
underground public toilets
is the Aitken Memorial
Fountain (Spalding 1994)

of shipbuilder William Pearce across the road serves to symbolise the fact that labour relations and private philanthropy were equally constitutive of the built environment at this time (**fig 5.47**). Philanthropy in industrial-era Govan, as the creation of the burgh itself, was intimately tied to the social politics, instabilities, and conflicts arising with industrialisation and urbanisation.

The Pearce statue was erected by public subscription in 1894 (**fig 5.48**), Pearce having died in 1888 (McKenzie 2002, 184; Williamson *et al* 1990, 592). Publicly sponsored, the statue is often held to symbolise gratitude to a benevolent industrialist. A brief consideration of Pearce's career, however, reveals tension in his relationship with the working population, giving a specific context to his benevolence and ambiguity to the statue's meaning.

Before 1885, Pearce was prominent amongst Clydeside anti-labour employers who combined to resist employers' liability, apprenticeship restrictions, and wage increases (Foster 1997, 24–5). Introducing this form of paternalism to Fairfield and moving away from the previous employers' attitude, he made himself a millionaire. He increased profits by targeting the lucrative market of Admiralty orders and, departing from established practice, reduced wages more sharply than profits when things were tight (*ibid*, 22–3; Slaven 1986, 229).

Pearce's approach to labour relations became particularly awkward when he sought election as Govan's first MP in 1885 – a move probably partly motivated by the prospect of new contacts and influence in his pursuit of Admiralty business (Foster 1997, 25–6). He needed to

FIGURE 5.47
Statue of William Pearce,
2007

FIGURE 5.48
Unveiling of statue of
William Pearce in 1894
(Reproduced by permission
of the Mitchell Library,
Glasgow)

secure the votes of Govan's overwhelmingly working class population and, despite his labour relations record, he was successful.

While standing as a Conservative and Unionist, he reinvented himself as a champion of the labour interest and played to Govan's Irish caucus with promises of devolution (Foster 1997, 20 and *passim*). Seeking credibility for his new position, he announced concessions to his stance on labour issues and was praised in the local press for his charitable donations. Subsequent labour disputes, his voting record and his platform at later elections confirm his opportunism (*ibid*, 25–30). Rather than indicating a simple harmony, Pearce's philanthropy and the statue celebrating him represent the ambiguity in worker-employer conflict at this time.

Pearce's opportunism contrasts with the more sustained philanthropy of Isabella Elder, who had more general concerns over the problems inherent in industrialisation and urbanisation (see McAlpine 1997 for a biography) (**fig 5.49**). This said, specific motives may underlie episodes of her work. So Elder Park, opened in 1885 and one of her major gifts to the town, was created at a time of significant economic depression (see Brotchie 1905, 203). Replacing Fairfield Farm, Elder Park was Isabella Elder's memorial to her husband, John, and his father (see Craig 1891; Gilmour 1996, 33–6; McAlpine 1997, 68–73, 167–9; McLellan 1894, 136–43; Spalding 1994, 4–6, 10; Williamson *et al* 1990, 591–2). She gifted the park 'for the use and enjoyment of the inhabitants in the way of healthful recreation by music and amusements' as defined in a series of by-laws (quoted in McLellan 1894, 141). As one contemporary added, it provided a 'breathing space [for the working classes] in a crowded industrial district' (quoted in McKenzie 2002, 96).

The Elder Park bandstand, since removed, and an adjacent platform for pipe band performances, provided a focus for musical entertainment

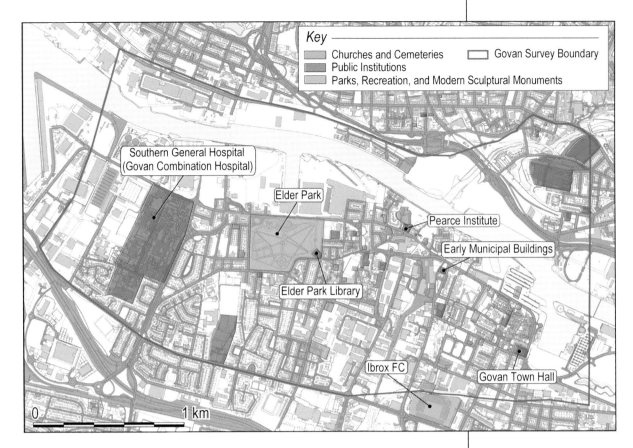

FIGURE 5.49
The churches, municipal institutions and philanthropic establishments are, not surprisingly, spread across the residential areas and away from the riverfront

(**fig 5.50**). The existing Fairfield farmhouse became the superintendent's offices, and rural connections were further referenced through a new deer park. In addition, a portico of the demolished eighteenth-century Linthouse mansion was erected in the park in 1921. A pond served for model boating, and the shipbuilding motif recurred in carvings on the bandstand. The Elder Park Library of 1903 carries carvings of a shipwright and draughtsman flanking the burgh crest over the entrance (**fig 5.51**).

The perception of the Elders as benevolent employers and innovative shipbuilders was promoted through two statues. The first, of John Elder, was erected through public subscription in 1888 (**fig 5.52**; Craig 1891, 106, 109–10; McKenzie 2002, 96–100; McLellan 1894, 141; Williamson *et al* 1990, 595). A paternalist, he had established an accident fund at Fairfield and funded evening class attendance for his younger employees (Craig 1891, 35; McAlpine 1997, 29–30). The second statue, of Isabella, was erected by public subscription and unveiled in 1906 (**fig 5.53**; Craig 1912, 1–4; Gilmour 1996, 34; McAlpine 1997, 175–6, 179; McKenzie 2002, 100–4; Williamson *et al* 1990, 595).

Beyond the park is other evidence of the diversity of recreation at this time and of attempts to control its form. The point is neatly made by the Cardell Halls and public house at Govan Cross (see Smart 2002, 91; Williamson *et al* 1990, 596). Built in 1894, the ground floor housed a

FIGURE 5.50
View of Elder Park looking east, *c* 1891. The bandstand can be seen in the background, while on display in the foreground is a llama, one of many animals kept in the park (Reproduced by permission of the Mitchell Library, Glasgow)

FIGURE 5.51
The portico to the Elder Park Library carries the burgh crest which features shipbuilding imagery and bears the motto *nihil sine labore*, 'nothing without labour' (Source: GUARD)

FIGURE 5.52
Unveiling the statue of John Elder in 1888 (Reproduced by permission of the Mitchell Library, Glasgow)

FIGURE 5.53
(top left) Statue of Isabella Elder

FIGURE 5.54
(top right) The Lyceum Theatre, built 1899, on Govan Road looking west (Spalding 1994)

FIGURE 5.55
(left) (a)The Lyceum Cinema in February 1939 (Reproduced by permission of the Mitchell Library, Glasgow); (b) Snow White and the Seven Dwarfs are among a number of Disney characters illustrated in a mural in the foyer of the Lyceum cinema that replaced the old theatre building on that site

FIGURE 5.56
(bottom left) The main stand of Ibrox Park, in 1935, from the Copeland Road end (Reproduced by permission of the Mitchell Library, Glasgow)

FIGURE 5.57
(bottom right) The Pearce Institute, photographed in 1959 by David Walker for the Scottish National Building Record (Crown copyright: Royal Commission on the Ancient and Historical Monuments of Scotland)

FIGURE 5.58
Postcard showing the British
Linen Bank, 1897, on the
south-west corner of Govan
Cross and the YMCA, 1905,
to the right (Reproduced by
permission of the Mitchell
Library, Glasgow)

pub, now Brechin's Bar, while the Halls served as a headquarters of the temperance movement.

Other entertainments were provided at the Lyceum Music Hall on Govan Road and at Ibrox Park. The Lyceum was constructed in 1899, but was replaced by the present cinema after it was destroyed by fire in the 1930s (**figs 5.54 & 5.55**; Spalding 1994, 30; Williamson *et al* 1990, 596). Rangers FC moved to Ibrox Park in 1899, although the earliest of the present buildings is the south stand of 1927–29 by engineer Archibald Leitch (**fig 5.56**; Williamson *et al* 1990, 592).

These symbols of working-class culture stand alongside two monuments to the ethos of self-improvement: the Pearce Institute on Govan Road and the former YMCA on Water Row. The Institute (1906) was designed by R Rowand Anderson, who had recently redesigned the parish church (**fig 5.57**; McKinstry 1991, 151–2; Spalding 1994, 28; Williamson *et al* 1990, 592). This was probably more than a coincidence, as the Institute was to be administered by the church. Erected in William Pearce's memory by his family and friends, the Institute provided the working population with reading rooms and clubs, a library, a gymnasium, retiring rooms, and cooking and laundry departments. With similar functions today, it also houses offices used by the minister of Govan Old, such that the church is integral to the Institute (Mitchell 2006). The YMCA was erected in 1898 (**fig 5.58**; Williamson *et al* 1990, 596), and would have had a similar remit.

The church in the industrial era
Up to the 1830s, the parish church was the only place of worship in Govan village. Matthew Leishman had become the minister in 1821 and served until his death in August 1874. A formidable personality and notable scholar, he

became leader of the 'Middle Party' at the time of the Disruption of the Church of Scotland in 1843, a division within the Presbyterian establishment that he believed could have been avoided had more compromises been reached between the opposing sides of Evangelicals and Moderates. By the end of his life, Leishman had come to symbolise the link between 'the teeming and busy burgh of the present, with the quiet and rural life of the last century' (Leishman 1921, 215). Rapid population growth in the Govan parish rendered his responsibilities particularly onerous; one evening in June 1870, he reputedly married 30 couples.

Leishman's successor, Revd John Macleod, arrived in 1875 and served as minister until his death in 1898. He was a member of the celebrated Highland preaching dynasty that included Revd Dr Norman Macleod of Glasgow's Barony Church. The family was noted for its commitment to improving working-class conditions, and so Govan was an appropriate destination for John Macleod. When he came, there were some 200,000 people in the parish, one of the largest in Scotland, and he made new church building a priority (Ferguson 1990, 94–5). A supporter of the Scoto-Catholic movement, which eschewed Calvinist austerity, Macleod's belief in mysticism, ritual, and the observance of the Christian year led to his nickname of 'Pope John of Govan'. He oversaw the building of a new parish church, opened in 1888, which included influences from Macleod's 'popish' visits to Italy (see below). George Macleod, later Lord Macleod of Fuineray, founder of the Iona Community, was yet another member of the family. He served as minister of Govan Old Parish Church between 1930 and 1938.

The years between the 1830s and 1870s were the great growth era for religious institutions in Govan. The movement started modestly, when the United Secession Church opened a small preaching station in 1837 (Brotchie

FIGURE 5.59
Norman-style church of Linthouse St Kenneth's by Peter Macgregor Chalmers opened in 1900, demolished in 1982 (Crown copyright: Royal Commission on the Ancient and Historical Monuments of Scotland)

FIGURE 5.60
The Romanesque-style tower
of St Anthony's RC church

FIGURE 5.61
Rowand Anderson's Govan
Old Parish Church, about
twenty years after it was
built in 1888, showing the
condition of the churchyard
prior to its modern decline
(Reproduced by permission
of the Mitchell Library,
Glasgow)

1905, 293–4). Ten years later, the Secessionists became part of the evangelical United Presbyterian Church, a denomination noted for its commitment to social outreach and enthusiasm for the temperance cause, which played such a prominent part in Scottish working-class culture during the Victorian period. The Free Church, another evangelical institution, emerged as a result of the 1843 Disruption. It attracted considerable support in Govan, and its first building for worship opened in 1844 on a site near Copland Road. A second church, Govan St Mary's, was built during the 1870s in Summertown Road. From 1908 to 1920 the minister of St Mary's was Revd James Barr, an outspoken, pro-temperance radical who was elected Labour MP for Motherwell in 1924 (Knox 1984, 61–5). The growing population placed huge demands on the established church and Govan Old responded by founding over 30 daughter churches during this period, the largest number by any church in Scotland (Davidson Kelly 2007).

Religion played a vital part in ensuring community cohesion and it often provided a sense of stability for incomers to the burgh from 1864. Significantly, a Roman Catholic chapel opened in Govan that year to serve the growing Irish community. The much more substantial edifice of St Anthony's designed in the Romanesque style by Honeyman, accommodating 1500, was erected in the 1870s (**fig 5.60**). Highland worshippers were catered for by two Gaelic-speaking congregations, one for the Church of Scotland, the other for the Free Church. Other Protestant denominations added to Govan's diverse religious profile by the 1900s: Episcopal, Free, Baptist, Wesleyan Methodist, United Free, and Congregational. Sectarianism represented another side of religious identity in Govan, with Protestant exclusiveness reinforced in the network of Orange Lodges and Masonic Halls that proliferated in the burgh by the late nineteenth century (Melling 1982, 92).

The considerable flux in religious provision had obvious effects on the built environment. One or two new churches were built in the period from the 1840s to the 1860s (Brotchie 1905, 293–7; MacDonald 1995, 53–5), but from the 1870s, the expansion in church construction increased dramatically. No fewer than seventeen churches built between 1870 and 1912 have been recorded during the survey (see Brotchie 1905, 295–8; MacDonald 1995, 50–5, 72–4; Williamson *et al* 1990, 586–91; Young 1899, 97). There was also a Salvation Army Citadel and a seaman's mission.

The architecture of Govan's surviving church buildings reflects the varying desires and needs of the congregations present (see, for example, Walker 1993). The earliest surviving

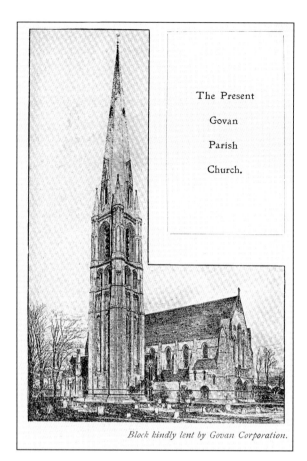

The Present
Govan
Parish
Church.

Block kindly lent by Govan Corporation.

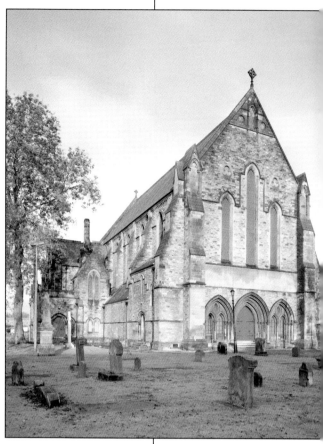

church in the survey area is St Simon's (RC) in Partick (1858). In Govan, the churches of St Mary's (now the New Govan Church of Scotland, originally Free Church) at Govan Cross (see **fig 5.46**) and St Anthony's (RC) on Govan Road date to the 1870s. Subsequently, we have St Saviour's (RC) in Merryland Street (1899), Linthouse St Kenneth's in Skipness Drive (1899) (**fig 5.59**) and St Columba's Free Gaelic in Briton Street (1910). The Salvation Army Citadel (1904) on Golspie Street still performs its mission.

Above all, Govan Old Parish Church saw renewed patronage. The manse was vacated in 1858 and demolished (Brotchie 1905, 161–2; Young 1899, 97 n.1). The church itself was dismantled in 1884 and re-erected in Golspie Street as the Elder Park Parish Church, since demolished (McKinstry 1991, 105; Young 1899, 97). A fund was raised for a new building, and Sir William and Lady Pearce, Isabella Elder and the Misses Steven of Bellahouston were major benefactors (McKinstry 1991, 107).

The new church was completed in 1888 and expanded out through the north wall of the churchyard, its orientation constrained by existing burial lairs (**fig 5.61**; Davidson Kelly 1994a, 12); an intended spire was never added (**fig 5.62**). R Rowand Anderson's design was heavily influenced by the incumbent Reverend John Macleod (see papers in Harvey (ed) 1988; McKinstry 1991,

FIGURE 5.62
Drawing of Govan Old Parish Church with the great tower that was never built (Brotchie 1905)

FIGURE 5.63
The Gothic appearance and enormous scale of the Govan Old Parish Church were intended to inspire worship, but perhaps also to emulate Glasgow's medieval Cathedral (Crown copyright: Royal Commission on the Ancient and Historical Monuments of Scotland)

105–7, 171; 1992; Thomson 1963; Williamson *et al* 1990, 586–7). Macleod believed in the beauty of worship as inspiration for the working classes, and hoped to transcend the darker side of industrialisation by creating a church geared towards a reformulated liturgy and the provision for daily worship (**fig 5.63**; see Bradley 1998 and Kirkpatrick 1915 for biographies of Macleod).

The graveyard continued in use, but burials eventually all but ceased; a recent survey has recorded 132 post-1809 nineteenth-century memorial stones in the churchyard, but only one dating to the twentieth century (Cutmore 1996; 1997; 1998; see also Willsher 1992). The nature of the memorials changed in terms of both their architecture and the epitaphs they bear, which became depersonalised. The profile of the burial population was also transformed. Before, a broad spread of the community had been commemorated, now, with the expanding population, many had to be buried elsewhere and the cemetery population came to represent a narrower segment of the population at large.

Discussion

From the mid-nineteenth century through to 1912 and beyond, the fabric and community of Govan underwent massive transformation, industrialisation and urbanisation. Govan and the neighbouring Clyde districts became a world-leading centre of shipbuilding and heavy industry, and there was a marked and related rise in population. In 1864, the police burgh of Govan was founded, primarily in order to manage the environmental and social problems arising from the creation of this large industrial population. Private employers, too, sought to reduce the potential for chaos, as they saw it, through programmes of philanthropy. In this period, Govan also became a significant base for the growing labour movement. The church, now catering for many diverse communities within Govan, retained something of its previous importance, but did so in a changed way.

Taking an overview of industry, population and housing, the burgh, and the social environment, it is clear that an understanding of Govan's industrial-period heritage necessitates a holistic approach. Recognising the connections between the numerous buildings and sites discussed in this chapter requires that we think of Govan's industrial-era heritage not just as a collection of individual sites and buildings, but also as a townscape. This means that the relationships between individual buildings, parks, industries, houses and other sites are as significant as the sites themselves.

The network of connections extends not just from one building to another, but from built environment to community. The social politics of this community were, in no small part, played out across this inter-connected built fabric. A key relationship was between employer and worker, but this relationship seeped out of the workplace and into the philanthropic works –

Elder Park, the statues, the Pearce Institute and other features – that still form a prominent part of the townscape today. This relationship is even evident in the long-established Govan Old Parish Church. The formation of the police burgh and its remit were intimately tied to the wider perceived problems inherent in industrialisation and urbanisation. Also, the elected representatives of the burgh – burgh commissioners, school board representatives and others – were very strongly connected to the employers, but only further detailed research will reveal just how closely and in what specific ways. At this stage, it is sufficient to note the close connections between built environment, burgh government, industry, education, philanthropy, and much besides.

These strong connections running between different elements in Govan's community have also seriously coloured past approaches to the history of the town. The nostalgia surrounding ancient and 'independent' Govan that emerged in the nineteenth and early twentieth centuries, and the related propaganda surrounding the benefits of industrialisation, municipal government, and the need to redress social ills, represents a specific view belonging to the Govan Commissioners, the employers, and the middle classes in general. It was from these groups that Govan's historians were drawn. Detailed historical research into the formation of Govan's capitalist and governing classes will not only further our understanding of those groups themselves, but inform us on the particular character of Govan's historiographical tradition.

Given the extent to which past histories have been geared towards the interests of the governing class, new research on the primary documentary and material evidence for industrial Govan is necessary in order to reassess fully the town's recent past. This new research must be extended to renewed insights into the relationships between all of the many diverse groups inhabiting the historic town, and should not simply be concerned with the role of the prominent few, famous names and industrial 'firsts'. The role of the built environment will be valuable in the genesis and continued transformation of Govan as an industrial and urban community. Extant buildings and other standing features, together with certain types of archaeological deposit, form a significant potential resource in this field.

This is a relatively well-documented period, and the potential value of the surviving documents is clear. But this documentary resource also has its own biases and partialities. Archaeological remains and the built environment in general can thus play a significant role in giving new historical insight. It is by taking these diverse sources together as a whole that we can maximise our understanding of Govan's recent past.

6 Developing Govan's cultural heritage

It is less than 100 years since Govan became part of Glasgow. In no small part because of the character of its built heritage, Govan maintains a distinct identity within the fabric of the city, but this is not to suggest that Govan has remained static since 1912 and it is the purpose of this chapter to carry the story of Govan forward from that date, through the twentieth century, to the present and the future.

New buildings and monuments continued to be built after 1912, and some of these have now become important heritage sites in their own right. We have seen, for example, how several important historic buildings, like the Luma Lamp Factory of 1939 or various structures within the Fairfield, Linthouse, and other shipyards, post-date 1912. Notable twentieth-century heritage structures extend beyond to a series of memorials erected to commemorate various events: the war memorial erected at the gate to Govan Old Parish Church; the memorial on the north side of Elder Park to the 32 submariners who lost their lives on 29 January 1917 during sea trials of the K-13 submarine, built at the Fairfield yard; and the recent memorial at Ibrox to the 1971 disaster there, when 66 fans lost their lives as crush barriers collapsed.

The twentieth century also saw important developments in the treatment of Govan's heritage. This was the era when 'heritage', as a concept, came fully into being and when the historic built environment came to be valued. It was also an era in which that heritage underwent a continual process of change. While efforts to protect and retain important ancient monuments and historic buildings advanced, there were also serious threats to the historic character of Govan resulting from de-industrialisation and subsequent redevelopment.

This chapter discusses the ways in which the heritage of Govan has been compromised or conserved in the last century, and considers the major heritage management issues that Govan faces today and in the future.

Historic Govan in the twentieth century

While many important features of Govan's pre-industrial settlement were retained during its expansion in the later nineteenth century, and thus survive into the present, its built environment, its society, and its economy were massively transformed through the linked processes of industrialisation and urbanisation. As has been outlined in previous chapters, new industrial works, tenements, churches, public institutions, rail and road systems, and much besides contributed to a changed townscape. The industrial economy was characterised by shipbuilding and other heavy industries, and established textile and victualling concerns were placed on a new footing. The social character of the town changed with population growth, in-migration, the emergence of wage-labour on a large scale, and the rise to prominence of the industrialist class. These changes gave rise to significant social tensions, leading in 1864 to Govan being constituted a burgh, with its own local government. It remained independent of Glasgow until 1912.

From the early twentieth century, despite a temporary resurgence at the time of the Second World War, Glasgow's industrial sector went into long-term decline. Once, numerous busy shipyards and docks lined the Clyde waterfront. Now, the only remaining shipbuilding activity is at BVT surface fleet, formerly the Fairfield Yard. Other heavy industries also suffered, with the result that a recent assessment argues that Greater Govan presents 'an image of vacant land and derelict buildings' (para. 10.89 of the Glasgow *City Plan*; see http://www.glasgow.gov.uk/en/Business/City+Plan/).

Urbanisation, industrialisation, and subsequent industrial decline have had tangible effects on Govan's social and occupational profile (the following information is derived from figures published by Glasgow City Council; see http://www.glasgow.gov.uk). For example, in the ward of Govan, *c* 65% of dwellings are rented from the Local Authority, Communities Scotland, or a housing association. The majority of homes are flats, with smaller numbers of detached, semi-detached, and terraced dwellings. Most of the working population falls in the skilled manual/non-manual and part-skilled/non-skilled groups for statistical purposes. There is a relatively high level of unemployment at 10%.

Industrialisation and urbanisation have also acted to transform the character of Govan's built heritage (see **figs 5.1 & 5.30**). Surviving traces of the pre-industrial town are of great significance, but few in number. Although the present-day Govan Old Parish Church dates to the 1880s, it contains an important collection of tenth- and eleventh-century sculptured stones. Burial monuments in the graveyard date from the fifteenth to twentieth centuries and archaeological excavations have uncovered evidence of burials dating back to the fifth or sixth century AD. Other visible fragments of the pre-industrial town survive in Elder Park. The park itself is, again, a product of the 1880s, but within it lies a pre-existing farmhouse and the portico of the demolished eighteenth-century Linthouse mansion. Perhaps the most extensive of survivals from the pre-industrial era are those elements of Govan's street plan and townscape, surviving in one or two important places, with a long historical genealogy. The most notable here is the public space around Govan Cross and its relationship to Water Row leading down to the ancient river crossing, to Govan Road, and to the parish church.

Alongside these visible survivals is an as yet largely unquantified buried archaeological resource. The origins of Govan Old Parish Church have been traced, through archaeological excavation, to the fifth or sixth century AD. Excavations around Water Row have demonstrated the survival of a section of the massive ditch that defined the base of Doomster Hill, an early assembly or court mound that once stood on the site. Elements of what may be an early nineteenth-century dye works, one of Govan's first industrial premises, also survive there. This is despite the fact that the site was first developed as a shipyard from 1839 and subsequently fell within the large Harland and Wolff yard. The level of archaeological survival throughout the rest of the pre-industrial town remains to be established, but the potential for further significant archaeological remains is certainly there.

While the growth of modern Govan had an adverse impact on the pre-existing built environment, it simultaneously created a new heritage, which is what most prominently defines Govan today. This period of the town's past, together with that of subsequent industrial decline, is significant in understanding Govan's present economic and social situation, and therein lies one aspect of its value: in understanding the past we can better understand the present. The history of the industrial period is complex and cannot simply be reduced to the story of the shipyards. Engineering, metal and textile works, and many others, grew up along the major rail and road links, while the Scottish Co-operative Wholesale Society had its main manufacturing premises at Shieldhall. To understand fully Govan's recent past and the character and significance of its built heritage, we must also take into account the buildings of burgh government, public order, and health care, tenements and other housing, schools, a proliferation of churches, a park, various public houses and other sites of recreation.

This industrial heritage came under serious threat with de-industrialisation. Govan was not unique in this regard: Glasgow's industrial heritage saw something of a crisis in the 1960s and 1970s, a process neatly summarised in the introduction to John Hume's *The Industrial Archaeology of Glasgow* (1974, xvii; see also Hume 1990, 85–6). When survey work for that volume began, and traditional industries were in decline, an intensive programme of redevelopment, involving the creation of industrial estates, and movement away to the new towns, was already underway (see Robertson 1998). It soon became apparent to Hume that most industrial buildings were no longer occupied by the firms for which they had been built and that the rate of demolition was likely to rise. In this context, the task of the industrial archaeologist was 'to record extant buildings, machinery and structures before the scrap-man, the incendiary and the bulldozer' came (Hume 1974, xviii). For Govan, the demise of the shipbuilding industry after the Second World War, together with the transfer of shipping downstream, has been particularly important (Williamson *et al* 1990, 585–6) and the scale of this decline is indicated by the fall in output from the Clyde yards from 18% of world tonnage in 1947 to 4.5% in 1958 (Slaven 1975, 218).

Other aspects of Glasgow's built heritage, especially housing, were also severely adversely affected at this time. The planning focus in the immediate post-war decades was on 'slum' clearance and the relocation of the population to both newly created peripheral housing estates, and to new towns (see, for example, Gibb 1989; Robertson 1992; Rodger 1989a). In this context, the large-scale demolition of inner-city tenements came to be seen as a necessity and 'the engine of destruction ran at full throttle' (Gibb 1989, 161). A conservation movement had begun to emerge, but this was targeted at buildings of 'architectural merit', not the general housing stock (Robertson 1992, 1118).

Attitudes to the treatment of older urban industrial areas began to change from the late 1960s, not least because the socially and physically disruptive effects of clearance and demolition programmes began to be recognised (Gibb 1989, 161, 169–70). Industry was disappearing from inner-city areas and social polarisation and distortion of the demographic profile became evident as families and the highly skilled and qualified were displaced, leaving a population skewed in profile towards the aged and unskilled. From this time, in general terms, consolidation and improvement of the existing fabric, including housing, was increasingly favoured and there was a marked decline in the demolition programme (see, for example, Gibb 1989; Robertson 1992; Rodger 1989a). The rehabilitation of tenements became a specific area of conservation activity promoted by a team of community architects under the banner *Assist* (Williamson *et al* 1990, 74), beginning in Elder Street facing the Fairfield yard. Despite these advances, however, the transformation in attitudes remains incomplete.

Govan's built heritage was affected by this pattern of events (Williamson *et al* 1990, 586), and industrial decline, decay in the existing housing stock, and falling population levels prompted radical changes in approach. In 1969, Govan was designated a Comprehensive Development Area, and the neighbouring areas of Elder Park and Kinning Park followed in 1975. This gave the local authority substantial demolition powers and, although some buildings have been saved, large areas of tenements were replaced with medium- and low-rise schemes of housing (see also Worsdall 1989, 143).

Today, the listed buildings in Govan broadly reflect these developments. The earliest listings were of buildings by a notable architect, R Rowand Anderson, and most listings since have been exceptional in architectural terms, although some more typical domestic architecture has been added more recently.

Although important parts of Govan's industrial-era heritage have already been compromised, a variety of significant buildings and other structures do survive. Also, many parts of the industrial townscape are still legible, and there is even potential for buried archaeological deposits in some places to reveal new aspects of the Govan story.

To some extent, past approaches to Govan in planning and redevelopment have had their own detrimental impacts on the historic environment: in altering the historic townscape through road design; in modern housing layout; in focusing on modern industrial over other development; in neglecting the historic public spaces of the district; and more besides (Robertson and McIntosh Consultants 2005, 87). But there have been successes and retentions too, with many aspects of the historic townscape surviving and some individual historic buildings having been redeveloped for new use.

Redevelopment following de-industrialisation has thus had both negative and positive effects, and it is particularly important now that, with a growing impetus for the regeneration of the area, due consideration is given to the future of Govan's archaeology and built heritage. Greater Govan, extending from Glasgow city centre to Shieldhall and from the Clyde south to the M8 corridor, has been identified as an Area of Focus in the *City Plan*. Areas of Focus are seen to be generally weak in socio-economic terms and characterised by vacant land and run-down and derelict buildings. Identification as an Area of Focus is intended as the first stage in targeting activity aimed at securing sustained regeneration, and a number of major issues which must be addressed in planning this regeneration have been identified in the *City Plan*. Many of these issues have potential implications for Govan's historic environment. A major aim of this *Scottish Burgh Survey* for Govan is to provide the information that will allow for the appropriate treatment of Govan's heritage – its historic buildings, archaeological resource and historic urban environment – as an integral part of the district's regeneration.

Following publication of the broadsheet that is enclosed with this Burgh Survey, Glasgow City Council was successful in obtaining in 2007 a Stage 1 Pass from Heritage Lottery Fund towards establishing a Townscape Heritage Initiative, and the Govan Conservation Area was designated in 2008.

Current statutory designations

Besides the conservation area designation, specific elements of Govan's built heritage are afforded statutory protection as scheduled ancient monuments or listed buildings. The one scheduled ancient monument is the churchyard and sculptured stones at Govan Old Parish Church on Govan Road (SAM number 10393). Excavations in and around the churchyard have established that this is an ecclesiastical site of great antiquity. Archaeological deposits extend back to the fifth and sixth centuries AD. The collection of sculptured stones largely dates to the tenth and eleventh centuries AD, and is remarkable for its size and quality. Medieval and post-medieval burial monuments range in date from the fifteenth to twentieth centuries. These monuments form a significant historical resource on the use of the churchyard, for which records survive only from 1855, and on the social history of Govan, Partick, and the surrounding area. The present church building is not covered by the scheduling, but it is A-listed. The churchyard is also B-listed.

In total, and including the church and churchyard, there are 48 listed buildings within the Govan survey area (see table below). The first listings were undertaken in the 1960s (5% of the total), while 15 listings fall in the 1970s (31%), 28 between 1987 and 1989 (58%), accelerated at the request of the city council in advance of the Glasgow Garden Festival, one in 1996 (2%), one in 2001 (2%), and one in 2004 (2%).

These listings cover a selected diversity of historic buildings, statues, and other structures, all of which are of significance to Govan's history and some of which have wider architectural significance.

Table of listed buildings within the Govan burgh survey area

As change is continuous, the precise statutory position should be verified with the Planning Authority, or Pastmap.

Name	Address/ Location	Listing Category	Date listed	HB Number
Auxiliary accumulator tower	Govan Road, west end of Prince's Dock	C(S)	15/05/1987	33347
Broomloan Road Public School	No. 71 Broomloan Road, return elevations to Summertown Road and Neptune Street	B	15/05/1987	33335
Brush factory	No. 140 Copland Road	C(S)	15/05/1987	33337
Cardell Halls and Public House	Nos 801 & 805 Govan Road; Nos 2 & 4 Burleigh Street	B	15/05/1987	33344
County Bingo Social Club, former Lyceum Cinema	No. 908 Govan Road and return elevation to Mckechnie Street	B	15/05/1987	33355
Drumoyne Primary School, janitor's lodge, gate piers, and boundary walls	No. 200 Shieldhall Road	B	12/10/1989	33312
Elder Cottage Hospital	No. 1a Drumoyne Drive and Langlands Road	A	15/12/1970	33300
Elder Cottage Hospital (west block)	No. 2a Drumoyne Drive and Langlands Road	B	15/12/1970	33301
Elder Park Library	Elder Park/No. 228a Langlands Road and Elder Park Street	A	15/12/1970	33310
Elder Park, cottage	Elder Park	B	12/10/1989	33302
Former Bishop Mills	Nos 206–12 (even nos) Old Dumbarton Road	B	22/03/1977	33096
Former British Linen Bank, and flats	Nos 816 & 818 Govan Road; Nos 1 & 3 Water Row	A	05/12/1970	33351
Former Govan Press Buildings	Nos 577–81 Govan Road	B	15/05/1987	33341
Former Govan Town Hall	No. 401 Govan Road, Summertown Road, Carmichael Street, Nos 1–11 Merryland Street (odd nos)	B	15/12/1970	33340

Name	Address/ Location	Listing Category	Date listed	HB Number
Former Hill's Trust School	Nos 65–9 (odd nos) Golspie Street	B	15/12/1970	33339
Former Hydraulic Pumping Station	Queen's Dock, No. 100 Stobcross Road	B	15/12/1970	33098
Former Luma Light Factory	Nos 470, 480, 490, 500 & 510 Shieldhall Road, Hardgate Road, Luma Tower	B	04/07/1988	33308
Former Savings Bank, Govan Branch	Nos 705 & 707 Govan Road, return elevations to Broomloan Road	B	15/05/1987	33342
Former YMCA	Nos 5, 7 & 9 Water Row	B	15/05/1987	33362
Fragments of Linthouse Mansion	Elder Park	B	12/10/1989	33303
Govan Cross drinking fountain	Govan Road	B	15/05/1987	33350
Govan Graving Docks	No. 18 Clydebrae Street	A	15/05/1987	33336
Govan Old Parish Church	Nos 866 & 868 Govan Road	A	06/07/1966	33353
Govan Old Parish Church burial ground	No. 868 Govan Road	B	15/12/1970	33354
Govan Police Building, former Govan Municipal Buildings	Nos 18 & 20 Orkney Street	B	15/05/1987	33361
Govan Shipbuilders Ltd, general offices	Nos 1030–1048 Govan Road	A	15/12/1970	33356
Govan Shipbuilders' Store, former Engine Works of Fairfield Shipbuilding and Engineering Co.	No. 1048 Govan Road	A	15/05/1987	33357
Govan Shipbuilders' Titan Cantilever Crane	No. 1048 Govan Road	A	14/04/1989	33364
Kelvin Hall, Arena and Museum of Transport	Argyle Street	B	11/07/2001	48034
Linthouse Buildings	No. 21 Holmfauld Road	B	12/10/1989	33309
Linthouse St Kenneth's Church, including original church hall and church officer's house	No. 9 Skipness Drive	B	12/10/1989	33313
Napier House	Nos 638–46 (even nos) Govan Road; No. 3 Napier Street; No. 35 Clydebrae Street	B	15/12/1970	33348
New Govan Church of Scotland, former St Mary's Church	Nos 2 & 4 Greenwell Street, Govan Cross	B	15/05/1987	33358
New Govan (formerly St Mary's) Church Hall and shops below	Nos 784–96 (even nos) Govan Road	B	15/05/1987	33349
Maritime House, former Glasgow Engineering Works	No. 143 Woodville Street	B	15/05/1987	33363
Partick Sewage Pumping Station	Nos 33 & 35 Dumbarton Road,	B	06/02/1989	32862
Pearce Institute	Nos 840 & 860 Govan Road and return elevation to Pearce Street	A	06/07/1966	33352
Pearson Hall	Nos 8–20 (even nos) Gilbert Street and Nos164–72 Yorkhill Street	B	15/12/1970	33024
Salvation Army Citadel	Nos 36–40 Golspie Street & No. 16 Garmouth Street	B	26/04/2004	49789

Name	Address/ Location	Listing Category	Date listed	HB Number
Scotway House	No. 165 Castlebank Street	B	15/07/1996	43569
Sir William Pearce, statue	Near No. 801 Govan Road, junction with Burleigh Street	B	15/12/1970	33343
Southern General Hospital	No. 1345 Govan Road	B	12/10/1989	33307
Southern General Hospital, Administration Block	No. 1345 Govan Road	B	12/10/1989	33306
St Anthony's RC Church	No. 831 Govan Road	B	15/05/1987	33345
St Anthony's RC Presbytery	Nos 62 & 64 Langlands Road and return elevation to Roseneath Street	C(S)	15/05/1987	33359
Statue of John Elder	Elder Park	B	15/12/1979	33305
Statue of Mrs John Elder	Elder Park	A	15/12/1970	33304
Tenement block	Nos 881, 883, 885 & 887 Govan Road; Nos 2 & 4 Shaw Street	B	15/05/1987	33346

The archaeological potential of Govan

Within Govan, Partick, and the other associated areas along the Clyde there are significant zones of archaeological potential. The nature of this potential can be discussed with reference to two broad themes. Firstly, there are the remains relating to pre-industrial Govan and Partick. They largely relate to a buried archaeological resource, the survival of which has been shown in some places by recent excavations. There are also a few important standing buildings. Secondly, there are the known and potential remains relating to the industrial era. Remains here occur across the whole of the survey area and take the form both of standing buildings and a buried archaeological resource.

For all the periods covered by this survey, the evidence of archaeology and buildings is complemented by a rich but varied historical resource. For the early historic and medieval periods, important documents do survive, and future research on these documents will be valuable in furthering our understanding. In the light of the relative rarity of these documents and their overwhelmingly ecclesiastical focus, however, it is through archaeology that the most significant advances will be made. The documentary record expands for the early modern period and becomes voluminous for the most recent past, and this early modern and later documentary resource is complemented by numerous historic maps dating from the sixteenth century onwards, along with archives of historic photographs and illustrations. For these periods, however, archaeology and buildings analysis remains significant, as will be discussed in more detail below. For these later periods, both new historical and new archaeological investigations are fundamental in furthering our knowledge of Govan's past, and it is in the combination of these various resources and disciplines that some of the most important steps forward will be made.

Few visible remains survive from the pre-industrial era of the district, but those that do are all the more valuable. Included here are the churchyard of Govan Old Parish Church, the Bishop Mills on the north side of the Clyde, and the portico of Linthouse and Fairfield farmhouse now lying within Elder Park. The churchyard, Linthouse portico, and the Bishop Mills are accorded statutory protection under ancient monuments and listed building legislation. Fairfield farmhouse has escaped redevelopment because of its inclusion in Elder Park from the 1880s, but is currently in a dilapidated state.

In terms of non-visible remains, assessment of the archaeological resources from the pre-industrial era has identified several principal areas of interest (see Broadsheet map). These are: Govan Old Parish Church; the area around Govan Cross and Water Row, including the site of Doomster Hill; the site of Partick Castle and the royal settlement that likely preceded it; the medieval and post-medieval villages of Govan and Partick; and the Clyde waterfront.

Together, these areas form a suite of interconnected historic sites of some significance. The recent appreciation of Govan's early historic political importance has implications for how these archaeological resources are managed. Govan appears to have been the *principal* centre of the last British kingdom in what later became Scotland. Partick may well be the only surviving British royal estate from this era, while Doomster Hill is likely to have been much more than the local court hill. It seems probable that Govan was a site of a 'national' assembly, perhaps the place where the British kings of Strathclyde were popularly acclaimed. Water Row and the ancient Clyde crossing are important to our understanding of how these different elements were linked, connecting a royal estate in the north with ecclesiastical and political monuments to the south. It is particularly unusual to be able to identify the key components of a major political centre from this period with such a degree of confidence. It is even more striking that the three interconnected royal structures at Govan are not sealed under modern structures, but are available for investigation. Taken as a whole, the early historic monuments of Govan and Partick are potentially amongst the most important of their kind in Scotland.

At some point, settlement began to build up around this early ecclesiastical and royal focus. Broadly, this process dates to the medieval period and the villages of Govan and Partick were well established by the post-medieval era. Given the notable lack of medieval documentation for these settlements and the limits of the more extensive archive record for post-medieval times, the archaeological resource is of particular significance. The processes whereby Govan and Partick were established and subsequently developed are major questions that will only adequately be addressed through the recovery of new evidence. For the more recent pre-industrial past, we can glean an outline image of a thriving craft settlement at Govan surrounded by country estates, but important details of everyday life and society are also likely to remain unknown until addressed through archaeological investigations.

Perhaps the most important surviving archaeological remains are found in and around Govan Old Parish Church, which was established in the fifth or sixth century and has been in continuous use ever since. Well-preserved and deeply stratified archaeological deposits have been excavated within and immediately outside the curvilinear churchyard boundary. Trial excavations in the 1990s have demonstrated the value of this resource and have done much to improve our knowledge of the archaeological integrity of medieval Govan. Housed within the church is a collection of 27 sculptured stones from the tenth and eleventh centuries. The majority are burial monuments decorated with interlace patterns in the form of a cross, but four of the pieces come from free-standing 'Celtic' crosses. The most outstanding piece is a sarcophagus decorated with interlace patterns and figurative panels. This is one of the most important collections of early historic sculpture in Scotland, partly because of the large number of pieces, which is only surpassed in Scotland by Iona and St Andrews, and partly because sculpture of this period is relatively rare. Learned opinion is that this collection points to royal patronage of the church and that the burial monuments are likely to represent a cemetery of the kings of the Northern Britons, who ruled this region until the twelfth century.

The churchyard and the sculpture within it are protected as a scheduled ancient monument under the *Ancient Monuments and Archaeological Areas Act 1979*, but it is important to recognise that the area of known archaeological survival extends at least 5m beyond the modern churchyard wall. The resource at Govan Old is finite and should be actively curated. Sites in Scotland which preserve evidence for continuity of use over almost 1500 years are rare and this value is enhanced by the quality of the buried archaeological deposits.

The ancient boundary ditch of the site lies beyond the churchyard wall, and is thus potentially more at threat. Although not equally preserved throughout its circuit, this infilled boundary ditch running around the outside of the churchyard represents one of the most vital areas of archaeological interest, because the silts within it preserve a long sequence of material which has not been disturbed by burials. On the western side of the churchyard, the ditch is likely to have been truncated by the construction of a car park in the 1980s. The degree of damage is unknown, but visual inspection suggests that the upper levels of the ditch fill are likely to have been removed. Despite this, it seems probable that the deeper deposits remain intact (some excavations are known to have been conducted in this area by Glasgow Museums in the 1970s, but no account of these investigations has been located). On the north side, the boundary ditch was not noted in either of the trial trenches, and it may have been removed by the action of the Clyde in this location. While it should not be assumed that all trace of it has been removed on the river side, it seems clear that the best-preserved sections of the ditch are to the south and east.

To the east of the church lies the important early area of focus around Govan Cross and Water Row. Lying to the east of Water Row, the area of greatest significance is that associated with Doomster Hill, which was built on a colossal scale: it was approximately 50m in diameter, 5m in height, and had a ditch over 5m broad (**fig 6.1**). As discussed above (see pp 42–4) the precise location, orientation and extent of the mound are unknown and significant questions, such as whether or not it began life as a prehistoric burial monument, remain to be answered. The excavations of 2007 make it clear that extensive areas of archaeological sensitivity survive to the east of Water Row. Survival of deposits relating to Doomster Hill is likely to be variable, so the archaeological resource requires careful management.

In the area to the west, formerly occupied by Water Row, the manse, and part of the Harland and Wolff shipyard, survival is variable and extensive areas have been disturbed by industrial construction work. Our knowledge of the survival of archaeological remains in this area is incomplete: only a small portion of the area was available for investigation in 1994–96 and 2007. There are two key areas where the discovery of archaeological remains should be regarded as particularly significant: Water Row and the buried riverbank behind the modern river frontage. Water Row's traditional buildings survived until modern times and this is one of the most likely place for the discovery of medieval settlement remains in Govan. It is also the place presenting

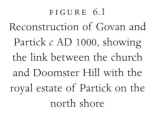

FIGURE 6.1
Reconstruction of Govan and Partick *c* AD 1000, showing the link between the church and Doomster Hill with the royal estate of Partick on the north shore

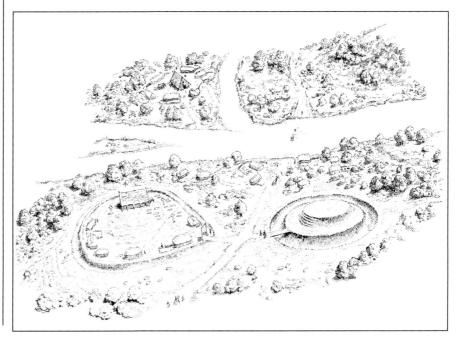

perhaps the best chance to build up a stratigraphic sequence linking the medieval settlement to the modern one. Archaeological interest in this area is not confined to the footprints of the old buildings, but includes the backlands where outbuildings stood, work was done, and refuse could accumulate. When Water Row was replaced by the Harland and Wolff works in the early twentieth century, the waterfront was transformed by the construction of a substantial vertical revetment. One purpose of this revetment was to contain the large quantities of soil required to construct a level floor right to the water's edge. There is, therefore, a broad stretch (perhaps 50m wide) behind the revetment where archaeological deposits may have been preserved under substantial levelling deposits. Both the buildings and the backlands to the west of Water Row could be preserved in this way. Moreover, the material used for levelling may be of archaeological interest, because it seems likely that the demolition rubble from Water Row and from the manse would have ended up in the levelling deposits.

The area to either side of Water Row is one where archaeological work relating to early deposits is difficult, because of its industrial legacy. Massive reinforced concrete crane braces are scattered across the former shipyard. Deep tenement foundations and demolition rubble encroach on the area towards Govan Cross and large pits have disturbed the site. These obstacles mean that early archaeological features will be difficult to interpret unless examined through large-scale programmes of investigation linked to major development works. Small-scale, piecemeal excavations will probably erode the archaeological resource without providing much new information.

Lying directly across the Clyde is the site of Partick Castle. During the early historic and medieval periods, Partick was considered part of Govan. Originally a royal *vill* ('estate'), Partick was acquired by the bishops of Glasgow, who maintained a residence there. After the Reformation, the site came into secular hands and a castle was built in 1611, presumably on or near the site of the bishop's residence and the earlier royal estate. Partick Castle was demolished in the mid-nineteenth century to make way for industrial premises, but the site of the castle itself appears to have escaped major development. The position of this seventeenth-century castle is known with a reasonable degree of precision from eighteenth- and nineteenth-century maps and drawings. These same sources indicate the position of the Bishop's Orchard, which is likely to represent the core of this ancient estate.

At present, the degree of survival of archaeological deposits on the site of the castle and estate at Partick is unknown. However, this is an area of considerable archaeological potential and, because deposits may only survive in isolated pockets, the area requires careful management. The grounds of the castle (represented by the Orchard) have been bisected by the Clydeside Expressway and the Milngavie railway line, while a graving dock cuts into the grounds to the south. Fortunately, the area occupied by the seventeenth-century castle itself has escaped these major destructive events. This said, the castle site has seen subsequent industrial use, which will undoubtedly have had an adverse impact on any near-surface archaeological deposits. Given the subsequent raising of the riverbank and levelling of the surface, the survival of important archaeological evidence for the castle and estate is a real possibility.

Between Partick and Govan lies the Clyde waterfront. Antiquarian sources suggest that this waterfront has archaeological potential because the improvements to the course of the river had a limited impact, with the process of land reclamation along the Clyde preserving archaeological deposits and structures behind the modern revetment wall. Unlike along some other stretches of the river, this reclamation process was not subsequently reversed at Govan to any great extent. Archaeological deposits and structures representing former shoreline activity, river crossings, and settlement may well survive, and wet conditions may promote the survival of organic objects, such as boats and timber water frontages.

Extending from the core of Govan Old Parish Church, Water Row and Doomster Hill and lying near Partick Castle were the two villages of Govan and Partick. The focus of discussion in what follows will be on Govan, as the core interest of this survey. However, several individual sites in Partick are discussed, and the general points made below largely apply to Partick as well.

The archaeological potential of the wider village of Govan is currently unknown. The town extended from the Graving Docks in the east to the eastern edge of the later Fairfield yard (BVT) in the west. It ran, approximately, from the river south to Golspie Street and the south side of Govan Road. A reasonable impression of its extent is given by the first edition Ordnance Survey map of the 1850s, surveyed at a time when industrial construction and the spread of tenements and other new forms of housing had only just begun.

Any domestic remains surviving from the medieval or post-medieval periods will be of great importance, as we currently know almost nothing about the processes of Govan's development and the daily lives of its inhabitants before industrialisation, other than the general descriptions in late sources. As well as elucidating daily routines and throwing light on the increasing involvement of Govan in the emergent textile industries, surviving archaeological remains from the post-medieval period may allow other key historical questions to be addressed. To what extent, when, and how did the townspeople engage with the wider market economy and how is this engagement evident in the artefacts recovered from domestic sites? What changes are evident in the structure of daily life, from the level of the family to the community? Archaeological deposits from this period could give valuable new insight into the social changes which led a farming community through the period of domestic manufacture to engagement in industry. This is an important, and to date little understood, aspect of the development of modern Govan and, indeed, Glasgow.

Remains of Govan's various inns may also prove important. Inn and tavern sites can produce large assemblages of artefacts, as well as evidence of demolished structures and other features (as has been demonstrated in Glasgow, for example, for the late eighteenth-century Saracen's Head inn; see Pollock 1992). Such material, especially inn clearance deposits and assemblages, is an acknowledged area of research (see, for example, Boothroyd and Higgins 2005; Fryer and Shelley 1997; Pearce 2000).

Important remains may also survive that relate to Govan's early economy and to the initial development of industry. It is likely that evidence of Govan's famous handloom industry will be found in domestic areas. Beyond this, excavations have shown that deposits probably relating to the early nineteenth-century dye works survive at Water Row. Morris Pollok's silk factory lay to the west and was an early example of its type; it has often been said that it was the first in Scotland. The site of this factory was later taken over by the Fairfield yard and the potential for archaeological survival there is currently unknown. Across the Clyde at Partick, noteworthy individual sites include the Bunhouse Mill, which was also redeveloped in the nineteenth century and is therefore of unknown archaeological potential. At all these sites, deposits may contain valuable information on the industrial processes undertaken and the resultant working environment.

Beyond the confines of the pre-industrial village, the potential for the recovery of remains of the various country mansions and their associated designed landscapes around Govan will have been limited by later industrialisation and urbanisation. But, again, the absence or presence and character of any archaeological remains are currently little understood. Some of these houses were new creations in the eighteenth and early nineteenth centuries, and we know little about their form beyond surviving photographs and map sources. Others incorporated elements of existing buildings, perhaps the houses of Govan's sixteenth- and seventeenth-century landed class. Should remains survive, some sites will therefore have a time-depth extending back from the modern era towards the medieval.

Considering all of the above, although the archaeological potential of the village largely remains to be established, excavations and other sources have shown that heavy industry and urban development have not acted to remove all deposits and that there is the potential for coherent remains to survive. Until otherwise demonstrated, the entire area formerly occupied by the village should thus be considered as having archaeological potential. Detailed, pre-development, site-specific assessments will enable more particular identification of areas with the potential for early remains, as many industrial-era buildings are fairly well documented in building control plans, maps, and other sources. In such areas of potential, the survival and character of any archaeological remains can be established through archaeological evaluation, providing a baseline of information leading to the formulation of an appropriate mitigation strategy for any given development.

As for the earlier material, elements of Govan's industrial-era heritage are of recognised importance, and a number of buildings and other structures are already afforded statutory protection as listed buildings. This group of buildings, however, only provides a partial representation of Govan's development from *c* 1850. For the industrial period, from the mid-nineteenth century to 1912, more general categories of known and potential archaeological remains are of significance despite the relative wealth of documentary sources, illustrations, maps, photographs, and other available sources.

Even where a particular archive is relatively complete, there will always be subjects that are 'beyond record', especially where these relate to routine, everyday life and to those numerous members of the population who rarely make it beyond the margins of the historical record. This is not to say that the archaeology of this period is simply an exercise in filling any gaps left by history. Historical and archaeological sources complement each other, giving different types of information or different levels of detail on the same subjects (Deetz 1996, 11). Combined, they can give a fuller picture of the past. It is accepted best practice in historical archaeology to pursue analysis of all the available data in order to achieve the fullest possible understanding of the past (*ibid*, 5–11). The value of using these different forms of data together also lies in the fact that, in some cases, they are in conflict and contradict each other, forcing refinement in our interpretations of the past, and pushing us to ask new questions and to reappraise all of our sources (*ibid*, 18–19, 26–7). The archaeology of the recent past is thus far from being 'an expensive way of learning what we already know' (*ibid*, 33), and there are good reasons for the proper treatment of recent-period archaeology in the development process (Gould 1999; West 1999, 10–11).

The archaeology of domestic sites has a great potential role to play here, but this is an area of knowledge yet to be fully explored in Scotland. Historical discussion often relies on official statistics, statements and analyses authored by concerned city officers and the philanthropic middle classes. These sources give a generalised and politically and socially biased view: 'Glaswegians were prone to publicise, examine and talk about their problems with zealous intensity, and this heightened public awareness, but it also singled out the city as being particularly damned'; moral reformers sought to emphasise Glasgow's shortcomings to justify and demonstrate the effectiveness of their own solutions (Fraser and Maver 1996b, 387; see also Fraser and Maver 1996c). Many archive sources responded to the depravity of working class and 'slum' housing and, while these sources are not entirely divorced from reality, Glasgow's domestic environment and the daily life of the city's inhabitants

FIGURE 6.2a
Taransay Street back court,
c 1970 (Raymond Young)

FIGURE 6.2b
Taransay Street tenements:
back courts after
reinstatement of drying
greens by ASSIST (Raymond
Young)

were undoubtedly much more diverse than these accounts suggest (**fig 6.2**; Maver 2000, 85–7). The use and experience of Scotland's tenements is not easy to reconstruct from historical sources (Glendinning 2003, 117).

Interpretative problems in relation to the everyday domestic environment are also not confined to our understanding of working-class life (Nenadic 1996). In the Victorian era, Glasgow's middle classes built their values around a series of myths in order to accommodate the profound ambiguities that were the normal experience of family, social and economic life (*ibid*, 295). The main implication of this process here is that sources detailing middle-class domestic life and the middle-class domestic environment cannot be considered objective. They present a certain image, an acceptable ideal; they elide variation, and they ignore conflicting evidence.

Even on the issue of housing in the twentieth century, historians have made clear that there are significant gaps in our knowledge and deficiencies in the archive resource. There is a recognised need for inter-disciplinary research in this area and calls have been made for studies that seek to balance our understanding of macro-scale processes with the peculiarities of different urban locales (Rodger 1989a, 21). There has been a general lack of research on significant themes like household composition, the family and social relations, working-class culture, and the nature of community (*ibid*, 21). The domestic arena will be one area, though not the only one, where the important historical issues of gender relationships and the role of women in society can be addressed. The history of Govan, as Glasgow, has a clear masculine profile with its concentration on shipbuilding, heavy industry, and industrial relations. The burgh historians and municipal governing class were overwhelmingly male, and this shows in the character of Govan's history as it has been written to date. The domestic environment is one of the key places for understanding, with subtlety, the relationships of gender and family, as well as those of class and other aspects of social life. As a whole, British historians have largely disregarded the experiential side of housing: 'personal interaction with the built environment therefore remains under-acknowledged ... the impact of grey stone tenements is confined to the physical, to their effect on light and ventilation, to public health . . . further attention could usefully be devoted to the interaction of resident and his/her home' (ibid, 22).

Further historical research is certainly required on established topics, on property ownership or on patterns of house building for example. A combined historical and archaeological approach is likely to yield valuable new insights into many major historical issues and the archaeological potential of Govan's nineteenth-century and later domestic heritage is, therefore, a significant one.

Consideration must be given here to the pockets of industrial-era housing that survive in places, and are mostly not protected by listing. The fabric of these surviving buildings is likely to yield evidence of changing attitudes to the use of space through time, changing needs, changing opportunities and constraints such as income, and much besides.

Most of the earliest tenements, built c 1850, have been demolished. Exceptions stand on Burleigh Street and between Copland Place and Summertown Road. Later nineteenth- and earlier twentieth-century examples survive in central Govan on Govan Road, Shaw Street, Langlands Road, Rosneath, Howat, Elder, Luath, Taransay, and Rathlin Streets. To the east and south, blocks survive on Southcroft and Clynder Streets and on Copland Road. West of Elder Park, a group lies on Govan Road, Cressy and Aboukir Streets, Peninver Drive and Burghead Place, and on Drive Road, Hutton Drive, Kennedra Drive, and Clachan Drive. To the south of Elder Park, seven blocks lie on Crossloan Road, Uist Street, Elderpark Street, Craigton Road and Langlands Road.

Govan's domestic heritage is also of significance in terms of the potential buried archaeological resource. We have some knowledge of the domestic architecture of this period from maps and plans, including the character and variety of ground plans, façades, and the layouts of interiors (as intended, not necessarily as built or used), but archaeological deposits will expand this knowledge significantly. The main interest here will extend beyond the building foundations themselves to include evidence of domestic activity available from features, deposits, and assemblages of artefacts in back courts and other adjacent spaces. Properly interpreted, the debris found on domestic sites – broken kitchen china, glass bottles, building debris, plaster samples – yields evidence of lives that barely enter the documentary record. Artefacts from former middens will allow us to consider such topics as: varying access to goods across the urban population; significant variation between the intended use of mass-produced items and their use in practice; wealth and poverty; and creativity in daily life under constraining circumstances. Depending on the nature of any surviving remains, we will be able to gain new insight into questions of diet and health. With such possibilities in mind, potential domestic archaeological remains of the period from the mid-nineteenth century have clear significance as a resource in understanding the social conditions of industrialisation and urbanisation. Such remains may lie across many parts of the survey area, but the survival of significant deposits requires clarification for specific sites through more detailed assessment and evaluation.

The significance of Govan's industries, particularly shipbuilding, has been the subject of much discussion. It is well known that Govan's yards were once at the forefront of the industry in global terms. Though much of the built heritage of this aspect of the town's past has now gone, significant elements do survive and the Clyde riverfront still bears many traces of its shipbuilding past. Most of the industrial concerns that grew up further back from the river have effectively been redeveloped, though this serves to make surviving buildings and sites all the more important.

The significance of surviving industrial buildings and of the archaeological remains of industry is generally acknowledged: 'many sites, which are not conventionally thought of as archaeological, have a great deal of information to offer: for example abandoned industrial complexes' (Scottish Office 1994, PAN 42 paragraph 3). The contribution of archaeology to an understanding of the industrialisation of Scotland is one of six research themes recently identified by Historic Scotland as being of over-arching importance and requiring particular attention in their Archaeology Programme (Barclay 1997), and there is much to be learned in this field:

> Comparatively little archaeological excavation has taken place on industrial sites in Scotland ... Little is known of the details of structures and processes used in individual industries, particularly the metallurgical and ceramic industries. It is a priority that industrial sites ... threatened by development should be recorded, both above ground and, where appropriate, through excavation or watching briefs ... Some industries ... do not survive significantly above ground today and excavation can contribute much here ... The importance of the remains of the infrastructure supporting industry should not be forgotten – transport systems (tramways, railways and canals) are little investigated as field monuments ... (Barclay 1997, 35).

Across the survey area, many industrial and related sites survive, some of them listed buildings. The former Meadowside and Pointhouse shipyards on either side of the Kelvin retain some buildings and riverside features, such as slipways. In Govan, numerous waterfront features survive, notably three dry docks, as does the 'Big Shed' of the Harland and Wolff yard on Govan Road. Much of the Linthouse yard has been redeveloped, but a 1914 office block remains. The Linthouse engine shop is now part of the Scottish Maritime Museum in Irvine. The Fairfield works retain the greatest coherence, with buildings dating from the late nineteenth century to the present preserved in the context of a still-operating shipyard (although the main office block facing Govan Road is currently out of use and falling into dilapidation). Some notable survivals are also to be found across the Clyde at the former Barclay Curle yard, including a distinctive engine works built before the First World War.

Other industries are represented by the British Polar Engines factory on Helen Street, a prominent survival in a heavily redeveloped area. On Broomloan Road, elements of the Ladywell Wire Works have also survived redevelopment. Carmichael Street is home to the remains of the Carmichael Works (chemical), and historic elements of the Clydeside Works and the Whitefield Works, both engine and boilermakers, may remain amongst the buildings presently on those sites. Also on Carmichael Street, elements of the Whitefield Brass Works may survive too. The brass foundry of Steven and Struthers lies in Eastvale Place in Kelvinhaugh and elements of the Scotstoun Mills remain on Scotstounmill Road, Partick.

Although partially infilled for the Glasgow Garden Festival (1988), part of Prince's Dock remains open. Yorkhill Quay and Basin has recently suffered through the demolition of its brick transit sheds, but the site retains much of its former character in its layout and the survival of the historic quayside. Govan Graving Docks used an extensive system of hydraulic pumps and tunnels to evacuate the water, and they, with Prince's and Queen's Docks, also used hydraulic power systems threaded through the made-up ground to open gates, and operate cranes, capstans and swing bridges. Four hydraulic accumulator towers remain above ground as evidence of this, but there will certainly be traces of the technology below ground as well. The Merklands Lairage in Whiteinch is currently being redeveloped. The SPT subway works on Broomloan Road are still operational.

The potential for buried industrial remains varies greatly depending on the impression made by the processes concerned below ground level. Some sites will undoubtedly have been compromised by redevelopment, but across the survey area there is still potential for significant surviving industrial archaeology.

Archaeology can provide genuinely new information on past production processes and technologies (Cranstone 2001, 184). Works operations can be detailed by mapping the elements of a site through excavation or survey and interpreting the location of different functions and the movement of materials from one part to another (Palmer 1990, 277). The operation of large sites in their entirety needs to be more fully understood, and particular processes within the site will require more detailed examination (Butterfield 1994, 198). It is also vitally important that we develop an understanding of the typology of industrial buildings and structures: how did these change through time; how did their form and use vary within and between industries and different regions, and for what reasons (Palmer 1991, 20)?

Thus, archaeology can further understanding of how different processes, operations, and structures evolved through time and varied across space, and the reasons for these changes and variations can be explored (Palmer 1990, 279–80). Archaeology can also help consider the labour required for different operations and processes, and the working practices of a given industry (Butterfield 1994, 202, 206–7). Technology, processes, operations, and work practices must be considered together if we are to understand production fully (*ibid*, 204). Consideration of work practices and the working environment also leads into another significant facet of archaeological understanding, and that is the daily lives and experiences of working people (Palmer 1991, 18).

It is vital, therefore, that the possibility of the survival of industrial remains is explored through further assessment and evaluation. Such a process will allow informed decisions to be taken on the value of known surviving remains for historical understanding.

Historic Govan: the significance of a place

There is a surprising level of latent interest in Govan's past, which was reflected in large numbers of visitors to an excavation open day held there in July 1994 (**fig 6.3**). A broad interest in Govan's archaeology has also been reflected in local media reporting (**fig 6.4**) and by the selection of the Govan Old Parish Church and Doomster Hill sites for an in-depth programme by a leading television archaeology series (**fig 6.5**). Govan's archaeology and built heritage have huge potential to contribute to improving the popular image of Govan and to enhancing local pride. In this, the great depth of history in Govan will be important, but it seems the recent industrial past is just as significant as medieval history. Given the existing interest in Govan and the future potential for Govan's heritage to form a focus for the community, cultural resources with the ability to make a positive contribution to the value of the place should be appropriately protected and developed.

The need to bring a new focus on the past has recently been laid out in Duncan MacLean's forward to a consultation draft conservation plan for Govan (Robertson and McIntosh Consultants 2005), commissioned by Govan Workspace Ltd:

Govan has had a bad press. For too long now the name of Govan has come to be identified with all that can go wrong in society – the complex array of human problems that beset an area seemingly in terminal decline. But for many of us who live and work in Govan the image presented to the outside world is grotesquely distorted. Undeniably there are problems and we would not wish to understate them. But the Govan that *we* know and recognise remains a vibrant community with a history as proud and distinguished as any in Scotland. It is time for

FIGURE 6.3
(above left) Visitors to the excavation open day 1994 contemplate a nineteenth-century burial (Johari Lee and GUARD)

FIGURE 6.4
(above right) Filming an evening news broadcast about the 1994 excavations (Johari Lee and GUARD)

FIGURE 6.5
Excavations undertaken in conjunction with Time Team in 1996 (GUARD)

people to switch focus and to look at the strengths and attributes that have made Govan the remarkable place that it is.

An important consideration for future management, promotion, and education efforts is the fact that Govan was a distinct place in the past and remains distinctive in the present. This distinctiveness relies in no small part on the character of the built heritage: Govan is a recognisable historic centre within the larger City of Glasgow. In order to retain and foster the identity of the place, due consideration must be given to the future of the historic built fabric.

The future investigation and promotion of important individual sites will add greatly to the perceived value of the place as a whole. It is important, however, to recognise that the heritage value of the place also lies in the connections between these buildings and sites in the townscape. One central aspect of Govan's present-day distinctiveness is the fact that the modern townscape remains heavily influenced by the past. The past is still legible in Govan's street plan, in the inter-relationships of one building to another, and in the connections between land and river. In concluding, the following paragraphs highlight some of the main aspects of this historic townscape that are worthy of consideration in defining the future shape of the place. Many of the areas highlighted below are also discussed in the draft conservation plan referred to above (Robertson and McIntosh Consultants 2005).

At the literal and metaphorical heart of Govan, the area including Govan Cross, Govan Old Parish Church, and Water Row still reflects the layout of the ancient settlement. The nationally important church and churchyard of Govan Old is now accessed from the main road, but the older access route leading from the south-east corner of the churchyard is preserved in Pearce Lane. The Lane issues on to the open square at Govan Cross and the site of Doomster Hill. An ancient assembly place, the Cross preserves its historic character in modern form (**fig 6.6**). From the Cross, Water Row leads down to an out-of-use ferry terminal and preserves the historic relationship of Cross and river crossing. Lying across the Clyde is the site of the early historic royal settlement and later castle at Partick. Taken together, these individual sites and areas relate in a way that retains a great degree of historical integrity. This historical integrity means that ancient relationships can still be appreciated, and it contributes to Govan's distinctive character today. The complex of features around Govan Cross and the old river crossing also have significance for the setting they give to the listed building and scheduled ancient monument of Govan Old Parish Church. A full appreciation of the church, churchyard, and striking collection of sculptured stones at Govan Old can only be gained by understanding this immediate townscape.

Govan Cross also forms a nodal point on the exceptional townscape that has grown up along the main artery of Govan Road, now a key part of the

FIGURE 6.6a
Govan Cross, 1969
(Rev David Orr)

FIGURE 6.6b
Govan Cross, 2007, shortly
before the Townscape
Heritage Initiative started

conservation area (**fig 5.46**). To the east of the Cross, the historic townscape has been somewhat compromised by modern development, particularly by the layout of housing at Napier Road, Terrace, Place, and Drive and by the bypass from Napier Road to Golspie Street. However, the old street plan can still be appreciated, with Govan Road following the line of the eighteenth-century turnpike road and with Clydebrae Street preserving a section of the line of the medieval and later Main Street. At the end of the old settlement, Govan Road still leads to Govan Graving Docks and then skirts around Prince's Dock, a rude interruption into the old street made by Victorian commerce on an enormous scale. As if to embrace that commerce, and proudly facing Glasgow, it was there rather than at the old core that Govan town hall was built in 1897–1901.

Moving west from the Cross and the long-lived river crossing at Water Row, the Victorian character of Govan is better preserved along tenement-lined Govan Road, and the complex of tenements and other buildings between Govan Road and Langlands Road immediately to the west of the Cross and lying beside the statue of William Pearce preserves an historic street plan. This and Govan's other main tenemented areas are important elements of the historic townscape that do not benefit from current individual statutory protection. But these ordinary, everyday buildings are fundamental to the historic character of the place, and have more recent significance, as it was in Govan that the idea that the Glasgow tenement was something worth preserving first took root.

Further west, the relationship between Elder Park and the former Fairfield Yard (BVT) is particularly significant. The park originated as a philanthropic bequest to Govan by Isabella Elder, wife of John Elder of Fairfield Yard. The still-existing juxtaposition of heavy industry and Isabella Elder's remedy to the ills of urban and industrial life neatly sums up many aspects of the social history of industrial-era Govan. The setting of the park is further enhanced by the survival of numerous coherent blocks of industrial-era tenements and rows of houses to the west and south, and by other features such as the Elder Park Library and the Elder Cottage Hospital. Together, these elements preserve a notable and largely intact example of Victorian town planning.

Shipbuilding is central to the history of Govan, and the Clyde and its crossing at this point is also of general importance. The waterfront of Govan, Partick, and Whiteinch retains some important historic characteristics. There are important survivals of groups of historic buildings, features, and machinery at Fairfield, across the river at the Barclay Curle yard, and at the Govan Graving Docks. But there are also individual industrial features, including various slipways, buildings, quays, and so on, and Yorkhill Quay and Basin is a good example here. Alongside the remains of industry lie the remnants of important ferry crossings at Yorkill Quay / Govan Graving Docks, Water Row / Pointhouse, and at the north bank at Govan Ferry West. Together, these features, if retained and sympathetically developed (**fig 6.7**), will still allow something of the industrial heyday of the Clyde to be appreciated. Piecemeal access to the waterfront still exists, and the inter-relationships of different historic elements on both banks of the Clyde and along the lower stretch of the Kelvin are still legible from a number of vantage points.

Away from these historic core areas, Helen Street and Broomloan Road are important reminders of the industrial expansion of Govan, representing the main arteries of that expansion. In these areas, individual historic buildings or features do survive, but there has been substantial modern development. However, the street plan tells an important part of the story of a shift from pre- and early industrial village to industrial and urban settlement. These roads also metaphorically preserve the more ancient relationship of Govan to its agricultural hinterland, even if they do not preserve their exact line.

All of these aspects of Govan's townscape, together with numerous important listed buildings and other buildings which are not listed, form a place of great historic interest. Govan was an early historic centre of some significance, not just in terms of local history but in terms of the history of Strathclyde and of Scotland as a whole. The character of this early historic centre can still be appreciated in the townscape today. Govan's identity as a renowned and world-leading industrial town is also still legible in many

important ways in the present-day built environment. This era of Govan's past is of exceptional interest from a variety of academic perspectives, including archaeology, architecture, shipbuilding and general industrial history, the arts, the history of religion, and social and political history. This period, as with the early historic, is core to the present-day identity of Govan itself – a place known for its industrial achievements and its legacy of political activism and of the search for social justice. This is a history of social tension, but also a story of achievement and of action leading to positive change. To appreciate, conserve, promote, and develop Govan's strong and distinctive identity it is necessary to take a holistic approach. The appropriate treatment of individual buildings and sites of particular significance will benefit greatly from a more encompassing treatment of the townscape as a whole. This townscape forms the historic setting in which Govan's listed buildings and scheduled ancient monuments sit and it also has value in itself, for the narratives it allows to be told about Govan past and Govan present.

Glossary

agricultural improvement	The process involving the commercialisation of rural Scotland, traditionally associated with the eighteenth and nineteenth centuries but with an ancestry extending back at least to the seventeenth. Prominent features of improvement were the enclosure of fields, the creation of single-tenant farms, the introduction of wage labour, and of new crops and fertilisers.
British	The native peoples of the Clyde spoke a form of British speech, akin to Welsh, and were the dominant social group until the collapse of the kingdom of Strathclyde in the eleventh century.
Bronze Age	Prehistoric period between the Neolithic and the Iron Age *c* 2000–500 BC in Scotland.
burgh	A legal term. Medieval burghs, where burgh status conferred privileges to a community including the right to trade, were created from the twelfth century. However, Govan was not created a burgh until 1864, and this was in a different legal context (see *police burgh* below).
carse	Low, fertile land; a river valley.
close	The common entrance and stair of a tenement (see *tenement* below).
commons	Ground held in common by a community, for the use of its members.
court hill	See *moot hill*.
cropmark	Discolouration of crops visible on aerial photographs and resulting from differential growth due to the presence of buried archaeological remains.
cross-slab	Recumbent burial monument bearing an incised cross.
crow-stepped gable	A form of building gable characterised by a stepped profile.
disestablishment	The programme pursued in the nineteenth century to sever the connection between church and state.
Disruption	In 1843, following conflict within the Church of Scotland over the issue of patronage (that is, control of the selection of the parish minister), the evangelicals split from the Established Church of Scotland in what has become known as the Disruption.

drumlin	Low, pear-shaped mound formed of glacial till. Such mounds form a prominent feature of the Glasgow townscape today, with examples across from Govan at Yorkhill and Partickhill (see *glacial till* below).
early historic	Period from *c* AD 400 to 1100, also known as the Dark Ages and the early medieval period.
façade	The front of a building.
feuing (feu-ferme/feuars/feu)	A process beginning in the medieval period in Scotland and accelerating in the sixteenth century, particularly after the Reformation. Feu charters granted ownership of lands, often previously rented, to a new class of owners known as feuers. In many areas, as Govan, a new class of small landowners was thus created.
fluvio-deltaic complex	A system of rivers, ending in a delta as rivers meet sea.
GIS (Geographical Information System)	GIS is a system for capturing, storing, manipulating, analysing, and displaying spatial or geographic data. It comprises both a database of information (such as archaeological sites or historic buildings) with specific capabilities for spatial data and a means of analysing and displaying that data.
glacial till	Deposits of sand, gravel, clays, silts, and other material laid down by retreating glaciers.
gothic	An architectural style popular in the nineteenth century, characterised by its reference to medieval architectural forms (gothic is usually used to refer to the pointed-arch style prevalent in the medieval architecture of Western Europe, in the period from the twelfth to sixteenth centuries, and nineteenth-century gothic might more properly be termed neo-gothic).
graving docks	Dry docks for the repair of ships.
Hearth Tax	In 1690, Parliament imposed a short-lived tax on every hearth payable by every landowner and tenant to raise money for the army.
heritor	A proprietor or landholder in a parish, with certain responsibilities in relation to church buildings and other aspects of the maintenance of the parish. Heritor was an old word that acquired new meaning in the post-Reformation period, when it implied a status based on property rather than feudal superiority.
historiography	The writing of history; a body of historical literature.
hogback	Tomb stone whose form may have been intended to resemble a house, found in those parts of Britain with Norse settlement or influence.

industrialisation	The process whereby an area is developed extensively with industries, industry becoming the predominant economic activity.
Iron Age	The final prehistoric period, running in Scotland from *c* 500 BC to AD 400, although the latter half is often termed the Roman Iron Age.
jamb	Often used to describe a vertical post at the side of a doorway, window frame, fireplace, or other feature, this term can also be applied to a part of a building adjoining the main fabric.
kirk session	The body of the Reformed church charged with maintaining church and moral discipline.
lair	A burial plot in a graveyard.
listed building	A building or other structure given statutory protection under the *Planning (Listed Buildings and Conservation Areas) (Scotland) Act 1997.*
moot hill	An artificial mound erected to serve as a place of popular assembly and where legal disputes were resolved, also known as a *court hill.*
muniments	Documents kept as evidence of rights or privileges.
nave	The long central part of a church, where the main congregation sits.
neo-classicism	A style of architecture, particularly popular in the eighteenth century, based on or influenced by the architecture of the ancient classical world, Greece and Rome.
Neolithic	Meaning 'New Stone Age' and in Scotland representing the period of human settlement between *c* 4000 and 2000 BC.
Norse	Cultural attribution referring to Scandinavian settlers from the Viking Age (AD 800–1000) to the thirteenth century.
pediment	The triangular portion of a building above the entrance, first used in the buildings of ancient Greece (see *neo-classicism* above).
police burgh	Govan was created a police burgh in 1864 under the *General Police and Improvement (Scotland) Act* of 1862 (commonly known as the 'Lindsay Act') which consolidated and extended previous legislation to allow for more efficient local government in hitherto unrepresented populous places.
portico	A roof supported by columns, especially one forming an entrance to a large building.

printfields	Open areas used for laying out linen or cotton cloth for the printing of patterns using blocks.
Quaternary	Geological period extending from around two million years ago until the present and characterised by repeated climatic fluctuations between temperate and arctic conditions.
Reformation	The movement in the 1550s and 1560s in Scotland that led to the replacement of the medieval Catholic church by the Protestant church.
Roman period	The period of Roman activity and occupation, occupying the first and second centuries AD in southern Scotland.
scheduled ancient monument	A monument given statutory protection under the *Ancient Monuments and Archaeological Areas Act 1979*.
single-end	A one-room flat in a tenement block (see *tenement* below).
Strathclyde (kingdom of)	This term is used to describe the kingdom based on the Clyde which replaced the kingdom of Dumbarton, following its destruction by the Vikings in AD 870. The kingdom of Strathclyde is poorly documented but appears to have survived well into the eleventh century (see Clancy 2006; Broun 2004).
tack	A form of lease.
tenement	A multiple-occupancy, multi-storey housing block. The smallest flats were of one room, but larger flats could extend to four rooms or more. Tenements were built in Govan from the mid-nineteenth century.
tube works	Industrial works producing iron tubes for gas, steam, and water.
turnpike	A road where a toll is levied for its use. Turnpike roads in the Glasgow area emerged from the 1750s, when the Turnpike Acts aimed to improve roads to aid commerce and ease the logistics of military movement.
urbanisation	The process whereby a place, especially a rural place, is changed into or absorbed into a town or city.
Viking Age	Period of Viking raiding and settlement AD 800–1000.
vill	Medieval term for an estate including the associated settlement.
wireworks	An industrial works manufacturing wire ropes, which were used in ship and crane rigging, amongst other things.

References

Primary sources

Cash book of the Govan poor fund (1703–27): *Glasgow City Archives, Mitchell Library, Glasgow; archive ref. CH2/1277/10*

Govan Heritors' Records (1791–1937): *National Archives of Scotland; archive series HR 702*

Govan Weavers' Society Records (1756–1968): *University of Glasgow Archives; archive ref. DC 52*

Hearth Tax records for Lanarkshire: *National Archives of Scotland; archive ref. E69/15*

Lindsay, J, 1912 Glasgow boundaries bill: brief for Counsel for the Promoters, unpublished typescript: *Glasgow City Archives, Mitchell Library, Glasgow; archive ref. A3/1/255*

Minutes of the Govan kirk session, nine volumes (1651–62, 1710–1821 and 1856–1907): *Glasgow City Archives, Mitchell Library, Glasgow; archive ref. CH2/1277/1–9*

Published primary sources

Adamson, D, 1981 *West Lothian Hearth Tax, 1691, with county abstracts for Scotland.* Edinburgh: Scottish Record Society

Bain, J, and Rogers, C, 1875 *Liber protocollorum M. Cuthberti Simonis, notarii publici et scribae capituli Glasguensis, AD 1499–1513. Also, Rental book of Diocese of Glasgow, A.D. 1509–1570,* 2 volumes. London: Grampian Club

Barrow, G W S (ed), 1999 *The charters of David I.* Woodbridge: The Boydell Press

Forbes, A P (ed), 1874 *Lives of S. Ninian and S. Kentigern.* Edinburgh

Fraser, W, 1863 *Memoirs of the Maxwells of Pollok,* 2 volumes. Edinburgh

Fraser, W, 1875 *The Cartulary of Pollok-Maxwell.* Edinburgh: privately published

Glasgow Boundaries Commission, 1888 *Report of the Glasgow Boundaries Commissioners, volume I: report, with appendix.* London: HMSO

Glasgow Corporation, 1911 *Report of the Medical Officer of Health of the City of Glasgow, 1911.* Glasgow: Glasgow Corporation

Innes, C (ed), 1832 *Registrum Monasterii de Passelet.* Edinburgh: Maitland Club

Innes, C (ed), 1843 *Registrum Episcopatus Glasguensis.* Glasgow: Bannatyne and Maitland Clubs

Leishman, M, 1845 'Parish of Govan', in *The New Statistical Account of Scotland,* volume 7. Edinburgh: Blackwood and Sons, 668–718

Marwick, J D, and Renwick, R, 1876–1916 *Extracts from the records of the Burgh of Glasgow AD 1573–1833,* 11 volumes. Edinburgh: Scottish Burgh Records Society (volumes 1–6). Glasgow: Corporation of Glasgow (volumes 7–11)

Marwick, J D, and Renwick, R, 1894–1906 *Charters and other documents relating to the City of Glasgow AD 1175–1707,* 2 volumes. Edinburgh: Scottish Burgh Records Society

Nicol, J, 1885 *Vital, social, and economic statistics of the City of Glasgow, 1881–1885.* Glasgow: James Maclehose, Glasgow

Pollock, J, 1973 'Parish of Govan', in Sinclair 1973

Renwick, R (ed), 1894–1900 *Abstracts of Protocols of the Town Clerks of Glasgow*, 11 volumes. Glasgow: Carson and Nicol

Simpson, G G, 1960 *Regesta Regum Scottorum*: handlist of the Acts of Alexander III, the Guardians, John, 1249–1296. Edinburgh

Secondary sources

Alcock, L, and Alcock, E A, 1990 'Reconnaissance excavations on early historic fortification and other royal sites in Scotland, 1974–84: **4**, excavations at Alt Clut, Clyde Rock, Strathclyde, 1974–75', *Proc Soc Antiq Scot* **120**, 95–149

Allen, J R, 1902 'The Early Christian monuments of the Glasgow district', *Trans Glasgow Archaeol Soc* **4**, 394–402

Allen, J R, and Anderson, J, 1903 *Early Christian Monuments of Scotland.* Edinburgh

Anderson, J, 1881 *Scotland in Early Christian Times.* Edinburgh

Anderson, J, and Black, G F, 1888 'Reports on local museums in Scotland, obtained through Dr R H Gunning's Jubilee gift to the Society', *Proc Soc Antiq Scot* **22**, 331–422

Annan, T, 1878 *The old country houses of the old Glasgow gentry*, second edn. Glasgow: James Maclehose

Arrol, W and Co, 1909 *Bridges, structural steel work, and mechanical engineering productions partly reprinted from 'Engineering'.* London: privately published

Ashmore, P J, 1996 *Neolithic and Bronze Age Scotland.* London: Batsford

Atkinson, M, 1904 *Local government in Scotland.* Edinburgh: William Blackwood and Sons

Barclay, G J (ed), 1997 *State-funded 'rescue' archaeology in Scotland: past, present and future*, with contributions by I Armit, P J Ashmore, G J Barclay, D J Breeze, S M Foster, D Hall, R Hingley, L Macinnes, and O Owen. Edinburgh: Historic Scotland

Barrow, G W S, 1981 'Popular Courts', *Scottish Studies* **25**, 1–24

Bluck, B J (ed), 1973 *Excursion guide to the geology of the Glasgow district.* Glasgow: Geological Society of Glasgow/University of Glasgow

Boothroyd, N, and Higgins, D, 2005 'An inn-clearance group, *c* 1800, from the Royal Oak, Eccleshall, Staffordshire', *Post-Medieval Archaeol* **39**(1), 197–203

Bradley, I C, 1998 'John Macleod centenary lecture', *Eighth annual report of the Society of Friends of Govan Old*, 14–24

Breeze, A, 1999 'Simeon of Durham's Annal for 576 and Govan, Scotland' *Nomina* **22**, 133–8

Brotchie, T C F, 1905 *The history of Govan.* Glasgow: The Old Govan Club (reprinted 1938)

Brotchie, T C F, 1908 'Old township of Govan', *Trans Old Glasgow Club* **1**(5), 219–23

Brotchie, T C F, 1916 'An old Govan advertisement', *Trans Old Govan Club* **1**(2), 7

Brotchie, T C F, 1921 'Notes on the Sheephead Inn', *Trans Old Govan Club* **2**(3), 82–3

Broun, D, 2004 *The Welsh identity of the Kingdom of Strathclyde ca 900–ca 1200*, *Innes Review* **55**, 111–80

Brown, A, 1916 'Govan industries of the 60s', *Trans Old Govan Club* **1**(2), 21–2

Brown, A M, 1921 'Govan in "The Forties"', *Trans Old Govan Club* **2**(3), 86–9

Buchanan, J, 1855 'Discovery of ancient canoes on the Clyde', *Proc Soc Antiq Scot* **1**, 44–5

Buchanan, J, 1877 'Notice of the discovery of a Roman bowl in Glasgow Green and Roman remains found at Yorkhill', *Proc Soc Antiq Scot* **12**, 254–8

Burnett, J, 1919 'Stepping stones at Linthouse', *Trans Old Govan Club* **2**(1)

Butt, J, 1967 *The industrial archaeology of Scotland*. Newton Abbot: David and Charles

Butterfield, R J, 1994 'The industrial archaeology of the twentieth century: the Shredded Wheat Factory at Welwyn Garden City', *Industrial Archaeol Review* **16.2**, 196–215

Cage, R A, 1981 *The Scottish Poor Law 1745–1845*. Edinburgh: Scottish Academic Press

Cameron, I B, and Stephenson, D, 1985 *British regional geology: The Midland Valley of Scotland*. London: HMSO

Carvel, J L, 1950 *Stephen of Linthouse: a record of two hundred years of shipbuilding, 1750–1950*. Glasgow: Alexander Stephen

Chalmers, G, 1824 *Caledonia: or, an account, historical and topographic, of North Britain, from the most ancient to the present times*, volume 3. London

Clancy, T O, 1996 'Govan: the name', *Eighth annual report of the Society of Friends of Govan Old*, 2–3

Clancy, T O, 2006 'Ystad Clud (Strathclyde)', in J T Koch (ed), *Celtic Culture a Historical Encyclopaedia*, Santa Barbara, California: ABC Clio, 1818–21

Clarke, D L, 1970 *Beaker pottery of Great Britain and Ireland*, volume 2. Cambridge

Clough, T H McK, and Cummins, W A (eds), 1988 *Stone axe studies, volume 2: the petrology of prehistoric stone implements from the British Isles*, CBA Research Report **67**. London: Council for British Archaeology

Coles, J M, 1960 'Scottish Late Bronze Age metalwork: typology, distributions, and chronology', *Proc Soc Antiq Scot* **93**, 16–134

Craig, A, 1891 *The Elder Park, Govan: an account of the gift of the Elder Park and of the erection and unveiling of the statue of John Elder*. Glasgow: Maclehose and Sons

Craig, A, 1912 *The statue of Mrs John Elder, Govan: a record of the movement for and unveiling of the statue. Together with some account of the Elder Free Library, the Elder Cottage Hospital, and the Cottage Nurses' Training Home and an obituary notice of Mrs Elder*. Govan: John Cossar for private circulation

Cramp, R, 1994 'The Govan recumbent cross-slabs', in Ritchie (ed) 1994, 55–63

Cranstone, D, 2001 'Industrial archaeology – manufacturing a new society', in R Newman, *The historical archaeology of Britain, c 1540–1900*. Stroud: Sutton Publishing, 183–210

Cullen, I S, and Driscoll, S T, 1994 *Excavations at Govan Old Parish Church, 1994*. Unpublished GUARD interim report **175**. Glasgow

Cunnison, J, and Gilfillan, J B S (eds), 1958 *The Third Statistical Account of Scotland, volume 5: Glasgow*. Glasgow: Collins

Cutmore, C, 1996 'Memorial stones in the kirkyard of Govan: a study of the early modern monuments and the interplay with the re-used early medieval "Govan Stones"'. University of Glasgow (Department of Archaeology): unpublished MA dissertation

Cutmore, C, 1997 'An archaeological study of the memorial stones in the kirkyard of Govan Old Parish Church', *Seventh annual report of the Friends of Govan Old*, 8–18

Cutmore, C, 1998 'An archaeological study of the memorial stones in the kirkyard of Govan Old Parish Church, part 2: index of monuments in the churchyard of Govan', *Eighth annual report of the Friends of Govan Old*, 1–7

Dalrymple Duncan, J, 1899 'Holmfauldhead House, Govan', *The Regality Club* **3**, 108–13

Darville, T, 2004 'Tynwald Hill and the "things" of power, in A Pantos and S Semple (eds), *Assembly Places and practices in Medieval Europe*. Dublin: Four Courts Press, 217–32

Davidson, G, 1923 'Recollections of old Govan', *Trans Old Govan Club* **3**(1), 13–22

Davidson Kelly, T A, 1994a 'The Prebend of Govan: 1150–1560', *Fourth annual report of the Society of Friends of Govan Old*, 12–24

Davidson Kelly, T A, 1994b 'The Govan collection in the context of local history', in Ritchie (ed) 1994, 1–17

Davidson Kelly, T A, 2007 *Living Stones: the daughter churches of Govan Parish, 1730–1919*. Govan: Friends of Govan Old

Deetz, J 1996 *In small things forgotten: an archaeology of early American life*. New York: Anchor/Doubleday

Dennison Torrie, E P, and Coleman, R, 1996 *Historic Hamilton: the archaeological implications of development*. Edinburgh: Historic Scotland

Donaldson, G, 1971 *Scotland: James V to James VII*, the Edinburgh History of Scotland, volume 3. Edinburgh: Oliver and Boyd

Dreghorn, Ex-baillie, 1919 'By-gone days', *Trans Old Govan Club* **2**(1), 20–3

Driscoll, S T, 1995 'Govan Old Parish Church', *Medieval Archaeology* **39**, 277–9

Driscoll, S T, 1997 'Govan Old Parish Church and Water Row', *Medieval Archaeology* **41**, 318–20

Driscoll, S T, 1998 'Church archaeology in Glasgow and the Kingdom of Strathclyde', *Innes Review* **49**, 94–114

Driscoll, S T, 2003 'Govan: an early medieval royal centre on the Clyde', in Welander *et al* 2003, 77–85

Driscoll, S T, and Mitchell, M, 2008 Pollok Park Ring-work Excavation 2007, unpublished data structure report. Glasgow

Driscoll, S T, O'Grady, O, and Forsyth, K S, 2005 'The Govan School revisited: searching for meaning in the early medieval sculpture of Strathclyde', in S Foster and M Cross (eds), *Able Minds and Practiced Hands*. Dublin: Four Courts Press, 135–58

Driscoll, S T, and Will, R S, 1996 Water Row, Govan. Unpublished GUARD interim report **175.2**. Glasgow

Driscoll, S T, and Will, R S, 1997 Govan Old Parish Church and Water Row. Unpublished GUARD interim report **175.3**. Glasgow

Driscoll, S T, Will, R S and Shearer, I, 2008 Water Row, Govan: Archaeological Evaluation 2007, GUARD data structure report **2497**. Glasgow

Duncan, J D, 1883 'Note regarding the ancient canoe recently discovered in the bed of the Clyde above the Albert Bridge', *Trans Glasgow Archaeol Soc* **2**, 121–30

Dunlop, D C, 1889 'The Bunhouse, Partick', *The Regality Club* **1**, 129–36

Dunlop, D, 1893 'Old Bridge Inn, Partick', *The Regality Club* **2**, 58–63

Ellis, C, 2000 'Braehead, Govan, Glasgow City (Govan parish), ?later prehistoric settlement', *Discovery and excavation in Scotland*, 43

Ellis, C, 2001 'Braehead, Glasgow City (Govan parish), prehistoric enclosure', *Discovery and excavation in Scotland*, 49–50

Fairbairn, T, 1885 *Relics of ancient architecture and other picturesque scenes in Glasgow*. Glasgow: Bryce and Son

Ferguson, A, 1919 'Sixty years ago', *Trans Old Govan Club* **2**(1), 15–18

Ferguson, R, 1990 *George Macleod, founder of the Iona Community*. London: Collins

FitzPatrick, E, 2004 *Royal Inauguration in Gaelic Ireland c. 1100–1600*. Woodbridge: Boydell & Brewer

Flinn, M W (ed), 1977 *Scottish population history from the seventeenth century to the 1930s*. Cambridge: Cambridge University Press

Forsyth, K S, 2000 'Evidence of a Pictish source in the *Historia Regum Anglorum* of Symeon of Durham', in Taylor (ed) 2000, 19–34

Foster, J O, 1997 'William Pearce 1833–1888, copper trousered philanthropist', *Seventh annual report of the Society of Friends of Govan Old*, 19–32

Fraser, W H, 1978 'Trades Councils in the labour movement in nineteenth-century Scotland', in I MacDougall (ed), *Essays in Scottish labour history: a tribute to W H Marwick*. Edinburgh: John Donald, 1–28

Fraser, W H, 1996 'Introduction: "Let Glasgow Flourish"', in Fraser and Maver (eds) 1996a, 1–7

Fraser, W H, and Maver, I (eds), 1996a *Glasgow, volume II: 1830 to 1912*. Manchester: Manchester University Press

Fraser, W H, and Maver, I, 1996b 'The social problems of the City', in Fraser and Maver (eds) 1996a, 352–93

Fraser, W H, and Maver, I, 1996c 'Tackling the problems', in Fraser and Maver (eds) 1996a, 394–440

Frodsham, P, and O'Brien, C (eds), 2005 *Yeavering People, Power and Place*. Stroud: Tempus

Fryer, K, and Shelley, A, 1997 'Excavation of a pit at 16 Tunsgate, Guildford, Surrey, 1991', *Post-Medieval Archaeol* **31**, 139–230

Fyfe, P, 1907 'Some old Glasgow mansions', *Trans Old Glasgow Club* **1**(4), 163–7

Galbraith, W C, 1958 'Transport and communication: historical development', in Cunnison and Gilfillan (eds) 1958, 308–25

Gibb, A, 1983 *Glasgow: the making of a city*. London: Croom Helm

Gibb, A, 1989 'Policy and politics in Scottish housing since 1945', in Rodger (ed) 1989a, 155–83

Gilfillan, J B S, 1958 'The site and its development', in Cunnison and Gilfillan (eds) 1958, 17–47

Gilmour, W, 1996 *Keep off the grass!* Ochiltree: Richard Stenlake Publishing

Glasgow International Exhibition, 1888 *The book of the Bishop's Castle and handbook of the archaeological collection*. Glasgow

Glasgow International Exhibition, 1901 *The official catalogue of the Glasgow International Exhibition*. Glasgow: Watson

Glendinning, M, 2003 'Tenements and flats', in G Stell, J Shaw, and S Storrier (eds), *Scottish life and society: a compendium of Scottish ethnology, volume 3, Scotland's buildings*. East Linton: Tuckwell Press/the European Ethnological Research Centre, 108–26

Glendinning, M, MacInnes, R, and MacKechnie, A, 1996 *A history of Scottish architecture: from the Renaissance to the present day*. Edinburgh: Edinburgh University Press

Gould, S, 1999 'Planning, development and social archaeology', in S Tarlow and S West (eds), *The familiar past? Archaeologies of later historical Britain*. London: Routledge, 140–54

Grant, I R and Withrington, D J (eds), 1973 (new edition) *The Statistical Account of Scotland 1791–1799* by Sir John Sinclair (ed), volume **VII**, Lanarkshire and Renfrewshire. Wakefield: E P Publishing

Greenhorne, W, 1914 *Old Partick: its schools and schoolmasters*. Glasgow: Thomlinson

Grosicki, Z, 1958 'Cotton and woollen spinning and weaving', in Cunnison and Gilfillan (eds) 1958, 240–51

Hanson, W S, 1980 'Agricola on the Forth-Clyde isthmus', in J Kenworthy (ed), *Agricola's campaigns in Scotland*, Scottish Archaeological Forum **12**. Edinburgh: Edinburgh University Press, 55–68

Harvey, J (ed), 1988 *Govan Old Parish Church, 1888–1988: a centenary celebration of its founder, its worship, its building and its people*. Glasgow: Wild Goose Publications

Hay, G D, and Stell, G P, 1986 *Monuments of industry: an illustrated historical record*. Edinburgh: RCAHMS

Henderson, W, 1938 'Scottish Late Bronze Age axes and swords', *Proc Soc Antiq Scot* **72**, 150–77

Hillhouse, P A, 1925 'Centenary of John Elder', *Trans Old Govan Club* **3**(3), 69–76

Hope-Taylor, B, 1977 *Yeavering: An Anglo-British Centre of Early Northumbria*. Edinburgh: HMSO

Horsey, M, 1990 *Tenements and towers: Glasgow working-class housing 1890–1990*. Edinburgh: RCAHMS

Houston, J A, 1922 'Govan in 1864: the birth of the Burgh', *Trans Old Govan Club* **2**(4), 125–42

Hume, J R, 1974 *The industrial archaeology of Glasgow*. Glasgow: Blackie

Hume, J R, 1976 *The industrial archaeology of Scotland: 1. The Lowlands and Borders*. London: Batsford

Hume, J R, 1990 'Industrial buildings', in Williamson *et al* 1990, 85–101

Jardine, W G, 1973 'The Quaternary geology of the Glasgow district', in Bluck (ed) 1973, 156–69

Jardine, W G, 1992 'Quaternary', in Lawson and Weedon (eds) 1992, 463–83

Jeans, J S, 1872 *Western worthies*. Glasgow: Evening Star

Johnson, A, 1959 Pollok estate, Glasgow, *Discovery and Excavation Scotland*, 25–6

Johnson, A, 1960 Pollok estate, Glasgow, *Discovery and Excavation Scotland*, 29–30

Johnston, C, and Hume, J R, 1979 *Glasgow stations*. London: David and Charles

Johnston, R, 2000 *Clydeside capital, 1870–1920: a social history of employers*. East Linton: Tuckwell Press

Jopson, C, 2001 A history of church buildings on the Govan Old Parish Church site: 700–2001 AD. Unpublished MA dissertation, Mackintosh School of Art, Glasgow

Kinloch, J and Butt, J, 1981 *History of the Scottish Co-operative Wholesale Society Limited*. Glasgow: Co-operative Wholesale Society

Kirkpatrick, R S, 1915 *The ministry of Dr. John Macleod in the parish of Govan*. Edinburgh: Blackwood and Sons

Knox, W (ed), 1984 *Scottish labour leaders, 1918–1939: a biographical dictionary*. Edinburgh: Mainstream Publishing

Kyd, J G, 1975 *Scottish population statistics; including Webster's analysis of population, 1775*. Edinburgh: Scottish History Society

Lang, J, 1994 'The Govan Hogbacks: a reappraisal', in Ritchie (ed) 1994, 113–22

Lavery, B, 2001 *Maritime Scotland*. London: Batsford/Historic Scotland

Lawrie, A C, 1905 *Early Scottish Charters prior to 1153*. Glasgow: James Maclehose and Sons

Lawson, J, 1990 'Topography and building materials', in Williamson *et al* 1990, 19–27

Lawson, J D, 1992 'Stratigraphical summary', in Lawson and Weedon (eds) 1992, 15–19

Lawson, J D, and Weedon, D S (eds), 1992 *Geological excursions around Glasgow and Girvan*. Glasgow: Geological Society of Glasgow/University of Glasgow

Leishman, J F, 1921 *Matthew Leishman of Govan and the Middle Party of 1843: a page from Scottish church life and history in the nineteenth century*. Paisley: Alexander Gardner

Leishman, J F, 1923 'Gleanings from old Govan', *Trans Old Govan Club* **3**(1), 8–12

Longworth, I H, 1984 *Collared Urns of the Bronze Age in Great Britain and Ireland*. Cambridge: Cambridge University Press

Loudon, J, Hanika, P, and Costain, G D, 1958 'Formative influences', in Cunnison and Gilfillan (eds) 1958, 141–52

Lynch, M, 1987 'Introduction: Scottish towns 1500–1700, in M Lynch (ed), *The early modern town in Scotland*. London: Croom Helm, 1–35

Macdonald, G, 1918 'Roman coins found in Scotland', *Proc Soc Antiq Scot* **52**, 203–76

MacDonald, I R, 1995 *Glasgow's Gaelic churches: Highland religion in an urban setting 1690–1995*. Edinburgh: The Know Press

MacFadyen, J F, Houston, J A, and Munro, Ex-baillie, 1926 'Personal recollections of Govan', *Trans Old Govan Club* **3**(4), 97–102

MacFarlane, J C, 1965 *An outline history of Govan Old Parish Church (565–1965)*. Govan: the Kirk Session, Govan Old Parish Church

MacGeorge, A, 1880 *Old Glasgow: the place and the people; from the Roman occupation to the eighteenth century*. Glasgow

MacGeorge, A, 1893 'The old Point-House', *The Regality Club* **2**, 54–7

MacGibbon, D, and Ross, T, 1892 *The castellated and domestic architecture of Scotland from the twelfth to the eighteenth century*, volume 5. Edinburgh: David Douglas

MacGladdery, C, 1990 *James II*. Edinburgh: John Donald

MacGregor, A, 1967 *Public health in Glasgow, 1905–1946*. Edinburgh: E and S Livingstone

MacLean, D, 1922 'Fifty years ago', *Trans Old Govan Club* **2**(4), 143–55

Macquarrie, A, 1990 'Early Christian Govan: the historical context', *Records of the Scottish Church History Society* **24**, 1–17

Macquarrie, A, 1993 'The kings of Strathclyde, c.400–1018' in A Grant and K Stringer (eds), *Medieval Scotland: Crown, lordship and community: essays presented to G.W.S. Barrow*, Edinburgh, 1–19

Macquarrie, A, 1994 'The historical context of the Govan Stones' in Ritchie 1994, 27–32

Macquarrie, A, 1997 *The saints of Scotland: essays in Scottish church history AD 450–1093*. Edinburgh: John Donald

Marvin, A W, 1958 'Other textiles, clothing and finishing, in Cunnison and Gilfillan (eds) 1958, 251–63

Matheson, A, 2000 *Glasgow's other river: exploring the Kelvin*. Ayr: Fort Publishing

Maver, I, 2000 *Glasgow*. Edinburgh: Edinburgh University Press.

McAlpine, C J, 1997 *The lady of Claremont House: Isabella Elder, pioneer and philanthropist*. Glendaruel: Argyll Publishing

McKean, C, 2001 *The Scottish château: the country house of Renaissance Scotland*. Stroud: Sutton

McKenzie, R, 2002 *Public sculpture of Glasgow*. Liverpool: Liverpool University Press

McKinstry, S, 1991 *Rowand Anderson: 'The Premier Architect of Scotland'*. Edinburgh: Edinburgh University Press

McKinstry, S, 1992 'The architecture of Govan Old Parish Church', *Second annual report of the Society of Friends of Govan Old*, 4–15

McLellan, D, 1894 *Glasgow public parks*. Glasgow: John Smith and Sons

Melling, J, 1982 'Scottish industrialists and the changing character of class relations in the Clyde region, c.1880–1918', in T Dickson (ed), *Capital and class in Scotland*. Edinburgh: John Donald, 61–142

Mitchell, A, and Anderson, J, 1890 'Scottish archaeology', in J Paton (ed), *Scottish national memorials: a record of the historical and archaeological collection in the Glasgow International Exhibition, 1888*. Glasgow: James Maclehose and Sons, 3–28

Mitchell, I R, 2006 'Govan's Pearce Institute', *History Scotland* **6.3**, 9–11

Mitchison, R, 1983 *Lordship to patronage: Scotland 1603–1745*. London: Edward Arnold

Moore, J N, 1996 *The Maps of Glasgow: a history and cartobibliography to 1865*. Glasgow: Glasgow University Library

Morrison, A, 1968 'Cinerary urns and pygmy vessels in South-West Scotland', *Trans Dumfriesshire and Galloway Nat Hist and Antiq Soc* **45**, 80–140

Moss, M S, and Hume, J R, 1977 *Workshop of the British Empire: engineering and shipbuilding in the West of Scotland*. London: Heinemann

Moss, M S, and Hume, J R, 1986 *Shipbuilders to the world: 125 years of Harland and Wolff, Belfast, 1861–1986*. Belfast: Blackstaff

Mowat, R J C, 1996 *The logboats of Scotland, with notes on related artefact types*, Oxbow Monograph Series **68**. Oxford

Murphy, S, 1920 'The story of "The Govan Press": an historical retrospect', *Trans Old Govan Club* **2**(2), 52–64

Murphy, W S, 1901 *Captains of industry*. Glasgow: William S Murphy

Murray, D, 1924–32 *Early burgh organisation in Scotland: as illustrated in the history of Glasgow and of some neighbouring burghs*, 2 volumes. Glasgow: Maclehose and Jackson

Murray, D M, 1996 'Matthew Leishman of Govan 1821–1874: the Middle Party and the middle way', *Sixth annual report of the Society of Friends of Govan Old*, 4–17

Murray, N, 1978 *The Scottish hand loom weavers 1790–1850: a social history*. Edinburgh: John Donald

Napier, H M, 1924 'Robert Napier: a great shipbuilder', *Trans Old Govan Club* **3**(2), 50–7

Napier, J, 1873 *Notes and reminiscences relating to Partick*. Glasgow: Hugh Hopkins

Nenadic, S, 1996 'The Victorian middle classes', in W H Fraser and I Maver (eds) 1996, 265–99

Neville George, T, 1958 'The geology and geomorphology of the Glasgow district', in R Miller and J Tivy (eds), *The Glasgow region: a general survey*. Edinburgh: T and A Constable, 17–61

Neville George, T, 1973 'Introduction: geology around Glasgow', in B J Bluck (ed) 1973, 9–25

Osborne, B D, Quinn, I, and Robertson, D, 1996 *Glasgow's river*. Glasgow: Lindsay Publications

Owen, O, MacSween, A, and Ritchie, M, 2000 *The future of the Scottish Burgh Survey*. Edinburgh: Historic Scotland

Palmer, M, 1990 'Industrial archaeology: a thematic or a period discipline?', *Antiquity* **64**, 275–85

Palmer, M, 1991 'Industrial Archaeology: working for the future', *Industrial Archaeol Review* **14.1**, 17–32

Park, J P, 1916 'Rural Govan', *Trans Old Govan Club* **1**(2), 30–3

Park, J P, 1920 'Memories of old Govan', *Trans Old Govan Club* **2**(2), 48–51

Pearce, J, 2000 'A late 18th-century inn clearance assemblage from Uxbridge, Middlesex', *Post-Medieval Archaeol* **34**, 144–86

Pollock, D, 1992 'The Saracen Head excavation 1980–1981', *Glasgow Archaeol J* **17**, 77–89

Radford, C A R, 1967a 'The Early Christian monuments at Govan and Inchinnan', *Trans Glasgow Archaeol Soc* **15**(4), 173–88

Radford, C A R, 1967b 'The early church in Strathclyde and Galloway', *Medieval Archaeol* **11**, 105–26

RCAHMS, 1978 Royal Commission on the Ancient and Medieval Monuments of Scotland, *Lanarkshire: an Inventory of the Prehistoric and Roman Monuments*, Edinburgh: HMSO

Riddell, J F, 1979 *Clyde navigation: a history of the development and deepening of the River Clyde*. Edinburgh: John Donald

Ritchie, A (ed), 1994 *Govan and its early medieval sculpture*. Stroud: Alan Sutton

Ritchie, A, 2004 *Hogback gravestones at Govan and beyond*. Glasgow: Friends of Govan Old annual lecture

Ritchie, J N G, 1970 'Beaker pottery in South-West Scotland', *Trans Dumfriesshire and Galloway Nat Hist and Antiq Soc* **47**, 123–46

Ritchie, J N G, and Shepherd, I A G, 1973 'Beaker pottery and associated artefacts in South-West Scotland', *Trans Dumfriesshire and Galloway Nat Hist and Antiq Soc* **50**, 18–36

Robertson, D S, 1992 'Scottish home improvement policy, 1945–75: coming to terms with the tenement', *Urban Studies* **29**(7), 1115–36

Robertson, D S, 1998 'Scotland's new towns: a modernist experiment in state corporatism', in S Foster, A Macinnes, and R MacInnes (eds), *Scottish power centres: from the Early Middle Ages to the twentieth century*. Glasgow: Cruithne Press, 210–39

Robertson and McIntosh Consultants, 2005 *A conservation plan for Govan: consultation document; a study commissioned, funded and published by Govan Workspace Ltd*. Glasgow: Govan Workspace Ltd

Rodger, R (ed), 1989a *Scottish housing in the twentieth century*. Leicester: Leicester University Press

Rodger, R, 1989b 'Introduction', in Rodger 1989a, 1–24

Roe, F E S, 1966 'The Battle-axe series in Britain', *Proc Prehist Soc* **32**, 199–245

Roe, F E S 1967 'The Battle-axes, mace-heads and axe-hammers from South-West Scotland', *Trans Dumfriesshire and Galloway Nat Hist and Antiq Soc* **44**, 57–80

Roger, J C, 1857 'Notices of the early history of the parish of Govan', *Proc Soc Antiq Scot* **2**, 212–16

Sanderson, M H B, 1982 *Scottish Rural Society in the Sixteenth Century*. Edinburgh: John Donald

Schmidt, P K, and Burgess, C B, 1981 *The axes of Scotland and northern England*, Prähistorische Bronzefunde **9**(7). Munchen

Scott, J G, 1996 'The ditched enclosure at Shiels Govan, Glasgow', in D Alexander (ed), *Prehistoric Renfrewshire: papers in honour of Frank Newall*. Renfrewshire Local History Forum, Archaeology Section, 65–70

Scottish Office, 1994 *Planning Advice Note 42: archaeology – the planning process and scheduled monument procedures*. Edinburgh

Sillars, J, 1924 'Glimpses of Govan', *Trans Old Govan Club* **3**(2), 39–42

Sinclair, J (ed), 1973 *The Statistical Account of Scotland 1791–1799, volume VII, Lanarkshire and Renfrewshire*. New edition I R Grant and D J Withrington (eds) (Wakefield 1973) Wakefield: E P Publishing, 356–71

Slaven, A, 1975 *The development of the West of Scotland: 1750–1960*. London: Routledge and Kegan Paul

Slaven, A, 1986 'Sir William Pearce', in Slaven and Checkland (eds) 1986, 229–30

Slaven, A, and Checkland, S (eds), 1986 *Dictionary of Scottish business biography, 1860–1960: volume 1, the staple industries*. Aberdeen: Aberdeen University Press

Slaven, A, and Checkland, S (eds), 1990 *Dictionary of Scottish business biography, 1860–1960: volume 2, processing, distribution, services*. Aberdeen: Aberdeen University Press

Smart, A, 2002 *Villages of Glasgow: south of the Clyde*, revised edn. Edinburgh: John Donald

Spalding, B, 1994 *Old Govan*. Catrine: Stenlake Publishing

Speller, K, 1995 Braehead: archaeological field evaluation and survey. Unpublished GUARD interim report **199.2**, Glasgow

Stirling Maxwell, J, 1899 *Sculptured stones in the kirkyard of Govan*. Glasgow

Stothers, T, 1911 *Stother's Glasgow, Lanarkshire and Renfrewshire, 1911–1912*. Hamilton: Stothers

Stuart, J, 1856 *The sculptured stones of Scotland*. Aberdeen: Spalding Club

Taylor, S (ed), 2000 *Kings, clerics and chronicles in Scotland 500–1297*. Dublin: Four Courts Press

Taylor, S, 2007 'Gaelic in Glasgow: the onomastic evidence', in S Kidd (ed), *Glasgow Baile Mòr nan Gaidheal City of the Gaels*. East Linton: Tuckwell Press, 1–19

Thomson, T B S, 1963 *A guide to Govan Old Parish Church, Glasgow*. Glasgow: Blackwood

Urquhart, R M, 1991 *The burghs of Scotland and the General Police and Improvement (Scotland) Act 1862*. Motherwell: Scottish Library Association

Walker, D M, 1993 'Govan Old: its place in nineteenth and early twentieth century church design', *Third annual report of the Society of Friends of Govan Old*, 4–20

Walker, F M, 2001 *Song of the Clyde: a history of Clyde shipbuilding*, revised edn. Edinburgh: John Donald

Watson, M, 2000 'Change for the better: Luma Lamp Factories, glass-clad Modernism and reworked textile mills', in D C Mays, M S Moss, and M K Oglethorpe (eds), *Visions of Scoland's past: looking to the future; essays in honour of John R Hume*. East Linton: Tuckwell Press, 156–72

Welander, R, Breeze, D, and Clancy, T O (eds), 2003 *The Stone of Destiny: artefact and icon*. Edinburgh

West, S, 1999 'Introduction', in S Tarlow and S West (eds), *The familiar past? Archaeologies of later historical Britain*. London: Routledge, 1–15

Whitelaw, C E, 1916 'Report on the old houses at Water Row, Govan Ferry', *Trans Glasgow Archaeol Soc* new series **6**, 280–1

Whyte, I D, 1997 *Scotland's society and economy in transition, c.1500–c.1750*. Houndmills: Macmillan Press

Williamson, E, 1990 'Medieval to twentieth-century Glasgow', in Williamson *et al* 1990, 38–85

Williamson, E, Riches, A, and Higgs, M, 1990 *Glasgow*, The Buildings of Scotland series. London: Penguin Books / The National Trust for Scotland

Willsher, B, 1992 'Govan Old Parish Church graveyard', *Second annual report of the Society of Friends of Govan Old*, 16–23

Worsdall, F, 1989 *The Glasgow tenement: a way of life; a social, historical, and architectural study*, paperback edn. Edinburgh: Chambers

Young, R, 2003 *No Ordinary Minister: Christian leadership and Community Change, Govan 1960–1980*. Govan: Friends of Govan Old

Young, W, 1899 'Govan', *The Regality Club* **3**, 95–103

Index

NB: numbers in **bold** refer to figures or their captions

Aboukir Street 80, 139
aerated water works 91
agriculture 20, 59–61
Aitken, Dr John 105, 111
Aitken Memorial Fountain 111, **112**, 129
Albion Works 91
Alexander and Sons 86
Alston, John Thomas 70
Anchor Line transit sheds 94, **96**
Anderson, R Rowand 117, 120, 126
archaeology
    contribution 48
    domestic sites 137–40
    excavations 124–5
        locations **36**
        reports 27
    industrial 125, 140–1
    potential 17–18, 50, 122, 125, 130–42
    prehistoric finds 14–17
    recent period 137–42
    Roman period 17
architecture
    post-industrial era 69–73
    pre-industrial 67–9
Arrol, Sir William 83, 86
Arthurlie Street 103
Artizan Machine Tool Works 91
Ascelin, Archdeacon 18
asylum 106

Baird, Thomas 69
bakeries 91
Barclay Curle shipyard 83, **84**, 89, 141
Barnwell Terrace 80, 103
Barr, Revd James 119
Barras, Dr James 105
Bellahouston Academy 108
Bellahouston House **69**
Benalder Street 56

Bennet, John 72
Bishop Mills 63–4, **64**, 91, 128, 131
Bishop's Orchard, Partick 48, 60, 134
Black Bull Inn 58
bleachfields 62
bleachworks 91
boiler works 89, 141
Braehead, prehistoric settlement **15**, 16
brass foundries 89, 141
Brechin's Bar 117
brewing 57
brick clay/brickworks 14, 64
Brighton Place 103
British Linen Bank 91, **117**, 128
British Polar Engines factory 89, 141
Bronze Age 15, 16
Broomloan **69**, 71
Broomloan Road 80, 89, 90, 99, 141
    school 109, 128
Bruce, Robert 31
brush factory 91, 128
bubonic plague 105
Buchanan's Waverley Tavern **62**
Buckingham Square 101
building materials 13–14
buildings, listed 126, 128–30
Bunhouse Inn 59, **59**
Bunhouse Mill 63, **63**, 91, 136
Burghead Place 102, **102**, 139
burial monuments 31–4, 49, 73–5, 121, 127, 132
Burleigh Street 102, 139
BVT surface fleet 86, 124

Caledonian Steel Foundry 89
Campbell, James 70
canals 20
canoes 14–15

Cardell Halls and public house 114–15, 128

Carmichael Street 89, 90, 91

Carmichael (chemical) Works 91, 141

Cassells, Robert 71

Castlebank Street 55, 91

cattle transport 95

Cessnock Dock (Prince's Dock) 84, 94, **95**, 141

Cessnock House **69**, 72

Chalmers, Peter Macgregor **118**, 120

chemical works 91, 141

church(es)

in industrial era 117–21

landholding by 66

post-Reformation 73–7

social functions 75

see also names of individual churches

Clachan Drive 102, 139

Clyde Navigation Trust 94, 96

Clyde Shipbuilders' Association (CSA) 110

Clyde shipyard 83–4

location **82**

Clydebrae Street 145

Clydeholm shipyard 83

Clydeside Engine and Boiler Works 89, 141

Clynder Street 101, 139

coal workings 13, 64

common land 60–1

Common Loan 60, 61

conservation plan 142, 144

Copland Place 103, 139

Copland Road 91, 103

subway station **99**

coppersmiths 90

cotton factories 91

County Bingo Social Club 128

court hills 45, 49

Craigton Commons 60, 61

Craigton Farm 61

Craigton House **69**, 71

Craigton Road 80, 91, 102, 103, 139

cranes, Titan cantilever 83, **84**, 86, **88**, 129

Cressy Street 80, 102, **102**, 139

Crookstonhall **69**

Crossloan Road 102, 139

David Elder Infirmary 107

David I, king of Scots 18, 19, 30, 50, 66

Dean Park 69

depression, economic 100

docks, off-river 94

documentary sources 18–21, 130

domestic environment, heritage / archaeology 138–40

Doomster Hill **12**, **23**, 28, 40–2, **43**, 45–6, 49, 61, 131, **133**

excavations 41, 42, 133, 142, **143**

location **2**, **3**, **15**, 22, **23**, **36**, 41–5

reservoir 44–5, 63

drinking fountain 111, **112**, 129

Drive Road 102, 103, 139

Drumoyne Avenue 103

Drumoyne Common 60

Drumoyne Drive 103

Drumoyne Primary School 128

Drumoyne Road 103, 106

dry docks 94, **95**, **96**, 140

dugout canoes 14–15

Dumbarton Road 56, 108

Dumbreck Villa **69**

Duncan, Robert 111

Dunsmuir Street 91

dye works **24**, 41, 44, 62–3, **62**, 63, 136

education 75–7, 108–9, 110

Elder family 85

David Elder Infirmary 107

Elder, Alexander 107

Elder, Isabella (Mrs John Elder) 106, 110, 113

statue 114, **116**, 130

Elder, John 69, 80, 84, 85, 86, 110

statue 114, **115**, 130

Elder Cottage Hospital 106, **107**, 128

Elder Park 70, 86, 103, 113–14, **115**, 124, **147**

cottage 128

Fairfield farmhouse 59, **59**, 114, 131
library **114**, **115**, 128
location **2**, **3**, **114**
Elder Park Church 73, 120
Elder Street 80, 86, 102, 139
Elderpark Street 102, 139
Elm Park House 69
engineering works 89–91, 141
estates, country 66–7, 74

Fairfield farmhouse 59, **59**, 114, 131
Fairfield House **69**, 70
Fairfield Shipyard 83, 84–6, **87–8**, 89,
    123, 140–1, **147**
    accident fund 110, 114
    location **2**, **3**, **82**
farming 59–60
ferry crossings **12**, **23**, 53–4, **58**, 95–6,
    98, **98**
Ferry Inn **56**, 57
feu fermes 66
fire service 105, 106
fishing 60, **60**
flood (1454) 19
flour milling 63, 91
footwear manufacture 93
fords
    River Clyde 12, 53, 54, **54**
    River Kelvin **55**, 56
Free Church 119
fulling mill, Partick 19

Geographical Information System (GIS)
    1, 5
geology 9–11
Gilbert Street
    drill hall 109, **109**
    school 109
Gilmourhill House **69**
Glasgow
    annexation of Govan 3, 7, 104, 105
    Govan's connection with 21
    records 19
Glasgow Cathedral 30

landholdings 18–19, 30, 78
Glasgow Engineering Works 129
Glasgow and Paisley Joint Railway 89,
    98
Glasgow Tramways Company 98
Golspie Street 109
Gorbals (Little Govan) **22**
Gordon, Martha 110
Govan **12**, **51**
    aerial views **7**, **147**
    archeological potential 135–42
    boundaries **2**
    as burgh 7, 80–122
    connection with Glasgow 21
    development
        environmental background 9–14
        map **3**
    early historic period 28–30
    historic significance 142–7
    histories of 80, 118, 122
    medieval period 30–1, 45–6, 48
    natural environment 9–14
    origins 28
    place name 28
    regeneration 127
    scope of study 6, 7–9
    since 1912 123–47
    sixteenth to early nineteenth
        centuries 51–79
    uniting with Glasgow 3, 7
Govan ale 57
Govan Combination Hospital (later
    Southern General Hospital) 105, 106,
    107
    location **3**, **114**
Govan Combination Poorhouse 106
Govan Conservation Area 127
Govan Cross **112**, **117**, 144, **145**
    Cardell Halls and public house
        114–15
    drinking fountain 111, **112**, 129
    school 75, 76, **76**
    shipyards 83
    subway station **99**
    tollhouse 55
Govan East shipyard 84

Govan Ferry 53, 95–6, 97
Govan Ferry West 96, 98
Govan Graving Docks 94, 95, 96, 141
Govan High School 108
Govan New Church (St Mary's) 112,
    119, 120, 129
Govan Old Church and churchyard 7, 8,
    12, 28–9, 53, 73, 117, 120, 127–8, 129,
    131, 144
    aerial photograph 29
    archaeological excavations 4, 27, 35–
        40, 37–40, 124–5, 132–3, 142, 143
        map 36
    in industrial era 119, 120
    location 2, 3
    manse 46, 46, 77, 77, 120
    position in churchyard 34
    sculptured stones/burial monuments
        31–4, 48, 73–5, 121, 127, 132
    sequence of buildings on site 35–7,
        38, 73
        1888 building 118, 119, 120–1, 120
Govan Press Buildings 91, 128
Govan Road 4–5, 55, 58, 87, 91, 145
    tenements 101, 102, 139
    town hall 105, 106
    see also under previous name of Main
        Street
Govan Ropeworks 90
Govan Shipbuilding Yard (Old Govan
    Yard) 58, 84, 85, 129
Govan Steel Works 89
Govan Victualling Society 91–2
Govan Weavers' Society 21, 61, 65
Govandale 68, 69
grain mills 63
graving docks 94, 95, 96, 129, 141
Greenfield Street School 109, 109
Greenhaugh House 69
Greenhead 69, 71

Hagart family 70
Harland and Wolff shipyard 46, 82–3,
    84, 86, 140
    graving dock 83

location 82
Harmony House 69, 71
Harmony Row 51, 61, 80
Harmony Row Commons 60–1
health services 105, 107
Helen Street 89, 91, 141
hemp ropeworks 90
Herbert, Bishop of Glasgow 18–19, 30
heritage
    industrial 125
    management 123–30, 142–7
heritors' records 20–1
Highland Lane 53
Hill, Abraham 109
Hillock see Doomster Hill
Hillock House 44–5, 69, 69
Hill's Trust School 77, 109, 109, 129
Hislop, Dr 69
Holmfauld Road 86
Holmfauldhead Drive 103
Holmfauldhead estate 70
Holmfauldhead House 69, 71
Honeyman, John 119
hospitals 106–7
houses/housing
    industrial and post-industrial era
        69–73
        19th century 68–70, 100, 101
        20th century 124, 126, 138–9
    local authority 124
    mansions 67, 69–72, 136
    pre-industrial era 67–9, 68
    suburban 102–3
    tenements 101–2
housing associations 124
Howat Street 102, 139
Hutcheson, George 48
Hutton Drive 102, 139
hydraulic power systems 94, 128, 129,
    141

Ibrox Park 116, 117
    location 114
    memorial to 1971 disaster 123
Ibroxhill 69, 72

Ibroxholm **69**, 71
Independent Labour Party (ILP) 105, 111
industrial archaeology 125, 140–1
industrial decline 124, 125
industrial heritage 125
industrial relations 110–11, 112
industrialisation 62–4, 81–99
    effects 80
        housing 101–3
        population growth 99–101
        port and transport infrastructure 93–9
inns 57–9, 136
Iron Age 16–17
iron deposits 13
iron industry 63, 89
ironstone 64

James VI, king of Scots 66
jetties, Clyde 52–3

Kelvin Hall 129
Kelvinhaugh
    ferry crossing 54, 96
    ford 53
    industry 91
    shipyards 82
Kelvinhaugh Primary School 109
Kennedra Drive 102, 139
Kerr, Alexander 70
King George V Dock 94
Kirk, Dr A C 84
kirk session minutes 20
Kittle Corner **51**

labour relations 110–11, 112
Ladywell Wire Works 91, 141
Lanarkshire and Dumbartonshire Railway 98
landholding 20, 66–7
Langlands Brick Works 64
Langlands Common 60

Langlands Road 55, 61, 107, 109
    housing 102, **102**, 103, 139
Leishman, Revd Matthew 117–18
limestone 13
Lindsay Act (1862) 104
Linthouse
    annexation by Govan 7, 101
    ford at **54**
Linthouse Buildings 102, 129
    location **3**
Linthouse estate 70
Linthouse Mansion **69**, 70, **71**, 114, 129, 131
Linthouse St Kenneth's Church **118**, 120, 129
Linthouse Shipyard 70, 83, 84, 86, **88**, 89, **90**, 123, 140
    location **82**
Lipton, Sir Thomas 91
listed buildings 126, 128–30
Little Govan (Gorbals) **22**
local government 103–9
lodging houses 103
logboats 14–15
Luath Street 102, 139
Luma Lamp Factory 93, **93**, 123
Lyceum Cinema **116**, 128
Lyceum Theatre **68**, **116**, 117

machine tool manufacture 91
McKechnie, John 80
McKechnie Street 80
Mackie and Thomson Shipbuilders 85
Maclean, Neil 111
Macleod, Revd George 118
Macleod, Revd John 73, 118, 120–1
Mafeking Street 80
Main Street (later Main Road and then Govan Road) 22, 55, 145
    houses 67, 68–9, **69**
    inns 58
manse 46, **46**, 77, **77**, 120
Manse (Pearce) Lane **4–5**, 46, 57, **57**, 144
mansion houses 67, 69–72, 136
    location of **69**

maps
    John Ainslie (1800) 22, **24**
    W D Barles 26, **27**
    development **3**
    William Forrest (1816) 22, **24**
    location maps **2, 3**
      industry **82**
    George Martin (1842) 22, **24**
    Ordnance Survey (1st–3rd eds) 23–4,
      25
    parish boundary **2**
    PASTMAP internet site 1
    Timothy Pont 21, **22**
    Thomas Richardson 22, 23
    River Clyde 26, **26**
    William Roy 21–2, **23**, 26, 43
    as sources 21–7, 130
marine engineering 89
Maritime House 129
Masonic Halls 119
Maxwell family of Pollok 19, 20
Maxwell, Sir William 92–3
Meadowside Granary **87**, 95, **97**, **147**
Meadowside shipyard 82, **82**, **83**, 140
Meikle Govan **22**, **23**, 103
Merklands Lairage 95, **97**, 141
Merryflats **69**, 71
Merryland Street 103, 107, 120
Middle Ages 30–1, 45–6, 48
Middleton Common 61
Middleton Yard 84
Mill of Partick 63
Mitchell, John 70
monuments
    burial 31–4, 49, 73–5, 121, 127, 132
    twentieth century 123
    see also statues
Moore Park estate 70
Moore Park house **69**, 70, **72**
Moorepark Boiler Works 89
Moses Waddell's Inn 57, **57**
Moss House **69**
municipal buildings 105–6, **106**, 129
    location **114**
Museum of Transport 129

name of Govan, origins 28
Napier, Robert 84
Napier Drive 145
Napier House 103, **103**, 129
Napier Place 145
Napier Road 145
Napier Street **44**, 45
Napier Terrace 145
Neptune Street 80–1, **102**
Nimmo Drive 103
North British Diesel Engine Works
    83
nursing home 107

Old Bridge Inn 59
Old Dumbarton Road 55, 56, **59**, 91
Old Govan Club 26
Old Govan shipyard (Govan
    Shipbuilding Yard) **58**, 84, **85**
Orange Lodges 119
Orkney Street 105–6, **106**
Oswald, Alexander 70
Oswald, Richard Alexander 70
Ovania 18

Paisley Road West 77
paper mills 64
Partick
    archeological potential 135, 136
    close association with Govan 7–8
    on early maps 21, **22**
    fulling mill 19
    orchard 48, 60, 134
    royal estate 8, 12, 30, 47, 131, 134,
      144
    sewage pumping station 129
Partick Bridge 21, **55**, 57
Partick Castle 19, 73, 134, 144
    archaeological potential 134–5
    on early maps 21, 22, **22**, 47–8, **47**
    site of **2, 3**
paternalism 110, 112
Pearce family 85
Pearce, William 69, 84, 85, 100, 110,

111, 112–13
  statue **3**, 112, **112**, **113**, 129
Pearce Institute **116**, 117, 129
  location **114**
Pearce (Manse) Lane **4–5**, 46, 57, **57**, 144
Pearce Street **4–5**
Pearson Hall 129
Peninver Drive 102, 139
philanthropy 110, 112, 113
plague 105
Plantation House **69**, 72
Point House **12**, **23**
Pointhouse
  ferry crossing 53, **58**
  ford 53
  mills 63
  tavern 57–8, **58**
Pointhouse shipyard 83, 89, 140
  location **82**
police 100, 104–5, 106
police burghs 103
politics
  national 111, 112–13
  social 110–11, 121–2
Pollock, Revd John 75
Pollok, Morris 62, **62**, **68**, 69
Pollok's Silk Mill 62, **62**, 136
  location **3**
poor, care of 20, 61, 64, 75, 78
poorhouse 75, 106
population 20, 65
  growth 99–101
  social profile 124, 126
pottery, prehistoric 16
prehistoric discoveries 14–17, **15**
Prince's Dock (Cessnock Dock) 84, 94,
  95, 141
print works 91
public health 105, 107

quarries 14, 64
Queen Street 81
Queen's Dock 94, **94**, 141

radicalism among handloom weavers
  65–6
railways 98
Randolph and Elder 84, 85
Rathlin Street 102, 139
recreation 113–14, 117
Regent Flour Mills 91
Reid family 69
Reid, Alexander 62–3
Reid's dye works **24**
religion 119
  see also church(es)
Renfrew Road 108
reservoir 44–5, 63
retail trade, 18th century 57
Ritchie family 71–2
River Clyde 11, **12**
  deepening and training 13, 52–3, 54,
    93
  fishing on 60, **60**
  fords 12
  navigation of 13
  reclaimed land 54, 135
  relationship with Govan 11–13
  surveys of 26, **26**
  as transport route 11–12
River Kelvin 12
riveters 111
roads 54–9, 61
Robert I, king of Scots 31
Robertson, John 72
Roman Catholic churches 119
Roman Catholic school 62
Roman period **15**, 17
ropeworks 90
Rosneath Street 102, 139
Rowan family 19, 70, 74
Rowan, Stephen 70

St Anthony's RC Church 119, **119**, 120,
  130
St Columba's Free Gaelic Church 120
St Constantine 28–9
St Kenneth Drive, terraces 103
  location **3**

St Kentigern 30

St Mary's Church (Govan New) **112**, 119, 120, 129

St Ninian's hospital 19

St Saviour's RC Church 120

St Simon's RC Church 120

Salvation Army Citadel 119, 120, 129

sandstone 9, 14

sarcophagus 31, **32**, 34, 132

Savings Bank 91, 129

schools 62, 75–7, 108–9

   see also names of individual schools

Scotstoun Flour Mills 91, 141

Scotstounmill Road 91

Scottish Co-operative Wholesale Society (SCWS) 91–2, 111

   Shieldhall site 92–3, **92**

     location **3**, **82**

Scottish United Trades' Council Independent Labour Party (STCLP) 111

Scotway House 82, **83**, 129

sculptured stones 31–4, 48

   hogbacks 31–2, **33**, 49

   plan of location **35**

     in churchyard **34**

   recumbent cross-slabs 32, **33**, 49

   sarcophagus 31, **32**, 34, 132

   Sun Stone **30–1**, 31

   upstanding crosses 32, **33**, 34, 132

seaman's mission 119

sewage pumping station, Partick 129

sewage system 107–8

Shaw Street **68**, 102, 139

Sheephead Inn 58, **58**, 59

Shield Hall estate 70

Shield Hall House **69**, 70–1

Shieldhall Lairage 95

Shieldhall sewage works 108, **108**

Shiels, prehistoric settlement **15**, 16

ship repair 94

Shipbuilding Employers' Federation 110

shipbuilding/shipyards 81–9

   archaeological potential of sites 140–1

   decline 124, 125

industrial relations 110–11, 112

map of yards **82**

Partick **56**

related industries 89–91

   see also names of individual yards

silk factories/mills **12**, 20, 62, **62**, 91, 136

Slit Mills 63, 64

slum clearance 126

Smith, James, of Jordanhill 73

Smithfield Iron Company 63

snuff mills 64

soapworks 64

social politics 110–11

sources

   antiquarian and archaeological accounts 27

   documentary 18–21, 130

   map 21–7, 130

Southcroft House 69

Southcroft Street 101, 139

Southern General Hospital (formerly Govan Combination Hospital) **107**, 130

   location **3**, **114**

Spreull, James 70

SPT subway works 141

Stag Inn 58

statues

   Isabella Elder 114, **116**, 130

   John Elder 114, **115**, 130

   William Pearce **3**, 112, **112**, **113**, 129

steel foundries 89

Stephen, Alexander 110

Steven family 74

Steven and Struthers foundry 89, 141

Stewart, Walter, of Arthurlie 66

Stewart, Walter, commendator of Blantyre 66

Stone Age 15, 16–17

stones, sculptured *see* sculptured stones

Strathclyde, annexation by Scots 50

street names 80–1

submariners' memorial 123

suburban housing 102–3

subway system 99, 141

Summertown Road 139

Taransay Street 102, **138**, 139
tenements 101–2, 130, **138**, 139
    demolition/rehabilitation 126
textile industries 13, 91
    dyeing 62–3
    handloom weaving 20, 61–2, 65–6
    industrialisation 62–3
    silk 62, 91
    textile-finishing 62
Thornbank **69**, 72, **72**
Titan cantilever cranes 83, **84**, 86, **88**,
    129
Tod and MacGregor 82
Toll-bar 20
tollhouse 55
town hall 105, **106**, 128
    location **2**, **3**, **114**
townscape 5, 81, 121–7, 144–7
trade unionism 110–11
Trades' Council 111
tramways 98
transport
    rail 98
    river 11–12, 93–8
        see also ferry crossings
    subways 99
    tramways 98
tube works 89

Uist Street 102, 139
unemployment 100, 124
United Presbyterian Church 119
United Secession Church 118–19
Upper Clyde Shipbuilders 86

Vale of Clyde Company (tramways) 98
Vicarfield House **69**, 71
Vicarfield Street 103
Victoria Street 81
victualling trade 91
Viking Age 13, 30, 49

war memorial 123
Water Row **4–5**, **8**, **12**, **43**, **53**, 55, **56**,
    144
    archaeological excavations 27, 46, 125
    archaeological potential 131, 133–4
    ferry crossing 53, **62**
    ford 53
    houses **56**, 57, 67, 68
    inns **56**, 57
    shipyards 83, 84
Watson, Robert 70
weaving/weavers
    handloom weaving 20, 61–2, 65
    industrialisation 62–3
    radicalisation among handloom
        weavers 65–6
White Inch 13, 21
    land reclamation 54
Whitefield Brass Works 90, 141
Whitefield House **69**, 71
Whitefield Road 61
    drill hall 109
Whitefield Works 89, 141
Whiteinch shipyards 83
    East Whiteinch 83
    location **82**
    Whiteinch Jordanvale 83
wireworks 90–1
Wishart, Bishop Robert 31
wood mills 64
Woodville Street 90, 91, 103

YMCA 57, 117, **117**, 129
Yorkhill **43**
    Anchor Line transit sheds 94, **96**
    mansion houses **69**, 72
    possible Roman fort **15**, 17
Yorkhill Quay and Basin 83, 141